Women in Ming China

Women in Ming China

Bret Hinsch

ROWMAN & LITTLEFIELD
Lanham • Boulder • New York • London

Published by Rowman & Littlefield
An imprint of The Rowman & Littlefield Publishing Group, Inc.
4501 Forbes Boulevard, Suite 200, Lanham, Maryland 20706
www.rowman.com

6 Tinworth Street, London SE11 5AL, United Kingdom

British Library Cataloguing in Publication Information Available

Library of Congress Cataloging-in-Publication Data

Names: Hinsch, Bret, author.
Title: Women in Ming China / Bret Hinsch.
Description: Lanham : Rowman & Littlefield, 2021. | Series: Asian voices | Includes
    bibliographical references and index.
Identifiers: LCCN 2020052106 (print) | LCCN 2020052107 (ebook) | ISBN
    9781538152966 (cloth) | ISBN 9781538181416 (pbk) | ISBN 9781538152973 (epub)
Subjects: LCSH: Women—China—History—To 1500. | Women—China—History—
    16th century. | Women—China—Social conditions. | Sex role—China—History. |
    China—Social life and customs—History. | China—Ming dynasty, 1368–1644.
Classification: LCC HQ1767 .H566 2021 (print) | LCC HQ1767 (ebook) | DDC
    305.4095109/024—dc23
LC record available at https://lccn.loc.gov/2020052106
LC ebook record available at https://lccn.loc.gov/2020052107

Brief Song[1]

Haven't you noticed—
   Flowers of radiant beauty
     on a bough in the breezes of spring,
And how, in a matter of days,
   spring breezes blow the flowers down?
Let us not glamorize
   the joys and sorrows of life;
Rosy faces will melt away
   in the heat of joys and sorrows.
There's no end to joys and sorrows
   but our lives will have an end,
Leaving only the moon at night
   to shed its pure and fluid light,
And among the flowers
   beneath the leaves
     mist in the vacant air.

Lu Qingzi (fl. 1590)

Contents

Chronology of Dynasties

Tang	618–907
Liao	916–1125
Northern Song	960–1127
Jin	1115–1234
Southern Song	1127–1179
Yuan	1271–1368
Ming	1368–1644
Qing	1644–1912

Introduction

China's circumstances during the Ming dynasty differed significantly from what came before and after, providing a distinct backdrop against which ordinary women had to live their lives.[1] The rulers of every dynasty always reacted to some degree against shortcomings of the previous era, and the Ming was no exception. When the dynasty began, the new establishment repudiated the hated Yuan regime that proceeded it. Yuan was just one component of the immense Mongol Empire that stretched across Eurasia. After conquering a huge swath of territory elsewhere, the Mongols turned their attentions to China. Although large and prosperous, China had been enfeebled by division. The Jin dynasty, founded by nomadic Jurchen invaders, ruled the north, while native rulers maintained the Southern Song dynasty in the south. In 1211 the Mongols invaded Jurchen territory, destroyed Jin, and added north China to their empire. Then they went on to attack the decayed Southern Song state, finally extinguishing it in 1279. China had been invaded many times before, but the Mongols were unusually savage. Rampaging horsemen massacred ordinary people and wrought terrible destruction, leaving behind depopulated wastelands.

After conquering China, the Mongols had to decide how they would govern such a large and sophisticated society. Out of necessity, they adopted a Chinese-style administrative system and named their regime Yuan. Although Mongol khans ostensibly presided over a Chinese dynasty, a long string of conquests made them confident in the superiority of their native culture. They maintained many Mongol practices that their subjects found alien, difficult to fathom, and deeply disturbing.

Chinese had long experience with life under conquest dynasties. Previous nomadic invaders had employed various combinations of native and pastoral practices to govern. However, the Yuan system was particularly exotic, and the Chinese found it difficult to accept. Most fundamentally, despite the size of their empire, the Mongols had never established a comprehensive bureaucracy. Although the Yuan government had bureaus staffed with officials in the Chinese fashion, Mongol overlords had little interest in systematic law or administration. They made spontaneous and unpredictable pronouncements, casting a pall of uncertainty over the government. Chinese regarded Mongol rule as a humiliating regression. Instead of being led by erudite literati steeped in classical learning, they had to obey the caprices of illiterate foreigners on horseback.

Kublai Khan (r. 1271–1294), the grandson of the famed conqueror Chinggis, chose Dadu (Beijing) as his Chinese capital and set down the basic institutions of the Yuan dynasty. A major problem was how a conquest dynasty staffed by both Chinese and foreigners would recruit talent. During the Song dynasty, the government had employed a rigorous examination system to select talented candidates for office. This method guaranteed that government functionaries had received a comprehensive humanistic education, enabling them to read regulations and draft complex bureaucratic documents. However, unlettered Mongol warriors could not possibly pass a written test, so Kublai relied on recommendations to fill government bureaus. This slapdash recruitment system enlisted many ignorant and illiterate officials. Overwhelmed by mediocrity, administration languished.

The Mongols may have been able to defeat their foes, but they were ill equipped to govern the conquered. The viciousness of the Mongol invasion earned them the hatred of their subjects, and the Chinese had a very low opinion of their rulers.[2] To make matters worse, the Mongols had little interest in routine administration. They delayed important decisions and often made bad choices. The Yuan dynasty only lasted as long as it did because efficient Chinese officials worked hard to hold the regime together, largely to stave off the anarchy that would inevitably accompany the dynasty's collapse. Even so, a string of natural disasters and famines eventually goaded peasants to rise up and overthrow their hated Mongol overlords.

Decades of chaos marred the decline of the Yuan, as various rebels fought to bring down this detested government of occupation. Although many insurgents were no more than bandits or petty warlords, a number of visionary leaders sought not only to overthrow the Yuan but also to establish a new dynasty in its place. Eventually the rebel commander Zhu Yuanzhang (r. 1368–1398) declared a dynasty called Ming ("bright"). He attracted widespread support, built up a large army, and battled Yuan forces. Zhu succeeded in expelling the Mongols from China, bringing the Yuan dynasty to a conclusion in 1368 after less than a century of rule.

Members of the elite founded almost all of China's dynasties. Only the Han and Ming were founded by commoners. Not coincidentally, in both of these dynasties, the humble origins of the founding emperors led them to ignore many precedents. The first ruler of the Ming rose up from particularly base circumstances. Born into a poor family, Zhu Yuanzhang was orphaned at a young age. Out of necessity, he became a Buddhist monk and begged to survive. His only assets were a quick mind and shrewd judgment. When the Yuan began to disintegrate, Zhu seized the opportunity. He threw himself into the fray, fought hard, and ultimately ended up the winner.

Zhu Yuanzhang, better known by the formal appellations Hongwu and Taizu, had several goals. Most importantly, he wanted to purify Chinese society by purging any traces of the hated Mongol occupiers. In many respects, the founding of the Ming marked a return to normality for China. The founding emperor established a capital in the prosperous south at Nanjing, reinstated traditional administration, and revived the examination system to recruit educated officials. Hongwu was an idealist. At first he planned to transform his traumatized nation into a Daoist utopia. However, his brash personality undermined his plans. Instead of creating heaven on earth, Hongwu established an oppressive and autarchic system of government.

Repressive institutions emerged unexpectedly due to the circumstances that clouded the dynasty's beginnings. Hongwu spent the early years of his reign fighting contenders in the south. Reunifying the world's biggest state was never an easy task, and Hongwu employed harsh measures to vanquish his opponents. This long period of violence conditioned Hongwu's general outlook toward administration, inspiring him to take oppressive measures when ruling his subjects. Mongol brutality had undermined many previous restraints on government power, and Hongwu filled this vacuum with despotic institutions.[3]

Confucian thinkers had traditionally emphasized that ruler and ruled are bound together with mutual ethical obligations. Hongwu's new system flouted this covenant. He promulgated a code of law but did not consider himself bound by it. The new emperor frequently intervened in the judicial process to hand down unusually severe punishments. Hongwu persecuted numerous officials and slaughtered tens of thousands of suspects in a series of bloody purges. He mistrusted his officials so much that he abolished the office of prime minister and ran the government himself. Senior officials did not dare act on their own initiative. Instead, they waited to carry out the ruler's commands, allowing the emperor to assume duties that normally came under the purview of the bureaucracy.

Under previous dynasties, officials had usually handled routine administrative matters. Disempowering the ruler in this way could help ensure long-term stability. Even if a mediocre emperor occupied the throne, an efficient bureaucratic system could still keep the government functioning smoothly. But because of the unusual centralization of power at the beginning of the Ming, the quality of administration depended largely on the capability of whoever happened to be monarch. Unfortunately, the Ming emperors showed little interest in the tedious minutiae of government. Some were utterly incompetent. When a succession of unqualified rulers personally made important decisions, the populace suffered through long episodes of bad government.

Following Hongwu's death, two factions wrestled for supremacy, each supporting a different successor. In the ensuing struggle, one of the claimants was murdered and his palace burned to the ground. The victorious Yongle emperor (r. 1402–1424) moved the capital back north to Beijing. Yongle thought that he could easily win the officialdom over to his side, but key members of the government refused to support a regicide. When Yongle ordered a high minister to draft the edict of accession, the outraged gentleman threw the brush to the ground and declared that he would rather die than legitimize the murder of an emperor. Yongle granted his wish and condemned him to death by a thousand cuts. He then slaughtered tens of thousands of opponents, real and imagined, in imitation of his father's reign of terror.

After Yongle's vicious reign, the throne was eventually inherited by the Zhengtong emperor (r. 1435–1449, 1457–1464). In light of the enduring acrimony that poisoned relations between the monarchs and officialdom, Zhengtong transferred power from the regular bureaucracy to a palace agency under eunuch control. This decision further degraded the quality of administration. The interests of castrated men conflicted with those of society at large. Although mainstream officials wanted responsible government, eunuchs only sought to enrich themselves. Zhengtong considered himself a formidable warrior, so his sycophantic eunuch minions encouraged him to lead a punitive expedition to punish the Mongols for recent incursions. The Chinese army suffered a terrible defeat, and the Mongols took Zhengtong prisoner, plunging China's government into crisis.

Normally, the emperor's son would accede to the throne, but Zhengtong's child was still an infant. The officials felt that with the nation so weak and exposed, an adult emperor was indispensable. Various factions at court worked out a compromise, enthroning Zhengtong's sibling as the Jingtai emperor (r. 1449–1457) and naming Zhengtong's child as the heir apparent. A year later, the Mongols released their hostage, hoping that his unexpected reappearance would foment chaos. Jingtai refused to yield the throne and forced Zhengtong to renounce his imperial title. However, seven years later, Jingtai died and Zhengtong ascended the throne for a second time. Because he had previously renounced the title of emperor, this time he felt obliged to take a new official appellation and called himself Tianshun.

The next two reigns went smoothly. Then the irresponsible behavior of the Zhengde emperor (1505–1521) brought yet more disorder. Zhengde had no interest in fulfilling his responsibilities, so he allowed a eunuch strongman and his henchmen to run the government. The eunuch faction was extravagantly corrupt and inept, and they harshly punished anyone who dared to condemn their malfeasance. Eventually, a relative of the ruler led a rebellion, hoping to restore normalcy. Although this uprising failed, this threat turned Zhengde against the eunuchs.

Even though the harem had hundreds of women, Zhengde had no progeny. After Zhengde's death, officials arranged for a relative to be posthumously adopted by Zhengde's father, thus making him eligible to succeed to the throne. However, the new Jiajing emperor (1521–1567) wanted state authorities to declare that his father had in fact been an emperor so as to make him a lineal heir to the throne. Principled officials firmly opposed this attempt to change the line of succession after the fact, as it threatened the fundamental legitimacy of the imperial institution. Jiajing responded by having numerous critics flogged, tortured, and exiled.

The subsequent reign of the Wanli emperor (1572–1620) was also mired in controversy. Wanli wanted to bypass the normal succession and name his third son as heir. When officials opposed this decision as a violation of precedent, the petulant Wanli punished them by refusing to carry out his responsibilities. Every morning the high officials dutifully filed into the palace for the requisite audience with their sovereign, but the emperor always failed to appear. Officials in the outer bureaucracy cooperated with palace eunuchs to keep the government functioning despite the bizarre situation. However, without a responsible emperor to maintain order, factions and intrigues destabilized the state.

The recurring failures of the Ming system eventually began to affect morale. As the educated gentry looked back on so many reigns marred by cruelty and ineptitude, they began to lose faith in the dynasty. When the Ming began, despite Hongwu's brutality, the state still managed to recruit talented men to serve in office. But in the later part of the dynasty, the elite began to regard government service as dangerous and futile. They felt no reason to rally around mediocre rulers who surrounded themselves with eunuchs and sycophants. Yet even as cynicism grew, the dynasty still managed to endure. Effective ideas and institutions that had developed over the centuries allowed determined officials to keep the decayed system running.

As the dynasty tottered, a series of natural disasters dealt the fatal blow. Alternating years of flood and drought, together with unusually cold weather, destroyed harvests. Peasants starved and epidemics raged, plunging vast regions into disarray. The Wanli emperor died during this run of bad weather. A child ruler succeeded him, so the government once again fell into eunuch hands. Manchu nomads took advantage of this turmoil to launch an attack. Simultaneously, rebels rose up around China, determined to unseat the Ming and establish a new dynasty. Battered by both foreign troops and domestic insurgents, the government collapsed. In 1644, the Manchus declared a new dynasty called Qing and reunited China under foreign rule.

In spite of the ambivalence that the decayed Ming had long evoked, many people nevertheless rued its extinction. They felt humiliated by the sight of crude nomads on horseback once again issuing orders to their countrymen. Some remained loyal to their government in spite of its failings, as they considered loyalty a moral obligation. The traumatic transition between Ming and Qing also brought terrible shocks. As untold millions perished from famine and disease, Chinese bandits and Manchu invaders terrorized the populace. Soon after the founding of the new Qing government, Huang Yuanjie wrote a poem of remembrance to her husband, who had disappeared the previous year and was never heard from again.[4] Although this poem expressed one woman's grief for a lost man, it also captures the pain and suffering of a generation of women who lived through the terrifying collapse of the Ming dynasty.

> Leaning against a pillar, I am overwhelmed with worries about the state.
> Others, as always, go to pleasure houses.
> My thoughts persist like unending drizzle.
> Tears fall like dispersing petals, without end.
> Since the time of parting, it's already a new year.
> Abstaining from burning fires is still an ancient custom.
> Thinking of my family I stare off into the white clouds.
> My small heart is overwhelmed by grief.

In spite of poor leadership, in many respects China flourished during the Ming dynasty. During the Song era, commerce had grown rapidly, setting down the foundations of a dynamic and prosperous society. Under the Ming, economic growth was accompanied by a population explosion. Over the course of the Ming dynasty, the number of people in China perhaps tripled, an increase fueled largely by the introduction of New World foods such as potatoes and corn that could be grown on hilly land. As the economy grew, the number of people increased even faster. These parallel trends had contradictory outcomes. Commercial activity increased, but the amount of income per person fell. Faced with spreading impoverishment, the autocratic Ming government intervened aggressively in economic matters, creating a command economy that operated alongside the private sector. A local official named Zhang Tao, active in the early seventeenth century, summed up these disorienting changes.[5]

> Those who went out as merchants became numerous, and the ownership of land was no longer esteemed. As men matched wits using their assets, fortunes rose and fell unpredictably. The capable succeeded, the dull-witted were destroyed; the family to the west enriched itself while the family to the east was impoverished. The balance between the mighty and the lowly was lost as both competed for trifling amounts, each exploiting the other and everyone publicizing himself.

While these complicated circumstances brought hardships and inefficiencies, they also offered opportunities to merchants, craftsmen, and consumers. The government fostered conditions generally favorable to commerce and maintained good transportation infrastructure, allowing trade to flourish. The economy also became increasingly monetized. Although China had minted money since antiquity, at the beginning of the dynasty, many people still used grain and cloth as de facto currencies. At this time, a huge influx of precious metal from mines in Japan and the Americas flooded China with silver, so cash became the standard medium of exchange. Monetization rationalized the economy and simplified buying and selling, further fueling economic growth. The resulting development was extremely uneven. Parts of south China became much more economically advanced than other regions. However, the south was also overpopulated, and peasants had to compete for insufficient resources, leading to widespread destitution.

Rising national prosperity continued to fuel the social transformations that had begun under the Song dynasty. For an increasing number of people, food was something to be bought, not grown. Cities became larger, more numerous, and different in character from before. Early Chinese cities were basically administrative centers where officials managed the surrounding countryside, which most people called home. As the economy grew, commerce came to dominate urban life, and the government had less control over merchants. Urbanization gave rise to a new social model. Under the traditional system, the rural gentry acted as local leaders. While this system may have been practicable in a nation of agricultural villages, urbanization rendered it obsolete in many places. The residents of cities became increasingly important. The hustle and bustle of thriving cities also gave rise to a diverse and exciting new urban culture. Most strikingly, the commercial economy turned almost everything into a commodity. People could live the lifestyle of their choosing and pursue distinctive personal interests. A wealthy man could purchase clothing in brilliant new colors, elegant furniture, antiques, and even talented concubines to sing and dance for his pleasure.

These fundamental shifts led people to reimagine China. Previously, self-sufficient peasants were not just the foundation of society, but also an ideal. The diligent farmer who plowed while his wife spun and wove were lauded as embodiments of naïve virtue. But during the Ming, ambitious and ambiguous new visions of the ideal life emerged. Many people craved success in the commercial urban world, which held out the possibility of earning a fortune and enjoying myriad pleasures. Even gentlemen educated in stringent Neo-Confucian platitudes felt the pull of the sophisticated urban lifestyle. However, the rising fascination with materialism also elicited concern. Confucius had warned about the moral threat by the pursuit of wealth. He feared that if people saw money as the prime goal in life, ethics would fall by the wayside, and they would be willing to commit immoral acts in pursuit of material gain. With these admonitions in mind, rising prosperity brought both exhilaration and apprehension.

As the economy developed, the basic structure of society altered in response. The commercialization of agriculture led to the rapid circulation of people and goods between villages and cities, undermining the established rural way of life. Traditional hierarchies became irrelevant. The Tang aristocracy and many Song literati families had already declined into obscurity, making room for a new elite. Most of the prominent men of the Ming had a sparse family tree, and their fortunes rose and fell more rapidly than before. As traditional social rankings became muddled, people interacted through relatively informal social groupings, such as networks of friends or people with the same occupation.[6]

Kinship consists of two major types: agnates and affines. As before, blood bonds held the agnatic family together, and they traced descent along the male line. Although the patriline provided people with their primary kin identity, the elite also valued affinal ties with the families of wives and mothers, as these connections could help ambitious men advance in their careers. However, female kinship status had undergone an important change. Traditionally a woman's ties with her natal kin had been the key to her identity, even after marriage. Over the centuries, however, wives had been growing steadily closer to their husbands' families. By the late imperial era of Ming and Qing, they had been firmly integrated into the families of their in-laws.

Beyond the family, lineages also helped hold society together. These large kinship groups traced descent from a common ancestor, real or imagined. When relatives owned property in common, their lineage became a clan. By cooperating and pooling resources, large kinship groupings could provide their members with useful support. The most active clans owned fields, ran businesses, built ancestral shrines and cemeteries, and established schools that allowed their boys to prepare for civil service examinations. Many clans imitated the organization of Buddhist monasteries by establishing formal administrative posts, setting down clear rules, and keeping meticulous records.

During the Yuan dynasty, the Mongols had tried to enforce a social hierarchy based on ethnicity. The Ming swept away this alien system and reinstated a traditional social organization that classified the emperor's subjects into four categories based on occupation—gentry, peasant, artisan, and merchant. Although these occupations theoretically constituted a hierarchy, economic development blurred relative status. The government considered merchants the lowest social group, yet wealthy tradesmen had a much higher standard of living than most landholding literati. A rich merchant sometimes paid out a large dowry to marry his daughter to the scion of a respected literati family, effectively buying his way into the elite.

The gentry were the most important social group, and they increasingly dominated local society. As the central government floundered, administration became a partnership between officials and local landed elites who helped maintain order in their districts.[7] Despite their importance, the gentry lacked noble title, making their position insecure. For a gentry family to maintain their privileged standing, members had to periodically pass the civil service examinations and take up government posts, bringing in regular infusions of wealth and reaffirming their prestige. The gentry also maintained their unique status by engaging in special activities that distinguished them from ordinary people. They intermarried with one another, spent their free time reading and writing, observed Confucian rituals, and socialized with their peers. The gentry shared an appreciation of the ancient classics, major works of history, and Neo-Confucian values.

In terms of culture, the Ming dynasty departed significantly from the Yuan. People looked back on the Mongol occupation with contempt. Emperors and literati extirpated nomadic influence from Chinese culture and tried to restore orthodox Song dynasty standards. This cultural cleansing ended up reinventing Chinese culture. Under the Yuan dynasty, China had been a multi-ethnic state within the much larger Mongol Empire. The Mongols emphasized ethnic difference as a fundamental social characteristic and built their system atop this foundation. In reaction, Ming dynasty authorities repudiated multiculturalism, restored native ideas and customs, and emphasized the cultural homogeneity of the Chinese nation. This is not to say that the Ming emperors were enthusiastic sponsors of cultural pursuits. To the contrary, unlike the great imperial patrons of the Song, most Ming rulers had little interest in the arts. Uncultured emperors were perhaps appropriate for a dynasty founded by an illiterate commoner. The famed dynamism of late Ming culture did not come from the top of society. It was propelled by popular entertainments that catered to the multitude.

⊶✦⊷

This book explores the history of women during the tumultuous Ming dynasty. Viewing this era through the lens of gender not only reveals significant details about the lives of women at that time but also provides a more comprehensive view of the Ming overall. Women built their lives around the circumstances of their particular settings, and they also affected the world around them. Gender conditioned power, wealth, and opportunity in myriad social relationships that were constantly negotiated.[8] An awareness of how gender affected people's behavior imbues it with deeper meaning and clarifies their motivations.[9]

Understanding Ming dynasty women is not a simple matter. People of the time did not have a singular view of womanhood. As before, they tended to see women not as unique individuals but as gendered actors playing out the key kinship roles of daughter, wife, and mother.[10] Genealogies recorded most wives and concubines according to their father's surname, not their given name, treating them merely as daughters instead of unique individuals. Many of these documents do not even bother to record daughters' names. It was thought sufficient to simply note the number of daughters born to each woman. For married daughters, a genealogy listed her husband's surname and place of residence. The wording of genealogies gives a sense of female anonymity, implying that women's personal identities were deemed irrelevant.

Although most men had little interest in female matters, Ming sources nevertheless include many detailed and insightful observations regarding women. Commercial printing flourished, and the number of printed books swelled in both number and variety. Prose fiction also came to maturity at this time. The resulting plethora of sources, both fact and fiction, provides varied and conflicting views of the feminine. At this time, writers explored provocative new female images. Long before, Tang dynasty authors had created a wide range of stock female types.[11] Although these stereotypes remained in vogue, sophisticated new literary techniques allowed people to write about various kinds of women with depth and detail. Ming authors entertained their readers with an array of compelling female characters that included martyrs, harlots, poets, beauties, and seductive ghosts.[12]

Each genre of writing had implicit conventions that guided how authors represented women, so they had different goals when writing about each female archetype.[13] Sometimes writers took a pragmatic viewpoint, while in other cases they could be highly ideological. Cultured men admired talented women and read their writings with interest. Epitaphs often emphasize a woman's useful contributions to her family, while moral biography stresses acts of martyrdom.[14] Readers also perused erotic stories, pictures, and songs that sexualized women and portrayed them as fundamentally licentious.

Even in biography, the author would carefully manipulate a text's organization, style, and content to produce a desired outcome.[15] Literature did not just disseminate diverse female images but deliberately emphasized the contradictory qualities of individual women. Rather than seeing people or events in simplistic terms, Ming authors tended to depict them as composites of opposite tendencies such as movement and stillness, elegance and vulgarity, happiness and sorrow, and so on. They considered an inclusive perspective subtle, comprehensive, and realistic. This bifurcated worldview influenced depictions of gender.[16] Rather than seeing women in simple unitary terms, Ming authors preferred to depict female nature as complex and ambiguous.

Each form of writing produced a different kind of female image. While epitaphs describe how a woman's life course conformed to Confucian platitudes, fiction depicts female characters transgressing norms by seeking romance and extramarital liaisons. And stage plays placed female characters in a wide range of situations that included weddings, celebrations, parting from loved ones, sharing a husband's achievements and setbacks, virtuous behavior, and romance.[17] Showing so many different sides to female life gave audiences far more diverse images than before, revealing the breadth and complexity of Ming views of womanhood.[18]

Overall, in comparison with their Song counterparts, Ming women suffered much more subjugation, and their rights clearly regressed.[19] Families observed the custom of female reclusion with greater stringency. Footbinding became extremely common, dooming women to unrelenting pain and reducing their mobility. Laws on inheritance and adoption became far less liberal. Stringent Neo-Confucian interpretations of female virtue entered the mainstream. And society increasingly looked askance at the remarriage of widows. The late Ming poet Shen Yixiu (1590–1635) summed up the challenges facing her sex.[20]

> I advise you: never be born a woman—
> Wealthy or humble, you will end sorrowful all the same;
> Why bother to consult Junping's soothsaying?
> One exerts no control over destiny.

Yet even though women faced growing difficulties, they had new opportunities as well. As the general level of education rose, more women became literate. They had opportunities to read poetry, popular fiction, Buddhist sutras, and even history and the Confucian classics. Female authors composed vast quantities of poetry and other writings. The rising commercial economy provided an unprecedented range of goods and services. Women also had many ways to enjoy their leisure time. They played ball and board games, traveled to scenic spots, enjoyed cultured pursuits such as painting or music, and engaged in worship.[21]

This book seeks to provide insights into various aspects of women's lives during the Ming dynasty, as well as the different ways that various sections of society viewed women, both true and imagined. This survey begins with family life (chapter 1). Unlike men, women usually spent most of their lives confined to the domestic sphere. When the circumstances of the family altered, the fundamental conditions of women changed as well. Chapter 2 explores the relation between women and government. During the Tang dynasty, Empress Wu Zetian (624–705) usurped the throne and ruled as the only female emperor in Chinese history. This episode traumatized powerful men, and they responded by imposing increasing restrictions on women in the palace. The reverberations of Empress Wu's unorthodox reign continued for centuries up to the Ming dynasty. Next, chapter 3 describes women's wealth, including their dowries, inheritance rights, and opportunities to work.

Chapter 4, on education, shows how rising educational standards allowed more women to learn about the world through books and to express themselves in writing, usually poetry. Chapter 5, on religion, describes the place of faith in the women's lives. Although Buddhism and Daoism had both declined in influence, religion still attracted numerous female devotees. Ideas about ethics also altered at this time, particularly views toward chastity and virginity (see chapters 6 and 7). Neo-Confucianism dominated academic discourse, leading to increasingly restrictive views of female virtue. Simultaneously, however, unconventional thinkers and writers explored the emotional side of the humanity. These conflicting views of human nature gave rise to debates over correct female behavior. The final chapter describes the variety of images of women that circulated during the Ming. In particular, views of the female body altered considerably, affecting how women lived and how society perceived them. When these various perspectives are all taken into consideration, they present the reader with a panorama of facts and imagery that conveys the richness of women's lives during the Ming dynasty.

Chapter 1

Family

While men interacted with a wide range of contacts, a woman spent most of her time inside the house. For this reason, her family's particular circumstances determined every aspect of her life. A girl lived under her father's roof until she married, at which time she moved in with her husband and in-laws. She usually remained with this new family for the rest of her life. Women's confinement within the home kept them under male control, as senior men had the final say in important matters. In societies throughout the world, people use family interactions to negotiate, maintain, alter, and socialize gender identity.[1] Likewise, in China the family was the social context where wives and mothers expressed their feminine identity, and daughters learned how to be a woman. Ming conceptions of family differed somewhat from those of previous eras. Starting from the Yuan dynasty, the state had embraced the Neo-Confucian view of family as a kin group grounded in inheritance and descent, with both passing down the male line.[2] At the popular level, people thought of the typical family as headed by a stern father and kind mother.[3]

During the late imperial era, lineages and clans regained prominence, making the family a subsidiary unit of a larger kinship organization. During the sixteenth century, the state allowed ordinary people to build large shrines to worship their ancestors. These halls served as focal points for forming lineages. Individuals and families who shared a common ancestor (real or imagined) could come together there, conduct rituals, and build solidarity.[4] The prevalence of lineages and extended families varied by region. Although these organizations were very common in parts of south China, the northern Chinese rarely constructed large formal lineages.[5] In some southern villages, every family belonged to the same lineage, so the local community functioned as a kinship organization. Single-lineage villages often developed into

clans whose members owned assets in common, including land and endow-
ments. Whereas partitive inheritance continually dispersed family estates by
giving each son an equal share, clan wealth remained intact over the generations. The stability of these holdings ensured a clan's longevity and provided
members with a sense of security. The rise of lineages also affected social
structure. Minor gentry tended to dominate lineage administration, increasing
their influence over local society.[6]

Large kinship groupings affected female members in various ways. Anthropologists have often assumed that the rise of strong patrilineal descent
groups, such as lineages and clans, tends to degrade female status. In some
regions of China, such as Guangdong, this may indeed have been the case.
However, these organizations did not always have such a clear and simple
impact on female kinship position. Women often played active roles in lineage life, exploiting these institutions to empower themselves, so in some
cases large kinship organizations could raise certain aspects of female status.[7]

Extended families, also referred to as communal families, also became
widespread during the Ming.[8] The members of these groups shared a mutual
ancestor and held productive assets together. Each nuclear family in the
group had their own house, but they resided in proximity. Most importantly,
extended-family members cooked together in a communal kitchen, attesting
to their unity. Extended families emerged as a pragmatic strategy to overcome
the fragmentation caused by partitive inheritance. Although family landholdings split up every generation, sometimes brothers remained together after the
deaths of their parents. In this way they pooled resources to maintain their
extended family's wealth and prominence. The size of a communal family
would inevitably increase over time. A growing domestic organization might
hold together for three or four generations before it finally became too un-
wieldy and had to split up.

Neo-Confucian thinkers lauded the communal family as an ideal arrangement that helped stabilize society and foster harmony. During the ancient
Zhou dynasty, extended families had been the norm. Neo-Confucians na-
ively looked back on that distant era as a utopian age. They believed that the
subsequent decline of extended families had caused atomized individuals to
become selfish and reckless. These thinkers encouraged people to imitate
the ancients and maintain large households as a way to raise the moral tenor
of society. Managing a large extended family could be complicated, so they
often managed their affairs by imitating the organizational techniques of Buddhist monasteries. Religious communities had developed workable rules that
allowed numerous members to live together in an orderly manner.[9] Extended
families also often employed the meticulous bookkeeping used by merchants
to manage their collective assets. While communal families elevated the so-

cial position of the kin group as a whole, this form of kinship organization likely had a negative impact on the status of women.[10] Extended households included larger numbers of senior men, thus depriving female members of the opportunities to exercise leadership and allocate resources that they would have had in a small nuclear family.

In spite of the rise of larger groups of relatives, the nuclear family remained the primary unit of kinship. More than two-thirds of families included between three and seven people.[11] The average family had four to six core members, with five people most common. A typical family included a wife and husband, one or two children, and perhaps a grandparent. Family size tended to vary according to wealth. Those with more resources could expand their families by taking in more members. Sons usually lived at home until both parents died, at which time male offspring divided up the estate and established separate households.

Over the course of Chinese history, a woman's primary kinship identity gradually shifted. In antiquity, women usually felt primary loyalty to their natal families. Ancient women felt only loosely integrated into the families of their husbands. The bonds with in-laws intensified through the centuries. During the Ming era, the focus of female identity shifted decisively toward the husband's family, completing the transition of female kinship identity.[12] The peasant origins of the Ming ruling house favored this change. Because the founder of the Ming came from the lowest rungs of society, the dynasty's culture and legal system put greater emphasis on conjugal ties, as was the norm in peasant culture. The state considered a woman's membership in her husband's family to be her primary legal and social identity. Although wives continued to maintain ties with their natal kin, from the official perspective these had become unimportant.

Wives and mothers retained a psychological presence in the family even after their death, particularly if they had gained a reputation for exemplary virtue.[13] In this era, it became very common for prominent literati to make money by writing elegantly composed epitaphs for deceased women. A family might even commemorate an exceptionally virtuous female family member by erecting a monument, such as a memorial arch or engraved stone stele, so that future generations would remember her moral achievements. Literati put great stock in appearances and strove to create a positive public image for their family. Commemorations of dead wives and mothers thus helped shape how gentry families understood themselves and how society at large viewed them.

Servants, wet nurses, and concubines were also considered family members, albeit of very low status. Although people today see the family as a unifying institution, the Ming household included people of different economic and social standing.[14] People living under the same roof held varied positions depending on their age, sex, and relationship with the male head of household. Families even extended the rubric of kinship to include people not related by blood or marriage. Kinship brought people together, so families extended the number of purported kin to gain useful allies. People exchanged gifts, participated in common activities, and employed titles of fictive kinship to strengthen their family by drawing in useful outsiders.[15]

The home was more than just a group of people. It constituted a set physical space as well. Women ideally spent most of their time demurely hidden within the innermost parts of the house, so builders designed domestic architecture to shield them from the embarrassing gazes of strange men.[16] A household's women did not necessarily feel close to one another. When a woman wed, she suddenly left her loved ones and found herself living among strangers who did not necessarily receive her amicably. The trauma of separation from blood family haunted many wives. Loving sisters who had grown inseparable might never meet again. A poem by Zou Saizhen (fl. 1496) to her younger sister captures the author's pain at being forced apart from a beloved sibling.[17]

> I seal my letter and ask the geese to deliver it.
> Despite many sicknesses we have remained inseparable.
> Wintry chestnut trees have encroached on your flesh of jade,
> Autumn raspberries have mussed your cicada curls.
> Your letter from the village had still not arrived,
> When flesh and bones had started to tug at each other.
> When will we return to our secret place,
> Light a lamp and talk of when we were young?

Even though women and men lived in proximity, they usually led very different lives. Men spent much of their day outside. Even within the home, it was considered proper for husband and wife to keep apart most of the time.[18] From today's perspective, women could seem almost like prisoners confined to a small space. To thrive, they had to find ways to make their isolation tolerable. A cloistered wife might create a cozy personal space, perhaps in the kitchen, where she spent much of her time together with her children.

In larger households, the female realm constituted the center of activity. Women and children often outnumbered men in the home, making their happenings virtually synonymous with family life. The frequent absence of men from home gave women the chance to pursue their private passions.[19] In Ming fiction, romantic and sexual encounters between women always occurred in the inner quarters of a large home. Whereas men could go outside in search of companionship, women mostly interacted with a constricted circle of domestic contacts. Concubinage sometimes brought women together in a small space, facilitating lesbian encounters. Fictionalized accounts describe a senior woman, older or higher in status, initiating a same-sex liaison. It seems that men did not mind discreet lesbian trysts in their homes. As long as women's intimate affairs remained hidden from the wider world, men did not take much interest in them. At most they might consider lesbianism strange or silly.

Whereas a man usually headed the family, under certain circumstances a woman could take charge. Tang and Song documents mention so-called female households (*nühu*). This term did not refer to a household composed only of women, but rather one overseen by a female head of household (*huzhu*).[20] Under Song law, a female household came into existence when it lacked a man to serve as head of household. A household had to have a designated head to pay taxes on behalf of the group, which is why the Song government allowed women to serve in this important role. Most often, a widow without sons managed a female household. Even if a widow had a son, she had to act as de facto household head until he reached adulthood and assumed responsibility.

Ming law followed Song precedent in this regard, allowing a woman to serve as household head when no man was available to fill the position.[21] As before, the government referred to these groups as female households, and the family head was responsible for tax payments. But whereas female heads of household had previously been fairly autonomous, Ming authorities supervised them much more closely. A local magistrate would not hesitate to intervene if he believed that one of these women was managing household affairs improperly. There were also a small number of special female households whose members worked in the palace. Women belonging to these households usually worked as servants, sedan chair bearers, or entertainers. When administrators selected a woman to work in the inner palace, they classified her family as a female household and subjected it to special regulations. Even if she performed a menial role, her connection with the palace elevated her domestic position. From the government's perspective, she became the most important person in her family.

◦═══╳═══◦

A wedding stood out as a momentous event for any woman, as it marked a turning point in her life. Marriage completely transformed the way she lived. A bride left her childhood home to take up residence with her husband's family, where she had to take on the unfamiliar roles of wife and daughter-in-law. Parents tended to arrange their children's marriages far in advance, and they formalized the engagement with a betrothal gift. Couples were usually engaged by the age of fourteen, and the wedding would take place two to ten years later.[22] Sometimes a young fiancée moved in with her future husband's family, and they raised her until she reached the age of marriage.[23] Song dynasty documents mention this arrangement, and it became common in parts of south China during the Ming dynasty. The minimum legal ages of marriage were sixteen for boys and fourteen for girls.[24] Grooms were typically several years older than brides, bolstering patriarchal authority within the home and generally depressing female status.[25]

Despite the importance of conjugal life, many men never married. Some could not afford the requisite betrothal gift, so they remained lifelong bachelors due to poverty. Moreover, female infanticide and concubinage lowered the number of available brides. Due to a shortage of marriageable women, many men could not find a spouse even if they could afford the cost of marriage. According to one study of local marriage patterns in Anhui, 26 percent of non-gentry men did not have a wife.[26]

As marriage required the exchange of betrothal gift and dowry, the union was usually arranged by the families of the bride and groom rather than by the couple themselves. Parents had the right to choose a child's spouse without the consent of the person being married off. In choosing a marriage partner, elders would usually seek to benefit the family as a whole rather than the two individuals directly involved. Also, a more powerful figure could sometimes marry off a low-status subordinate without her consent. For example, the master of a bondservant could arrange a marriage for her, and she did not have the right to refuse.[27]

During the mid-Ming, overpopulation and economic difficulties plunged many families into poverty. Some families at the bottom of society felt compelled to sell off their children to make ends meet.[28] Although bridewealth and dowry had long been customary, this practice degraded marriage into a blatant financial transaction. Marriage documents record the sale of daughters and sons into marriage. Occasionally an uncle sold his nephew or an employer sold a servant. In most cases, the people being sold into marriage were very young and unable to resist.

Even the gentry arranged the marriages of children to maximize wealth, prestige, and connections.[29] The Neo-Confucian authority Zhu Xi stressed the importance of a couple's compatibility and cautioned parents to shun financial marriages. Nevertheless, even the elite saw marriage as a pragmatic arrangement. Most importantly, they used it to forge a connection with useful in-laws. The ideology of Chinese kinship may have downplayed the importance of affinal relations, but in fact the elite found these ties extremely useful. The gentry sought in-laws of high standing and talented sons-in-law with good prospects. The families of brides paid out large dowries to attract the best marriage partners, making the exchange of wealth a major factor in marriage negotiations.

Ming marriage law and custom observed ritual propriety.[30] The government enforced monogamy, so minor spouses had the status of concubines rather than true wives. As before, people of extremely different social status could not marry. And even though the betrothal gift had become far less valuable than the dowry, it continued to symbolize a proper marriage. The law required families to employ a matchmaker, even if elders had negotiated the marriage themselves. Matchmakers were considered untrustworthy and had a poor reputation, but the ancient rites demanded their involvement to formalize a marriage, so people continued to employ them.[31]

People put so much stress on engagement that it was almost akin to a marriage ceremony in importance.[32] Once the marriage contract had been finalized and betrothal gifts exchanged, for all practical purposes the couple was considered united. The law enforced the validity of engagements, and these promises were difficult to break. Authorities allowed an engagement to be annulled only in extraordinary circumstances, such as one of the betrothed committing a crime prior to the wedding.

Filial piety helped make children amenable to arranged marriage. Children were taught to defer to parental authority so that they would meekly accept the spouse chosen for them, regardless of their own feelings on the matter. Because couples had no say in their marriage, people tended to have a fatalistic view of the matter. During the medieval era, writers began to depict marriage as fated by supernatural forces. A couple had no choice but to accept this sacred mandate. Popular literature shows that people often considered marriage to have been decided by heaven, karma, or folk deities such as the matchmaker god or moon god.[33] Shifting supposed responsibility for marriage from parents to supernatural forces helped ensure a couple's acquiescence.

The ancients had assumed that a wife would reside with her husband's family. Husbands felt embarrassed to move in with the families of their wives, as they considered this sort of union unorthodox and humiliating. Nevertheless, matrilocal marriages were not uncommon.[34] If a couple lacked a son, they might marry their daughter to a man willing to adopt his father-in-law's surname, become his surrogate son, and carry on the family line. Popular fiction also describes childless men adopting a daughter who would then enter into a matrilocal marriage, bringing in a male heir to perpetuate the family line. Even though men found it demeaning to live with their wives' families, some of them acquiesced to these arrangements to achieve upward mobility. However, it seems that prejudice against matrilocal marriages had eased somewhat from before, making it easier for people to enter into these unconventional unions.

Elite marriage patterns departed from those of the previous dynasty. The Yuan had been a multi-ethnic state. Although Mongols dominated the government, their numbers were relatively small, particularly in the south. Mongols residing in China often had to marry ethnic Han for lack of native marriage partners. Because the Mongols and their foreign allies wielded so much power, important Han families willingly intermarried with influential Mongols to bolster their positions, even though they looked down on their in-laws as barbarous.[35] In contrast, important Ming dynasty families married exclusively within their own ethnicity.[36]

The lengthy and difficult reunification of China at the beginning of the dynasty elevated the importance of the military, so initially many gentry families sought out army officers as marriage partners. After the situation stabilized, civil officials took over many duties that had previously been performed by the army. As the status of military families declined, the gentry no longer considered them premium marriage candidates. Instead, they revived Song dynasty marriage strategies and sought out affines with high educational achievements likely to excel in the civil service. The gentry usually married counterparts from the same region. In many cases, a group of elite families intermarried repeatedly for several generations, producing a closed marriage circle that bound influential local families together into a tight faction.[37]

In many respects, female rights reached a highpoint during the Southern Song. In contrast, the *Great Ming Code* (*Da Ming lü*) restricted the autonomy of women and put them more fully under the control of their husbands. Family law became increasingly thorough, clarifying the official status of each spouse. Ming jurists used Neo-Confucian metaphysics to justify these changes, arguing that gender relations ought to conform with the cosmic order. According to this reasoning, just as heaven and earth constitute a hierarchy, so the law ought to enforce the husband's authority over his wife. In some circumstances, a husband even had the right to kill his spouse. Yuan dynasty authorities allowed a man to kill an adulterous wife or concubine and also their lover if he caught them in flagrante, and Ming law maintained this provision.[38]

The *Great Ming Code* prioritized keeping women under the control of their fathers and husbands. To this end, a woman convicted of all but the most serious crimes would likely avoid incarceration. Officials feared that removing a woman from her family would devastate her reputation and disgrace her male kin.[39] Instead of incarceration, authorities usually placed a female convict under her family's supervision and made them responsible for her actions. The law endeavored to keep wives together with their husbands in other ways as well. If a man committed a crime and was punished by exile, his wife was to accompany him.[40] And if a wife committed adultery or absconded and was subsequently caught, her husband could either keep her or sell her into a new marriage.[41] The law also included provisions intended to protect women from domestic abuse, thereby preserving family harmony and keeping wives from divorcing or fleeing.[42] Because women were expected to remain under the control of their husbands or fathers, they effectively had limited criminal liability. Only if a woman's husband was away from home and her sons were still minors did she become fully responsible for her actions under the law.

Ming divorce law adhered to Tang and Song precedents. As before, a woman could not initiate divorce without her husband's consent. If he refused to agree to a separation, she had no legal recourse to end the marriage. A man could divorce his wife, but the *Great Ming Code* followed earlier standards by enforcing ancient ritual rules regarding divorce. A husband had to cite one of seven reasons as grounds for separation: disobedience to parents-in-law, not bearing children, immorality, jealousy, illness, loquaciousness, or theft. He was not allowed to divorce his wife under three circumstances: she had no family to which she could return, she had mourned his parents for a full three years, or the man had been poor when they married and later became rich. While these provisions followed the divorce system of earlier dynasties, women lost ground in one key respect. Unlike during the Tang or Song, when a man divorced his wife, he would confiscate her dowry. This made it almost impossible for the divorcée to marry well, as a groom's family expected his bride to enter their home with a dowry. Divorce constituted a terrible financial blow to women, impoverishing them and reducing their position in society. Wives rightly feared divorce, and their insecurity empowered husbands. A man could likely force a wayward wife to obey him by threatening to divorce her.

Despite the inequities of the marriage system, an increasing number of people came to believe that the conjugal bond should ideally resemble friendship or even romance. Ancient documents had depicted marriage as an important duty and solemn ritual tie. Love did not factor into marriage. In fact, ritual specialists feared that this emotion might even distract from the more important aspects of the relationship. In the medieval era, romantic fiction emerged, spurring writers to explore the emotional relationships between the sexes. Initially they positioned romance outside of marriage. In fact, the characters in these stories often could not possibly marry because they were separated by a wide gulf in social status or because one was an ordinary person and the other an immortal and ghost.

Ming writers put forward more inclusive depictions of romance. A poem by the sixteenth-century writer Zheng Ruying describes her playfully exchanging letters and presents with her beloved.[43]

> You sent me a bright mirror
> That reflects my tangled hair.
> I require you with curdled cassia grease
> And fragrant oils to smooth your hand.
> You gave me gold-dusted ink,
> I requite you with hibiscus paper.

Eventually people found it conceivable that a married couple could share romantic sentiments. Even as the laws governing marriage became increasingly unequal, more people thought that spouses should share an intense emotional bond. Over time, the educational level of women from elite households had risen, allowing couples to communicate with greater sophistication. Although spouses were still not equal, many couples hoped that they could become devoted companions.[44] Literature held up the companionate marriage as an ideal relationship. Even if marriage began as a dutiful relationship between strangers, love might blossom. Scripts of popular dramas written by women promoted emotionally intimate marriage. These works commended the cultivation of a romantic bond between spouses as an important achievement worthy of admiration.[45]

Commemorations of deceased spouses displayed intensifying conjugal feelings. As before, when men wrote remembrances of their dead wives, they usually employed standardized language and moral stereotypes.[46] Even so, at this time, bereft husbands more often broke free from these polite conventions and expressed their true feelings. Their intense grief sometimes exceeded the accepted bounds of mourning set down by ritual. The inclusion of emotionally charged language in epitaphs transformed them from polite hagiographies into more realistic and sentimental portraits. The injection of sentiment into funerary commemorations also elevated the importance of the lost conjugal relationship.

The talented fiction writer Song Maocheng (ca. 1559–1620) composed an extravagantly demonstrative epitaph for his wife, Madame Yang.[47] Although they had only been married for three years before she died from complications from pregnancy, his passionate encomium shows how intensely some men mourned their wives. The epitaph opens in a conventional manner but quickly takes on an impassioned tone. Song blames himself for having treated his wife badly. In particular, he regrets spending so much time away from home and flirting with courtesans, which his wife rightly resented. Overall, he condemns himself for being self-absorbed and inattentive. Song Maocheng used his literary talent to transcend established stylistic constraints. The epitaph genre had traditionally consisted of respectful praise for a deceased woman's virtues. In this case, a guilt-ridden survivor took the opportunity to write a shockingly candid confessional.

Women rarely wrote formal epitaphs for their husbands. Instead they used poetry to express grief for a departed spouse. Soon after the death of her husband Shen Cheng (d. 1625), Bo Shaojun (d. 1626) composed one hundred quatrains of lamentation, of which eighty-one survive.[48] The intensity and authenticity of these expressions of grief made this poem cycle rightly famous. Bo was born into a gentry family and received a good education, but her husband failed in his career, reducing the couple to genteel poverty. The heartbreak of her husband's early death added to Bo's tribulations. She soon followed her husband to the grave, making it seem as if she died from a broken heart.

Bo Shaojun's poems of mourning address various aspects of her marriage. She loved her husband passionately and emphasized the instant sense of connection they felt at their first meeting. "Those events, twelve years ago at Rainbow Bridge, / Now seem, looking back today, just like a dream."[49] In spite of her husband's failures, she nevertheless expresses admiration for his integrity, elevating the nature of their relationship. She emphasizes that it was not just love that bound them together but a shared commitment to virtue as well. Bo rues the untimely end to a relationship that in retrospect seems to have been almost too good to have been true.

Even though literature lauded emotional attachment, the intensity of actual relationships varied considerably. Burial customs help reveal the relative intimacy of various marriages. Among the prominent Wu family of Huizhou, 45 percent of their burials during the Ming dynasty consisted of joint interments of husband and wife.[50] Second and third wives were rarely buried with their husbands. Even if a wife was not buried in the same tomb as her spouse, she would still usually be laid to rest in the cemetery of his lineage. These arrangements imply that in spite of the attention given to companionate unions, the actual intensity of marriages varied. People regarded first marriages as more orthodox and presumably closer than subsequent unions. But even among first marriages, spouses related to one another with varying degrees of intimacy.

Women were not blind to the way that expectations of companionship and romance conflicted with the realities of hierarchy and obedience. This clash could even give rise to cynicism. Many women realized the futility of seeking intimacy when such a deep gulf separated the sexes. However much a wife might yearn for an emotionally fulfilling marriage, the relationship had been arranged by others, and her husband did not necessarily have any feelings for her. In spite of all the talk about love and emotion, many people continued to see marriage primarily as a duty. A woman who hoped for a soul mate often ended up bound to a respectful but apathetic partner.

◦══╪══◦

Isolated within the home, a mother's relationship with her children often constituted her primary social bond. Society considered raising children and seeing them thrive as a woman's primary achievement. The average childbearing age varied according to social background, with women in elite families giving birth earlier. In most cases, a wife became a mother not long after her wedding. Motherhood elevated a wife's standing within her husband's family, so it was to her advantage to bear a child as soon as possible. Most women had their first child between the ages of twenty-one and twenty-three. They typically bore four children who survived infancy, two or three of whom might survive to adulthood.[51]

Although the bond between mothers and children had always been important, over time this relationship received increasing attention. During the Han and Six Dynasties, many people held large funerals for their mothers and undertook extensive mourning for them, even though such extravagant observances exceeded the bounds of orthodox ritual.[52] The ancient rites held that children ought to mourn longer for a father than a mother, but during her reign, Empress Wu Zetian (624–705) ordered sons to mourn for mothers and fathers equally. Although this change attracted criticism at first, over time it became the norm. At the beginning of the Ming, the law mandated extended mourning for mothers.[53] A son was to mourn his mother for a full three years even if she had remarried, implying that he did not mourn her as his father's wife, but due to a direct kinship bond. Moreover, the law specified that daughters were to mourn parents equally, and to the same extent as their brothers, another violation of orthodox ritual. It seems that the humble background of the Ming dynasty's founder made him uninterested classical mourning rules advocated by the educated elite. Instead the dynasty promulgated new regulations based on realistic emotions.

Overall, however, changes to the legal system steadily increased the distance between mothers and children.[54] Tang dynasty law did not allow children to accuse their mothers of a crime, as such a condemnation seemed grossly unfilial. During the Song, such an accusation became possible, and by the Ming, mothers had lost legal immunity from denunciation by their children. The authoritarian Ming state prioritized allegiance to the state over family loyalty.

Mothers confined to the home could not participate in the prestigious male-dominated activities taking place outside. However, they could bask in the glow of a son's success. A mother enjoyed some of the credit for her son's triumphs, and men gladly acknowledged the debts they owed to the mothers who lovingly nurtured them and prepared them to flourish in a competitive world. A poem by the sixteenth-century writer Yang Wenli offers a glimpse of how mothers urged their sons to succeed.[55]

> Your talents are fine, your name should resound,
> Though lowly your post, your way is unbounded.
> For a hundred years you must drive yourself on,
> For pure and clean are our family's ancient ways.

Raising a child was never easy, and many mothers failed. In the late imperial era, many writers focused on the theme of maternal suffering.[56] They detailed the pain and danger of childbirth as well as the inconvenience of nursing squealing infants, performing tedious childcare, and caring for sick offspring. The image of the maternal martyr sacrificing herself for her children became a common stereotype, and people came to regard motherhood as almost saintly. The only way that a son could possibly requite such immense sacrifice was to become a success, thereby proving that his mother had not suffered in vain. When a man obtained an official position, he often wrote an essay commemorating his mother's sacrifices and acknowledging her role in his achievements.[57]

Although Ming culture sacralized motherhood, the real situation was far more complicated. Due to overpopulation and widespread poverty, infanticide was widespread. A bride had to receive a generous dowry, so it was not uncommon for parents to murder a newborn daughter in order to preserve family wealth. The dangers of abortion made it much safer for a mother to give birth and then kill the infant, usually by drowning, than terminate an unwanted pregnancy in the womb.

Buddhists also strongly opposed abortion and infanticide.[58] Monks and nuns warned that mothers who killed their children would eventually suffer terrifying karmic retribution. Popular culture spread Buddhist teachings about the sanctity of life, increasing their impact. Dismay over widespread infanticide also induced the government to take measures to prevent the murder of infants.[59] Infanticide was strictly illegal, and officials spoke out against it and tried to convince people not to kill their children. The state also founded a system of orphanages so that parents could rid themselves of unwanted infants without having to commit murder. During the Song dynasty, the government had set up an agency called the Love of Youth Bureau (*Ciyou ju*) dedicated to child welfare. Amid widespread concern about infanticide, the Ming revived this system, and local bureaus helped care for vulnerable children. Besides taking in abandoned children and raising them to maturity, these organizations also provided aid to keep vulnerable infants alive, such as hiring wet nurses to feed babies whose mothers did not produce breast milk.

○══✦══○

Concubines were also a kind of family member, albeit of marginal status. The changing relations between concubines and their masters altered the dynamics of family relations over time. A man purchased a concubine from her family or a broker, so these women traditionally had very low status. During the Tang dynasty, concubinage had been seen as a kind of servitude. The status of these women steadily rose, however, and they had a more intimate bond with their masters during the Ming era. At the beginning of the dynasty, Hongwu elevated the status of concubines.[60] Previously, these women had been distinguished from true family members in accordance with the classic rites, but Hongwu put great stress on the emotional dimension of family life. The intimate relationship between a man and his concubine made it reasonable to treat her as a kind of family member. Ming law recognized the intimacy of the relationship between concubines and their children. Previously, the children of concubines had only been legally required to mourn their mothers for one year, but Hongwu had them carry out three years of mourning, akin to a father's wife.

In spite of greater official sympathy for concubines, some laws tightened.[61] Officials schooled in stringent Neo-Confucian ethics saw concubinage as morally dubious and unregulated by the rites. Some moralists wanted to abolish it except when absolutely necessary to produce an heir. Officials also worried that concubinage fueled human trafficking. Criminal gangs abducted vulnerable women and sold them to wealthy men as concubines. To address these concerns, in 1533, the government prohibited a man from purchasing a concubine until he reached age forty. Even then, a man could only legally buy a concubine if he had no male heir. However, authorities never enforced this law, and the Qing government abolished it in 1740. Throughout this time, concubinage remained very common among the wealthy.

Some concubines were vocal about the suffering and humiliation they endured. A poem written on the wall of an inn by an anonymous writer known only as the Woman of Kuaiji sums up the anger of a proud woman who had been degraded into a wealthy man's plaything.[62]

> I sit silently, not showing my bitterness that knows no end.
> Heaven had its reasons for giving me this life—
> To make me an entertaining topic of conversation!

In spite of the contradictions between institutionalized concubinage and conventional ethics, not to mention the suffering of so many victims, this practice also had some positive aspects. Concubinage allowed poor women to benefit from wealth accumulated by the elite, ameliorating some of the era's gross economic inequality. This custom also helped stabilize rural society by ameliorating poverty and providing tangible relief to victims of natural disasters. In times of hardship when the poor faced starvation, a woman might become a concubine to save her own life and those of the family members who sold her. If an impoverished woman ended up as the concubine of a rich man, her new standard of living might represent a kind of social mobility. Although no one saw concubinage as the best possible path, it was sometimes better than other options.

Concubinage blatantly commoditized women.[63] Given the dynamism of the commercial economy, there was considerable demand for concubines. Various factors determined a woman's cost.[64] A young beautiful virgin skilled at music and poetry would fetch a much higher price than someone who lacked those advantages. When a man purchased an accomplished woman, he would want to nurture her talents and put her on display for his friends. Some concubines received excellent training and went on to distinguish themselves as notable poets and painters.[65] Women born into good families that had fallen on hard times also fetched a higher price, as they were considered refined and respectable. Professional brokers licensed by the government bought and sold woman using written contracts. Binding a concubine to a master required a titular matchmaker in imitation of a marriage ceremony. The sale also had to be registered with the local government.

Concubinage affected household dynamics. De facto polygyny had complex consequences.[66] A concubine entered the home with depressed status, so her presence elevated the status of the wife in comparison. But as people emphasized emotion as the basis of relationships, the distinction between wife and concubine eroded.[67] Moreover, the sons of concubines had inheritance rights akin to those born to wives. A concubine whose son inherited part of a large estate could achieve a respectable social position.[68] Even so, the law continued to distinguish wives and concubines. From the perspective of the state, the wife was superior by far. As in so many respects, the government tried to maintain order by enforcing clear hierarchies, while a dynamic society generated nuances and contradictions that challenged simplistic ideals.

Chapter 2

Power

According to the patriarchal ideology that structured Chinese society, all public matters were the purview of men, who expected women to remain hidden and passive. However, actual circumstances were not nearly so simple, as women also exercised various types of power. Most obviously, they had a say in many domestic matters. The family constituted the basic building block of society, so authority within the home allowed wives and mothers to influence matters central to the lives of those around them. And because kinship formed the basis of the monarchical system, the domestic power of elite women sometimes extended to influence government policy as well.

Power relations are never absolute.[1] Although human relations are usually organized as hierarchies, people constantly renegotiate dominance and submission. This fluidity sometimes provided openings for women to gain authority. In its most basic form, power can be defined as the possibility of influencing the behavior of others.[2] According to this broad definition, all social relationships involve power relations to some degree. China's political system specifically forbade women from overtly exercising power, so ambitious palace ladies had to find ways to circumvent these strictures to gain prestige and influence. To empower themselves, they manipulated kinship bonds, employed wealth strategically, and displayed charisma to win support and deference.

Over the course of Chinese history, women had managed to participate in government in various ways. Some past empresses dowager had taken control of the state apparatus and reduced the emperor to a symbolic puppet. Most notably, Empress Wu Zetian (624–705) ruled as the only self-proclaimed female emperor (*huangdi*) in China's long history. Attitudes toward her unorthodox reign shaped subsequent ideas about female political power in general. Over time, views toward Empress Wu shifted.[3] Initially, historians expressed only mild criticisms of her, but her reputation declined over time. By the Ming, Wu Zetian's popular image had become extremely negative. Authors of historical fiction had no compunction about distorting and exaggerating past events, and they frequently introduced erotic and violent content to attract the attention of readers. Although Wu had in fact been a capable ruler, Ming novels portrayed her as foolish and sexually depraved. These fictionalized portraits influenced powerful men, who reacted with revulsion. Ming officials took steps to prevent other women from following in her footsteps and usurping supreme power.

In reaction to the reign of Wu Zetian, eleven of the remaining Tang emperors did not even dare to name an empress, lest a woman use this exalted position to seize power.[4] Song dynasty emperors revived the custom of granting their primary consort the title of empress, and nine of these women even ruled as regents. However, Song officials steadfastly opposed female power. They responded to any hint of ambition with fierce criticism, so in spite of the numerous female regencies in this period, by and large Song empresses behaved very cautiously and directed their energies toward uncontroversial activities. Instead of aggrandizing themselves politically, they sought praise by displaying virtue and piety, and patronizing art and religion.

The high-profile participation of women in Mongol politics alarmed Chinese men.[5] Prior to the establishment of the Yuan dynasty, the daughters and wives of Chinggis (Genghis) Khan had played key roles in governing conquered territories, thereby freeing up high-ranking men to undertake distant campaigns. After the conquest of China, Mongol palace women did not bother to conceal themselves and appeared openly at court. They continued to practice nomadic martial pursuits such as archery and riding. Yuan empresses controlled considerable wealth and received income from personal domains. Some advised male leaders or tried to influence the imperial succession.

When the Ming dynasty began, some ethnic groups in China's southern border region had female leaders.[6] These women usually inherited a leadership position from their fathers. In some societies, if a leader died without a male heir, a wife or daughter might assume his position. In other instances, a woman took over leadership because a ruler had become old or sickly. Chinese literati looked askance at the female rulers in neighboring tribes and kingdoms. They considered these unapologetic displays of female power alien, unorthodox, and emblematic of barbarism.

Ming fiction popularized negative stereotypes of powerful women. Authors rewrote some historical vignettes to associate infamous beauties of the past with malevolent fox spirits. In these stories, a fox assumes the guise of an alluring temptress to lure a powerful man to his doom.[7] The infamous royal consort Daji had long been blamed for contributing to the fall of the ancient

Shang dynasty. Ming fiction intensified her evil image by turning her into a malicious fox who had assumed human form. As authors introduced a fox element into these sorts of stories, they made powerful women seem strange and sinister.

The founder of the Ming considered palace women a potential threat to the stability of the dynasty, so he set down rules to restrain empresses and other imperial consorts. For example, Hongwu repudiated the Mongol custom of allowing women to openly attend court audiences. He also forbade women from serving as regents to keep them from the center of power. These regulations successfully checked the ambitions of palace women, and Ming empresses were generally passive.[8]

Hongwu set down other safeguards against female aspirations as well.[9] Although he believed that an emperor should name his wife as empress as a way to promote marriage, which he valued as a constructive institution, the dynasty's rulers deliberately recruited their wives from relatively unimportant families. In doing so, they reduced the prestige of empresses and made it difficult for consort kinsmen to accrue power. Moreover, Hongwu declared that only an emperor's son by a principle wife could inherit the throne. Due to this provision, Ming emperors frequently deposed a childless empress and replaced her with the mother of the eldest son. Five rulers deposed or divorced their empresses. The ease with which emperors switched empresses degraded them, making them very insecure. They behaved very cautiously to avoid being deposed.

Changes in the nature of government reduced the chances that an empress or her kinsmen could dominate the government. The adoption of professionalized bureaucratic government during the Song dynasty had shifted the balance of power.[10] Henceforth, links to the throne did not guarantee high office. Overall, power shifted toward bureaucrats unrelated to the ruler. Political marriage thus became a less effective strategy for emperors to gain allies, so they took their empresses from low-ranking families. Because the kinsmen of emperors were no longer politically useful, it made sense for emperors to select wives from a modest background, whose relatives would be least likely to cause trouble.

More broadly, the ruling elite of the early Ming strove to enforce gender hierarchy among the populace. Placing men definitively above women would help contain female power in society at large and also discourage female participation in affairs of state. Accordingly, Ming law and administration systematically identified women not as unique individuals, but according to the major kinship roles of daughter, wife, and mother, all of which were theoretically subservient to a male kinsman. Officials expected women to behave in ways appropriate for these standardized personas.

Scholars used historical discourse to thwart the ambitions of palace women.[11] In 1403 the Jianwen emperor, second ruler of the dynasty, wrote the preface to a collection of women's biographies. Since the beginning of the imperial system, the biographies of empresses in the historical annals had been composed in a standardized format that depicted them according to moral stereotypes. The same held true for the Ming. Canonical accounts depicted the dynasty's early empresses as virtuous to the point of sainthood. However, when an emperor displayed partiality to a woman other than his empress, these favorites ended up being portrayed as vicious and depraved. The Confucian scholars writing history considered imperial favorites unorthodox and potentially dangerous, and they manipulated the dynasty's historical accounts to illustrate their point of view.

Given this intolerance of female ambition, any woman who tried to participate in politics ended up being roundly condemned. Such was the fate of the Xuande emperor's wife Empress Sun (1399–1462). Although Sun does not seem to have been immoral or ill intentioned, because she tried to influence certain government matters, imperial historians censured her. This historiographic custom acted to restrain palace women. Every empress knew that if she tried to exercise power, she would go down in history as a wicked monster. The desire to be praised by future generations served as an incentive for palace ladies to keep a low profile.

The education of palace women also encouraged them to be passive and benign. In spite of Hongwu's low opinion of scholarly activities, he ordered the compilation of a work called *Admonishments for Women* (*Nü jie*).[12] Although this book had the same title as one by the famous Han dynasty polymath Ban Zhao (45–ca. 116), the contents differed. While Ban had targeted her ethical guide to ordinary wives, Hongwu intended this homage as a textbook for palace women. The authors drew together examples from previous dynasties to argue that women should refrain from participating in government affairs. They also denigrated women other than empresses who gained imperial favor, depicting them as devious and dangerous. The text put particular stress on the negative example of Wu Zetian, portraying her as the archetypal evil consort. To provide women with a positive alternative, Empress Xu (1362–1407), wife of the Yongle emperor, wrote *Instructions for the Inner Quarters* (*Nei xun*). This book declared the author's commitment to virtue and set down contemporary understandings of female ethics.[13]

Early Ming rulers weakened palace women in a far more violent way as well. In a stunning violation of Confucian principles, the first five emperors of the dynasty practiced human sacrifice.[14] Despite official denunciations of the Yuan regime as foreign and unorthodox, the early Ming rulers followed

Mongol custom in sacrificing minor palace women to follow a deceased emperor to the afterlife. Perhaps they used human sacrifice as a way to emphasize their supreme rank. The peasant origins of the Ming emperor were a perpetual source of embarrassment, and human sacrifice dramatically demonstrated the social preeminence of the ruling line. Moreover, killing palace women reduced them to chattel, degrading them to such a degree that they would be unlikely to influence important matters.

When the Hongwu emperor's second son died prematurely, two of his concubines were sacrificed and interred with him. When Hongwu himself later died, he was accompanied to the grave by forty sacrificed minor consorts. Eventually Yingzong abolished this cruel practice. Besides wanting to observe Confucian dictates and bring Ming mortuary practices in line with those of previous native dynasties, it seems that Yingzong also had personal reasons for ending these murders. His grandmother Empress Dowager Zhang (1379–1442) had given Yingzong sage advice in his youth, and he became a capable ruler by putting her teachings into practice. Yingzong considered his grandmother prudent and virtuous. Her beneficent influence seems to have given him a high opinion of palace women in general, so he did not want to see them murdered. But after Yingzong put an end to human sacrifice, this practice still affected people's thinking. The early Ming emperors had shown their contempt for palace women and permanently degraded their position.

Although the Ming political establishment feared strong empresses, weakening them gave rise to unforeseen problems. In most eras, empresses dowager usually worked together with high officials to keep eunuchs from accruing too much power. Negating the powers of palace women thus created a vacuum when the ruler was young or weak. During the reigns of weak emperors, eunuchs repeatedly usurped authority and effectively took over the government.[15] Historians consider the periods of Ming dynasty eunuch rule some of the most terrible episodes in China's political history. Eunuchs gained authority by weakening the legitimate mechanics of good government, so their ascendency was always synonymous with corruption and despotism. Moreover, when castrated men dominated the government, the gentry had fewer opportunities to serve in high office, so they withdrew their backing for the dynasty. Deteriorating administrative competence coupled with a loss of support hastened the eventual collapse of the Ming. Although the dynasty's emperors feared the consequences of female power, the rise of eunuchs demonstrated the problems that could arise when the position of palace women declined too much.

The Ming palace mostly used systems and rules set down in previous eras. These time-tested institutions had proven effective, so employing them was the surest way to make palace administration a success.[16] As before, the emperor had a large harem, as befitted his unique status.[17] These women did more than just provide amusement. Sexual encounters with multiple women made it more likely that the emperor would produce an heir. Although the inner palace housed numerous concubines, the emperors of previous dynasties had often focused their attentions on just one woman. In contrast, Ming officials, eunuchs, and empresses dowager all encouraged the ruler to spread his attentions widely among the harem.[18] Usually one woman served as empress, another was the emperor's favorite of the moment, and a third was mother of the heir. Dividing prestige among three or more women helped prevent one of them from seizing control of the government. However, this strategy had drawbacks. Pitting palace women against one another provoked jealousy and intrigue. Moreover, this arrangement meant that most empresses did not bear sons, complicating the succession.

Various titles marked the specific ranks of consorts. The principle wife of the emperor was titled empress (*huanghou*). In the early part of the dynasty, only the wife of a deceased emperor could be elevated to empress dowager (*huang taihou*) upon his death. Later, the birth mother of a reigning emperor also received the appellation empress dowager. Due to this change, two women could hold this title simultaneously. In earlier eras, competition between two or more dowagers had sometimes given rise to political instability. However, Ming empresses dowager were relatively weak, so they rarely caused problems. They had largely devolved into icons of universal motherhood. The emperors treated them with respect in public, as a way of demonstrating their filial virtue, but did not usually allow them a voice in policy matters. Only three women ever held the title grand empress dowager (*taihuang taihou*), which they obtained when a grandson ascended the throne. Lower ranking consorts also had numerous titles. From the mid-fifteenth century, rulers designated one favorite as imperial honored consort (*huang guifei*).[19] The holder of this title ranked above her peers and was almost equal in status to the empress. The unusual practice of giving a lesser consort so much prestige undermined the empress.

Thousands of people resided in and around the palace, so this huge establishment required a sophisticated bureaucratic system to manage routine matters. The numerous ranks of minor consorts established a clear hierarchy among them.[20] A consort's rank determined every aspect of her life, from the size of her quarters to the clothing she wore. Unlike previous dynasties, the titles of Ming consorts were not considered equivalent to grades in the male bureaucracy. The Ming rulers thus reduced the importance of consorts by avoiding comparisons between palace ladies and government ministers.

Seven major departments oversaw palace administration. Earlier dynasties had successfully used female officials to help run the palace, and the Ming continued this custom. Whereas uncastrated men and eunuchs still took care of many matters, women could move freely throughout the inner palace, so it made sense to put them in charge of tasks within the female quarters. Women accordingly staffed the seven palace departments.[21]

Two types of women served as palace administrators: unmarried commoners and talented palace women.[22] In the early Ming, the palace recruited female officials from the region around the southern capital. After the seat of government was moved to Beijing, most female officials came from the north. As in the regular civil service, a female palace official could be promoted to a higher rank. This possibility inspired ambitious women to study and work hard so that they could become eligible for promotion. A particularly competent woman might be assigned to manage a specific palace compound of a prince, princess, or consort. If a woman handled the living arrangements of a prince, she received the title madam (*furen*), which placed her just below an imperial consort in rank. However, female officials were usually of relatively low birth, so the emperor's consorts often treated them rudely. During factional battles, female palace officials were considered expendable and often ended up as victims.

Although the myriad consorts usually had little to do with important matters, emperors sometimes used the harem to achieve practical ends. Hongwu employed this institution to further his foreign policy objectives.[23] To help stabilize China's northern borders, he followed Yuan precedent and took Mongol and Korean women into the palace. In this way, he built direct links with potentially troublesome Mongol khans and the king of Korea, bringing these regions more firmly into China's sphere of influence. However, xenophobic officials disliked the presence of foreign women within the symbolic center of the state. They argued that Chinese and foreigners were fundamentally incompatible and should not mix so intimately. Eventually the Ming abandoned this policy in the face of widespread criticism.

While ordinary people may have envied the luxurious lifestyle of palace ladies, the elite did not want their daughters to become imperial consorts. A gentry family usually had more to gain from in-laws in the civil service who could provide educational assistance and useful connections. The Zhengde emperor, notable for his dissipation, abused the palace concubine system to extort money from wealthy families.[24] Starting in 1517, he began taking unusually large numbers of women from highborn families into the palace. Some became consorts, but most were mere captives confined on the palace grounds until their families ransomed them. If a woman's family failed to redeem her, she would be sent to work in the palace laundry. Conditions there were grim. Laundry women worked hard and received little food. Some died of starvation.

Women outside the palace could also receive titles. Biographies and epitaphs often refer to women as madam (*furen*), a polite appellation for a highborn lady. When a man assumed a post in the bureaucracy, his wife received a specific honorific title commensurate with his rank.[25] There were seven grades of female title, with further distinctions within each level. Women considered these titles extremely prestigious. Some biographies call a woman by one of these official titles even though she had not formally received it. In such cases, the author was simply using the appellation as a polite honorific. Titled ladies constituted the female elite of Ming society. Their unusually low mortality rate reflects the lifestyle of privilege that accompanied their exalted status. In an age when many people died young, titled women lived until age 75.36 on average.[26]

⚬━━✦━━⚬

Although Ming empresses were generally unimportant, the choice of the ruler's spouse nevertheless remained a weighty matter. In many respects the emperors observed standard Chinese marriage customs.[27] For example, they avoided marrying someone of the same surname, as this was traditionally considered a form of incest. In other ways, however, imperial marriages were distinct. Unlike the gentry, who used marriage to bind together two families of roughly equal status, emperors always had to marry down. While the rulers of previous native dynasties had usually married women from official or aristocratic families to forge connections with powerful political allies, Ming emperors took the opposite approach and selected wives from low backgrounds.[28] The dynasty's founder ordered his successors to take lowborn wives as a way to limit the power of empresses and their kinsmen.

Hongwu chose his own wife, Empress Ma (1332–1382), when he was still a commoner. Ma belonged to the family of one of the rebel leaders who helped overthrow the Yuan dynasty, and he had been Zhu Yuanzhang's superior for a time. This marriage connection helped Zhu take over leadership of the rebel army and eventually ascend the throne. After Hongwu became emperor, his wife received the title of empress in line with tradition. However, once he felt secure, Hongwu realized the dangers that wives from important families posed to the imperial house, so forbade his descendants from following his example of taking an empress from a politically significant family.

The Ming was the first native dynasty to routinely select empresses from a modest background. Most of the emperors' wives were born into low-ranking military families in the capital region. Representatives of the ruler selected a suitable candidate based on her personality and appearance. Several empresses came from families so poor that they had previously been forced to sell their daughters into concubinage. A few emperors refused to heed the injunctions of the dynasty's founder and married women from important families. As Hongwu predicted, these women's kinsmen became politically active. However, these were exceptional cases. The Ming stands out for the unusually low origins of most of the dynasty's empresses. A key dynastic principle held that the emperor's power could not be delegated to another, thus limiting the powers of the women around him. Their base background helped enforce this provision.

Because empresses mostly came from humble backgrounds, their families experienced a dramatic rise in status.[29] Close male relatives of the empress received a noble title and land grant. Initially, consort kinsmen did not receive a large domain, but over time the size increased. The family's new position depended entirely on their kinship association with the current empress. As soon as an empress died, her family's status fell considerably. Everyone knew that the elevated rank of consort kin was fleeting, so these transient gentry were not true members of the upper elite. The father and brothers of an empress knew that they would not enjoy their good fortune very long, so they used the opportunity to enrich themselves as quickly as possible. If consort kin quickly obtained enough wealth, they could become major landlords and permanently join the elite. The urgent desire to accrue wealth earned Ming consort kin a bad reputation. Some even used underhanded means to make money, such as stealing land and soliciting bribes.

The most striking fact about the Ming empresses is their overall unimportance.[30] Only Empress Ma, the first empress, had much influence over government matters while her husband was still alive.[31] Ma gained prominence largely due to her husband's limitations. Because Hongwu came from such a low background, he was illiterate. He relied heavily his trusted wife, as she could read and also had a basic familiarity with classical learning and history. Hongwu respected his wife's knowledge and sought her advice on policy and legal cases.

The official history of the dynasty describes Empress Ma in very unrealistic terms, using a litany of stock language and stereotypical images to portray her as a paragon of female virtue. They constructed this idealized portrayal in accordance with mandate-of-heaven ideology. Since antiquity it had been assumed that the first ruler of a dynasty and his wife would be extremely virtuous, while the dynasty's final ruler and his consort would display gross wickedness. Historians manipulated their accounts to assert that a dynasty's virtuous first emperor earned heaven's mandate while the final ruler lost it. They paired both of these men with women who were equally good or evil.

Historians used this model to explain the rise and fall of dynasties in moralistic terms. While historians today appreciate Empress Ma for her competence, imperial writers depicted her as a moral exemplar.

Other than Empress Ma, few Ming empresses stand out for achievements of note. One gained attention for her exotic background. Empress Ji (1451–1475), called Li Tangmei in popular stories, has a brief biography in the dynasty's official history.[32] She came from the Yao people of Guangxi in the far south and was the only ethnic Yao ever to become a Chinese empress. Li's uncommon ethnicity captured the popular imagination, and she became a character in literature. Writers spun fanciful tales of the imaginary adventures of this colorful southern beauty.

Because Hongwu forbade formal female regencies, few empresses dowager achieved much prominence at court. In spite of this injunction, one woman nevertheless managed to assume control of the government for a time. Empress Zhang (1379–1442) was the wife of the Hongxi emperor (r. 1424–1425) early in the dynasty.[33] Like most other empresses, Zhang came from a modest background, yet she was unusually well educated and informed about political matters. Her husband reigned for less than a year, and when he died, Zhang became the dynasty's first empress dowager. The lack of dynastic precedents for the conduct of empresses dowager gave Zhang considerable room to maneuver. Her son, the Xuande emperor (1425–1435), was already an adult, so she could not have declared a regency even if it had been permissible. However, Zhang had an extremely close bond with her son and she guided his actions. Xuande preferred amusements to statecraft, so he turned over authority for civil and military matters to his mother. Empress Dowager Zhang effectively ran the government for a decade under Xuande. This era stands out as one of the most peaceful and successful eras of the Ming dynasty.

After Xuande unexpectedly died, a child ascended to the throne as the Yingzong emperor (r. 1435–1449, 1457–1464). Empress Dowager Zhang and Empress Dowager Sun (1399–1462), the wife of Xuanzong, openly vied for supremacy. Ultimately, Zhang prevailed and sidelined her rival. During previous dynasties, in this sort of situation an empress dowager would have declared a regency and formed a government. Officials even invited her to become regent. However, Hongwu had strictly forbidden female regencies. Zhang knew that she would face open hostility if she became regent, so she decided to assume the powers of a regency without formally invoking one. Empress Zhang's decision to forego a regency set an important precedent, as subsequent empresses felt obliged to follow her example.

Although Zhang was not officially a regent, she behaved like one. The empress dowager solicited the cooperation of powerful forces at court to cobble together a workable coalition. Bureaucrats and eunuchs worked together to draft policies and submit them for her approval. If she agreed, Zhang would stamp the document with the type of large jade seal usually reserved for the emperor. As before, Empress Dowager Zhang handled matters prudently. In particular, she avoided criticism by limiting of her family's powers. Although her father and brothers received titles and important military positions, she kept them from accruing much authority.

The death of Empress Zhang allowed the incompetent Yingzong to manage matters himself. He foolishly decided to lead a military expedition against the Mongols and ended up being captured. The officialdom despised Yingzong, so rather than ransom him, they decided to make his younger brother the Jingtai emperor (r. 1449–1457). The Mongols soon released Yingzong, knowing that the presence of two emperors would cause instability among their enemies. Yingzong was initially placed under house arrest. Six years later, Empress Dowager Sun and her brothers led a coup that unseated Jingtai and put Yingzong back on the throne.

Empress Dowager Sun's coup and the de facto regency of Empress Dowager Zhang stand out as anomalies within the larger sweep of Ming history. In general, the dynasty's empresses and dowagers had little authority. Barred from exercising power openly, they sought respect in other ways. Many tried to construct a positive public image. An empress knew that she could gain praise by behaving in ways that appeared conspicuously virtuous. Empress Ma set an important example with her supposedly saintly behavior. She had been born into poverty, and after she became empress, she led an unusually frugal lifestyle. Ma even helped make clothing for soldiers. Observers interpreted her modest way of life as the result of virtuous restraint. Empress Ma also observed basic virtues referred to as the "way of women" (*fudao*), such as filial piety. In addition, she undertook cultured leisure activities, such as reading histories and the ancient classics, which gave her a reputation for seriousness.

Other consorts followed the example of medieval empresses and devoted themselves to religious patronage. Many Tang and Song palace women had been enthusiastic Daoists. During the Ming, however, only the formidable Empress Zhang had a close connection with Daoism.[34] Zhang was even ordained as a Daoist nun. A scroll painting that depicts her ordination shows her surrounded by supernatural figures. Notably, the emperor is absent from this scene. This deliberate omission put the emphasis on Empress Zhang herself, highlighting her independent religious identity. Cultivating an otherworldly religious persona allowed her to seem virtuous and even holy without appearing ambitious.

Pious Ming consorts usually participated in Buddhist activities.[35] Empress Xu (1362–1407), the Ming palace's most prolific author, wrote works on

Buddhism. More commonly, palace women used their wealth to build and repair temples and support monastic communities. It was also common for empresses to pay for the copying of Buddhist sutras. Empress Xu even copied them by hand herself to gain merit. Empress Li (1546–1614) was perhaps the dynasty's most enthusiastic Buddhist patron. The reign of her son Wanli stands out as the highpoint of Ming Buddhism, largely due to Li's enthusiastic patronage activities. She sponsored the construction of an impressive number of temples, singlehandedly altering China's religious landscape. However, her building spree was ruinously expensive and depleted the treasury. Although Buddhist devotees remember her fondly, historians blame her for wasting state resources at a time when many people lived in poverty.

In addition to imperial consorts, emperors' daughters had a significant presence in the palace.[36] Under some previous dynasties, princesses had many privileges. Tang princesses enjoyed great wealth, ignored ritual decorum, dominated their husbands, and even led factions at court. Song officials realized that such powerful and uninhibited women could cause problems, so the emperors of that dynasty demanded that their daughters keep a low profile. The Ming system reduced the status of princesses even further.

At the beginning of the dynasty, Hongwu used marriage as a political strategy. He married his twenty-five sons to brides from the families of generals and other important figures. Likewise, Hongwu married off his sixteen daughters to prominent officials and the sons of key supporters. After conditions stabilized, rulers no longer needed to use marriage politics to attract support. The emperors began to see their daughters not as useful assets but as potential troublemakers, so they reduced the standing of princesses. Also, important families disliked having a princess as a daughter-in-law, as they feared that she would be haughty and jealous. Rather than pairing a princess with the scion of an important official family, Ming emperors ended up marrying off most of their daughters to men of middling status in the capital region. After a princess married, she lost her privileges and lived like an ordinary commoner. Even so, when a princess died, she received a special funeral that reflected her imperial background.[37] Although marriage had reduced her status while she was alive, in death she deserved respect due to her imperial blood.

Chapter 3

Wealth

Economic transformation stands out as one of the defining characteristics of Ming history.[1] Rapid economic change forced people to quickly adapt to new and unfamiliar conditions, giving rise to new forms of social organization. When the dynasty began, the Hongwu emperor initially dreamed of realizing the utopian vision of a society made up of self-sufficient villages, as described by the ancient sage Mencius. Hongwu saw the market economy as a source of instability and inequality, and considered replacing it with a simpler system. In the end, however, he realized the futility of casting off centuries of progress. Moreover, he needed economic growth in order to rebuild his shattered nation. China's population plunged 15 percent or more under Mongol rule. Chaos at the fall of the Yuan had disrupted agriculture and commerce, leading to widespread impoverishment. Faced with these problems, Hongwu had no choice but to prioritize economic recovery.

Hongwu's officials may have been conversant with the ancient classics, but they knew almost nothing about commerce and industry. However, ignorance of practical matters did not deter them from interfering in the economy. When the dynasty began, government ministers frequently meddled in economic affairs, setting an unfortunate precedent. Henceforth, prodigal Ming emperors regarded the commercial economy as a state resource to be pillaged at their pleasure. When rulers of the dynasty needed funds to finance wars and expensive pet projects, they might persecute southern merchants and expropriate their wealth. The government also issued too much paper money in an effort to gain revenue. The currency steadily lost value, destabilizing economic life. As a result of these ruinous policies, production languished and people left the cities.

Population growth compounded these problems. China's population swelled to an unprecedented size during the Ming, and by the middle of the dynasty, some regions had become seriously overcrowded. Peasants had no choice but to work their land more intensively, and they managed to coax impressively high yields from their fields. However, due to partitive inheritance, family landholdings were subdivided into increasingly small plots every generation. Over time, the average peasant owned less and less land, and many fell into destitution.

Officials belatedly recognized the damage caused by maladministration, reversed course, and worked hard to stimulate the economy. As the state retreated from the economic sphere, private enterprise took the lead. Manufacturing became increasingly sophisticated, and production rose. Merchants knit the entire nation together into a single domestic market, allowing diverse regions to exchange a plethora of products. Moreover, exports brought in a massive infusion of silver from abroad that allowed more people to participate in the monetary economy. The resulting economic changes were so dramatic that some historians have compared the importance of the late Ming to the momentous Tang–Song transition that gave rise to modern China.

New economic and social conditions forced people to abandon time-tested assumptions and explore new ways to think and act. They adopted novel perspectives toward money and status. In the past, certain kinds of poverty had been considered acceptable and even virtuous. As society became more materialistic, however, people came to look on poverty as a disgrace. In addition, intensifying economic competition forced the gentry to contend with wealthy merchants for supremacy. Parvenus could even purchase the accoutrements of the literati lifestyle, such as antiques and elegant gardens, threatening the traditional elite's monopoly on high culture. Competition with savvy merchants made the gentry feel insecure. They had to find new ways to maintain their privileged position within an increasingly dynamic society.

While many individuals fell into penury, society as a whole became increasingly prosperous. What had previously been considered luxuries were now quotidian items. The ready availability of so many goods sparked a consumer revolution. Rising consumption altered women's lives. Craftsmen produced numerous consumer items specifically for female consumers.[2] The new materialistic ambiance made female life increasingly comfortable and even sumptuous. Wealthy women found themselves on the vanguard of the late Ming consumer revolution, and they became an important economic force. Female demand for quality products spurred further economic development. The culture of consumption also affected women's social identity, allowing them to manipulate their clothing and surroundings to construct a carefully tuned public image.

Because women had fewer opportunities than men to engage in productive labor, they usually obtained the bulk of their wealth from their families.

Historians have long debated the basic nature of the Chinese property system and have yet to come to a consensus. While some scholars allege that all family members, female as well as male, owned household wealth in common, others insist that it belonged only to men.[3] Song dynasty Neo-Confucians such as Zhu Xi had envisioned the family as centered on the patrilineal line of descent. During the Yuan dynasty, the state had embraced Neo-Confucian views regarding family matters, and the Ming government maintained similar values. This restrictive view of kinship justified restricting inheritance to men as much as possible to prevent the withdrawal of wealth from the male line.

In spite of growing Neo-Confucian influence, Hongwu considered daughters to be integral members of their natal families. Because of his peasant origins, he had little interest in rarified philosophy or the classical rites. Instead, he viewed family matters from a grassroots perspective grounded in emotion and pragmatism. Hongwu accordingly ordered major changes to official regulations on mourning, decreeing that daughters were to mourn their parents in the same manner as sons.[4] This shift had considerable significance. People relied on the elaborate and carefully calibrated mourning system to distinguish the precise degree of propinquity among family members. For daughters to extensively mourn their parents incorporated them more firmly into the heart of the family of their birth.

Contrary forces affected female kinship identity. Even as ritual raised the position of daughters, other forces drove the state to disinherit them. Women's inheritance rights had reached an apex under the Song dynasty.[5] During the Northern Song, an unmarried daughter inherited a sum equal to half the value of a brother's betrothal gift to provide her with a decent dowry. Under Southern Song law, daughters exercised an even greater claim on family wealth. A woman inherited half the value of a brother's total share of her parents' estate. This arrangement assumed that a daughter had a claim to her parents' estate independent of dowry.

The inheritance rights of daughters plummeted during the Yuan dynasty. Authorities embraced Neo-Confucian family concepts favoring men, leading them to believe that daughters had no right to family wealth. If a woman had brothers, she normally did not inherit anything from her parents.[6] The dramatic disjunction in inheritance law between the Southern Song and Yuan abruptly deprived Chinese women of the most generous inheritance rights they had ever enjoyed. Instead, they were left with nothing. During the Ming, officials once again allowed daughters to inherit a share of their parents' estate sufficient to fund a suitable dowry.[7] Otherwise, Ming inheritance law followed Yuan system precedents regarding women. Other than dowry, a daughter who had brothers did not receive any family wealth.

If an unmarried woman had no brothers, when her parents died, the government classified the family as an "extinct household" (*juehu*). This seems to have been the fate of between 6 and 12 percent of families each generation.[8] During the Tang dynasty, when the state declared a household extinguished due to lack of male heirs, relatives oversaw disposal of the estate. They were to sell off all the main assets, including land, and pay for the funeral of the deceased. By the late Tang, all remaining assets were to go to the extinct family's daughters.[9] However, women's claim on an extinct household's assets declined substantially during the Yuan era.[10] At that time, daughters received only one-third of the extinct household's assets, and the state confiscated the remainder. Ming law was more generous toward daughters.[11] As during the Tang, daughters inherited the entirety of an extinct estate. Moreover, all daughters received an equal share of the assets, regardless of whether they had already married. Only if an extinguished family had neither sons nor daughters would the government confiscate the estate.

The inheritance rights of wives also declined over time. A Song dynasty widow could inherit from her husband under certain circumstances. Women lost this possibility under Yuan law, and Ming authorities maintained these reduced rights.[12] If a widow had a son, he would inherit the entire estate. However, a son was legally obligated to obey his mothers and care for her. Nor could sons divide up the family patrimony as long as their mother remained alive. They had to continue living with her until her death.[13] Moreover, if the son was a minor at the time of his father's death, the widow would act as the estate's custodian until her son came of age. Some surviving contracts for the sale of family land note that a boy's mother had approved the transaction, demonstrating her active stewardship of the estate. In theory, if a widow remarried, she had to cede control of her deceased husband's property to his relatives. Occasionally, however, a widow managed to bring a new groom into her deceased husband's home to serve as a foster father (*yifu*) to her son.[14] Regardless of law, custom, and kinship rules, women sometimes found ways to circumvent convention and arrange matters to favor their own interests.

About one-fifth of families lacked a son.[15] In such cases, the widow still did not inherit the estate. If she declined to remarry, she would serve as custodian of her deceased husband's property for the rest of her life. The law required her to select one of her husband's nephews as the heir who would eventually receive the property when she died. The designated heir had to be approved by the head of her husband's lineage. A nephew was posthumously adopted to maintain the husband's family line and hold the estate together. This procedure reduced the inheritance rights of daughters by preventing them from inheriting, even if they lacked brothers.

A young widow might live on for decades. Her ambiguous position as custodian of the estate, but not owner, could be awkward. In spite of the legal obligation to appoint an heir, some women resisted taking this step for fear that the heir might seize the estate while she was still alive. If a widow had a particularly bad relationship with her in-laws, she might pass over her husband's kinsmen and adopt an unrelated boy as his heir. This was illegal, however, and her husband's kinsmen would likely bring a lawsuit to expel an illegitimate heir. A deceased man's kinsmen often fretted that the widow might fritter away the estate or covertly pass it on to others, and disagreements about property managed by widows frequently gave rise to litigation. Documents record cases in which a widow sold off land from her husband's estate, so these concerns were not groundless.[16] Sometimes a man's relatives simply seized land from his widow by force.[17]

The position of concubines in the inheritance system changed over time. Although concubines could not inherit from their masters under the Tang system, they gained some basic rights during the Song.[18] At that time, if a deceased man left behind neither child nor wife, his concubine could take the place of a spouse. She did not inherit the estate, but she could manage it as long as she lived. Like a widow, she was expected to designate an heir who would receive the property after her passing. The standing of concubines declined during the Yuan, and the *Great Ming Code* lacks this generous provision, in line with Yuan precedent. Ming law took great care to distinguish concubines from wives, as jurists did not want to the two roles to be confused.[19]

The rising cult of chastity affected concubines' property rights. If a man lacked a wife and his concubine declared herself chaste after his death, she might take on the role of widow and obtain custodial rights over his estate for the remainder of her life.[20] In theory, a concubine's son was the child of his father's wife, not his birth mother. Because of this useful fiction, a concubine's son was entitled to the same share of his father's property as sons born to the wife. A widow sometimes adopted the son of her husband's concubine and made him heir to the estate.[21] This way she maintained the continuity of his family line, assumed the honored role of mother, and had a male offspring to manage the family property and support her in old age.

<hr/>

Aside from inheritance, an unmarried woman might also receive a share of her natal family's estate to finance her dowry. The amount and significance of dowry changed over time. In antiquity, dowry was considered unimportant. The classical rites stressed the betrothal gift as essential for a proper wedding but did not even mention dowry. Initially bridewealth (a gift from the family of the groom to that of the bride) far outweighed dowry in value, but the relative amounts of these two sums switched during the Song dynasty. At that time, the gentry offered large dowries to attract a son-in-law with good prospects, and dowry remained far more valuable than bridewealth during the Ming. By that time, betrothal gifts were often merely symbolic items without much tangible worth.

Dowry endowed women with their own resources. A woman who entered marriage with her own assets had higher status and more autonomy within her husband's family.[22] However, this custom had negative consequences as well.[23] Some anthropologists see dowry as a justification for disinheriting women and excluding them from co-ownership of family wealth.[24] Weddings were preceded by intense haggling over the dowry, and many women had their marriages delayed while their families struggled to come up with the requisite sum. This problem affected not just the poor but those of middling means as well. If the groom's side was disappointed with the amount the bride brought with her, they might sue their new in-laws. The crushing expense of dowry drove many parents to kill newborn daughters, eliciting widespread alarm.[25]

While dowry had been the most important factor in marriage finance during the Song era, the Yuan government had a very different perspective on the matter. The Mongols traditionally did not dower their daughters. Instead, a wife received a share of a husband's property to manage, often after the birth of her first child. When Mongol conquerors established the Yuan legal system, they stressed only betrothal gifts in compliance with native customs.[26] Ethnic Han continued to dower their daughters generously during the Yuan, but they did so outside of the official marriage system endorsed by the state. The Ming state subsequently revived Song practices and assumed that brides would receive a generous dowry.

Song dynasty law gave a woman permanent ownership of her dowry. If she returned to her natal home or remarried, she could take this wealth with her.[27] The situation changed drastically during the Yuan. Mongol custom held that a widow should enter a levirate marriage with a husband's relative.[28] Traditionally, the Mongols considered it unthinkable that a woman would remove valuables from a family, and this assumption shaped Yuan law. In that era, if a husband expelled his wife without cause, she could bring her dowry. However, in 1303 it was decreed that a widow who remarried could not take her dowry with her.[29] She had to leave it behind, and it became the property of her deceased husband's family. Whether intentional or not, this provision made it very costly for a widow to remarry, and thus helps account for the notable increase in widow chastity from the Yuan dynasty onward. The Ming maintained this Yuan provision regarding dowry.[30] If a widow remarried, her in-laws not only gained control of her deceased husband's estate but took her dowry as well.

Because the rites did not regulate dowry, the amount and contents varied considerably, depending on social status, wealth, and region.[31] The couple's parents carefully negotiated the precise details prior to announcing the engagement and set down their agreement in a written marriage contract.[32] The most significant dowries included arable land.[33] Families valued dowry land because they could farm these fields or rent them out to produce a reliable return. Eventually, the land would be passed down to a woman's children. If a family dowered their daughter with land, she would have to marry someone nearby so that she could manage it. This practice encouraged intermarriage of the landed elite in each place.

Women owned their dowries and could use this wealth however they wanted. Some sold off land for cash, while others bought more land as an investment.[34] The wording of contracts of sale shows that women had full ownership of dowry land. They could buy and sell this property themselves without having to use a husband or son as an intermediary. Women used their dowry wealth in various ways.[35] Some invested their capital in a shop or set up a small business. Many kept the sum intact to guarantee their future security. A widow with a sufficient dowry could forego remarriage and remain chaste. Women often drew on their dowries to pay for emergency expenses, such as medicine or funerals. Many spent their dowries on their families. Gentry wives often used dowry wealth to finance the education of a husband or son, hoping that he might gain an official post and raise the family's standard of living. If a woman took over responsibility for a household, she might have to use her dowry to pay taxes on behalf of the entire household.

In addition to receiving assets from their natal families as inheritance and dowry, women earned money on their own. Although gentry ladies did not have to do productive labor, the average woman worked very hard. Even though the commercial economy grew rapidly in this era, China was still overwhelmingly agricultural, and working women usually labored on farms. Rapid population increase led to the fragmentation of landholdings, so most farming families had to struggle very hard to survive on a small plot.

Changes in the land-use system had altered women's relationship with farmland. During the medieval era, the government allocated land-use rights. Under the so-called equal field system, women received a share of arable land, so they regularly performed all sorts of agricultural tasks. However, as the economy developed and productivity rose, female labor was no longer essential to support the agricultural economy, so fewer women labored in the grain fields.[36] Instead, textile production became the most important type of female domestic labor. This shift turned out to be economically rational.[37] Beginning in the late Ming era, the demand for homespun cloth increased. As a result, the value of women's labor rose, making their families more prosperous and helping to integrate them into the cash economy.

In spite of the overall shift toward spinning and weaving, some women continued to participate in agriculture. The female members of peasant families often helped process the family's crop by threshing and milling grain.[38] Some Ming dynasty gazetteers even mention women working in the grain fields.[39] Families with the fewest resources made the most demands on their female members. If a family was too poor to afford a water buffalo, women might even help with the laborious task of manual plowing.[40] Ideas about the propriety of women working in agriculture varied considerably by region. While some places considered agriculture solely a male preserve, others expected women to work in the fields. Hakka women in particular were known for doing all sorts of agricultural work.[41] Because Hakkas expected their women to perform demanding labor in the fields, they rarely bound their daughters' feet.

Textile work was traditionally considered the most important type of female labor. People expected women to spin thread, weave cloth, and sew garments. In earlier eras, when households strove for self-sufficiency, women rarely sold what they produced. The rise of the commercial economy provided them with new opportunities to profit from their labor.[42] Not only could more people afford to buy cloth and clothing, but also urban women working in specialized professions did not want to make their own clothing, as they could use their time more profitably. These trends increased the demand for readymade cloth. It became much easier for women to sell the textiles they produced, enabling them to earn cash. Even as women began to profit from spinning and weaving, literati continued to depict this activity as a virtuous expression of diligence and frugality.[43] By making cloth, women could simultaneously earn money and also garner praise.

Cotton became a more popular material at this time, affecting the nature of textile production.[44] Although Chinese farmers had produced small amounts of cotton in antiquity, it did not become a major commodity until the twelfth century. The Yuan government successfully promoted the cotton industry, and by the Ming dynasty, farmers across China were growing this cash crop. Peasant women did most of the spinning and weaving that turned raw cotton fibers into salable cloth. The countryside also constituted the main market for inexpensive cotton garments. Women produced cotton textiles to clothe their families and sold excess cloth to earn money. Small-scale production suited the social conventions of the time. Women were becoming increasingly reclusive and wanted to hide from the humiliating gazes of strange men. Making thread and cloth at home allowed them to participate in the commercial economy while remaining demurely concealed. Women in some places, such as the region around the mouth of the Yangtze River, specialized in the production of cotton cloth, and this female household industry became central to the local economy.

In the late Ming dynasty, economic advances altered the structure of the textile industry. The emergence of a prosperous consumer class created immense demand for readymade cloth and garments. Eventually women ended up becoming the victims of their own success.[45] Because they built up this industry and made it highly profitable, male artisans entered the field to take advantage of these new opportunities. Male labor altered the structure of textile production. Men introduced large sums of capital, professional management, expensive technology, and economies of scale. Production shifted away from rural women working part time to male professionals laboring in urban workshops. Male entrepreneurs did not hire female workers, nor did women want to leave their homes and place themselves under the authority of unknown men. As men encroached on textile manufacturing, women gradually lost control over the most profitable type of traditional female labor.

Even as women lost ground in cloth manufacture, they could earn money by ornamenting clothing with detailed embroidery.[46] Technological innovations made Ming embroidery more varied and delicate than before. Women had access to finer threads in a wider range of colors, and they invented a larger repertoire of stitches. These improvements allowed Ming embroiderers to elevate their craft to an unprecedented level of excellence. Women did most embroidery, allowing them to dominate a highly skilled line of lucrative work. Embroidery was far more than just a trivial pastime or a way for girls to prepare their dowry. It was an extremely valuable commodity. A richly embroidered piece of cloth could fetch a high price. When a woman created an elaborate piece of embroidery, she was adding to her store of accumulated wealth. She knew that if she ever needed money for an emergency, she could sell off some embroidered items and earn ready cash. Moreover, women who devoted their spare time to embroidery also earned respect. Poets lauded embroiderers as models of female talent and virtue. And many women seem to have enjoyed creating beautiful handwork. Even though needlework could be tedious, it allowed housebound women an outlet for their creativity.

Custom excluded women from most forms of work, and female reclusion was on the rise. Nevertheless, women performed many sorts of labor outside the home.[47] Numerous female vendors hawked goods in urban markets. Unlike

male merchants, who often traveled widely and engaged in wholesale transactions, female commerce was usually confined to small-scale peddling. Yet
even if a woman just wanted to hawk inexpensive goods by the roadside,
she needed some capital to get started. Most women had few assets at their
disposal, so they usually worked in the service sector if they needed to make
money. For example, they might cook food and attend to customers in restaurants and tea houses, as this required little capital.

People looked askance at many stereotypical female professions and
regarded them as morally dubious. Traditionally many shamans had been
female. Although this sort of popular religion was increasingly derided, it
could still provide income.[48] Other women worked as midwives and healers.
Female medical professionals did not receive the systematic training expected
of male physicians. Instead of reading medical texts, they usually learned
about disease and medicine by listening to oral lore. Male physicians looked
down on female healers and considered them ignorant and dangerous. Match-
making was another job for women.[49] Ancient ritual texts demanded that the
ceremonies solemnizing a marriage include a matchmaker. Go-betweens
played more than just a symbolic role. Although families actively negotiated
marriages, a well-connected matchmaker might provide useful information
and introductions, expanding the possible range of marriage partners. Although matchmakers could be useful, they had a bad reputation. Ming fiction
portrays them as untrustworthy liars.

In fact, most female professions carried a stigma, as women who worked
outside the home appeared greedy and licentious. By crossing the threshold
of the house, they transgressed the bounds of propriety. Although a woman
could earn money by leaving home, defying social norms earned her oppro-
brium. When a woman decided whether or not she would work outside, she
had to weigh the value of her potential earnings against the damage that her
behavior would inflict on the reputations of herself and her family.

Nevertheless, there were ways for women to earn money without endan-
gering their social standing. Some talented women monetized their mastery
of cultured activities. During the late Ming dynasty, Zhou Zhibiao became a
successful editor and publisher, putting out books in various genres that sold
well.[50] She understood women's taste in literature and made money by issuing works that appealed to a female audience, such as the scripts of popular
dramas and collections of women's poems.

The talented painter Wen Shu (1595–1634) also managed to turn a profit,
even as she remained cloistered. Her distinguished family had fallen on hard
times, so she sold her paintings to help her family maintain a respectable
standard of living.[51] Wen also taught painting to other gentry women to earn
money. She specialized in stereotypically feminine paintings of flowers and

insects done in a delicate and colorful style. Unlike the paintings of literati amateurs, she rarely added dedications or poems, marking these pieces as commercial works. Wen avoided landscapes and other literati genres to avoid criticism from jealous male rivals. She became so successful that she eventually brought in assistants to maintain a steady output. Forgeries of Wen's works were already being made while she was alive, testifying to her works' monetary value.

Wen Shu's family enthusiastically promoted her as a model woman of talent. Her father and daughter marketed paintings on her behalf. They cleverly branded her works, raising the price and ensuring steady demand. Wen was marketed not as an anomalous genius, but as the most recent representative of a long tradition of painters in her family. The family's beautiful garden was declared the source of her inspiration. She carefully legitimized her work by linking it to the traditions of a respected literati family. Moreover, by publicly promoting the family's beautiful garden and their long dedication to refined activities, she managed to raise their collective social standing. Wen Shu stands out for having successfully positioned herself as a talented woman who worked in the public eye without attracting criticism. Even as her paintings circulated freely and garnered praise, she prudently secluded herself at home, thereby maintaining a reputation for integrity.

Very few people possessed such outstanding talent. More commonly, working women assumed lowly positions in the economic order. Although the number of bondservants seems to have been decreasing, there were still considerable numbers of people with this servile status, and many were women.[52] Bondservants constituted a debased class with restricted rights. Although they had been purchased, unlike slaves, their status was temporary. After a set period of time, a bondservant became free. Policies toward female bondservants (*binü*) changed over time. During the wars leading up to national reunification and the founding of the Ming dynasty, soldiers captured many free women and sold them as bondservants. Other women were sold into servitude by family members in response to war, destitution, or natural disasters.

Early Ming authorities considered the large numbers of servile women a potential source of social instability. They tried to liberate female bondservants and return them to their families. To do so, the government decreed that only officials could legally own bondservants, making this a perk of government service. In theory, the number of bondservants an official could own depended on his rank. Because of these regulations, people associated the ownership of bondservants with high status.

The Ming government failed to limit the number of bondservants, as the wealthy continued to purchase them. As the economy developed, the number of rich merchants able to afford bondservants increased. It became common for affluent men to buy large numbers of bondservants as a way to flaunt their wealth. Ming fiction describes rich men attended by retinues of bondservants at all times. The government eventually accepted the inevitable presence of bondservants in homes of the wealthy. Authorities even used Buddhist doctrine to justify bondservents' debased status. They argued that karma determines a person's social position, so a bondservant's lowly state constituted punishment for sins committed in a former life. They also defined the relationship between master and bondservant using Confucian ethical concepts, arguing that people interact as superiors and inferiors.

Masters treated their bondservants in various ways. Some were very strict and others kind. Although bondservants had very low status, they rarely did productive work, so their lives were not necessarily difficult. Most were just displayed as status symbols. In fact, becoming a bondservant could elevate a woman's status. A woman from a destitute family who entered servitude would likely enjoy a better standard of living and light workload. Sometimes masters treated these women with empathy and affection, despite their difference in status. Mistresses wrote poems that described their bondservants as vivacious, innocent, and loveable. Owners sometimes even mourned the death of a favorite bondservant. Some wealthy ladies took a benevolent interest in the welfare of these dependents. They saw that their female bondservants received a basic education and were eventually married off to a decent husband. A bondservant did not have the right to arrange her own marriage. If her master decided that she should get married, she would have to wed the person selected for her. She did not have the right to refuse.

In the demimonde of entertainment and sexual services, women worked in various capacities, ranging from ragged prostitutes to refined courtesans skilled at music and dance. It seems that many poor women worked as prostitutes, and brothels were probably ubiquitous. However, these women lived in the shadows. The sort of people who wrote about their society ignored people of such a lowly station, so not much is known about them.[53] In contrast, skilled courtesans had a high profile, hobnobbed with the wealthy and educated, and influenced the development of Ming culture.

Originally, performance was not a commodity in China. In antiquity, people entertained themselves and those around them by playing musical instruments and singing. The wealthy could enjoy the performances of trained slaves or concubines in their homes. During the medieval era, the performing arts became linked to prostitution, and professional entertainers performed for customers in restaurants, bars, tea houses, and bordellos. During the Ming dynasty, economic growth increased the demand for skilled courtesans and other female performers.[54] There were probably more than one million prostitutes, courtesans, and professional entertainers in China at the time. The late Ming marks the highpoint of courtesan culture, which was most sophisticated in the prosperous lower Yangtze River delta region.

Courtesans stood at the apex of the entertainment world, performing in luxurious surroundings for wealthy clients.[55] The commoditization of entertainment raised the level of female artistry. These women underwent years of intensive training, and they were required to master music, dance, and perhaps poetry composition. They also learned the art of small talk, allowing them to put their customers at ease and create a convivial atmosphere. Famous courtesans were considered celebrities, and meeting one was no simple matter. A potential client had to gain an introduction from a trusted contact to enter this mysterious realm.

As before, the law continued to classify people as either good (*liang*) or base (*jian*). Officials considered entertainment a degrading profession, so they regarded courtesans as base people. Even the most famous performer suffered low legal status and reduced protections. Officials also tried to regulate courtesans' behavior to keep them from overstepping the boundaries of their station. In theory, courtesans could not dress like respectable gentry wives or entertain government functionaries. However, these measures proved unenforceable. Literati could raise their profile by socializing with famous courtesans, so they were constantly attended by ambitious men who treated them with respect and shielded them from indignities. Courtesans dressed in expensive clothing, hobnobbed with the elite, and presented themselves as women of privilege.

In spite of the glamorous façade, courtesans had hard lives. They had been born into poor families. Their parents had sold them to the manager of an entertainment establishment at a young age, so they were akin to bondservants. These women suffered through a long course of rigorous training, had little personal autonomy, and could be beaten for unsatisfactory behavior. Even so, in an era of widespread poverty and exploitation, many women would have considered the courtesan's life a decent option. It was certainly not the worst possible path in life for a poor woman. An atmosphere of glamor and exclusivity helped compensate for the hardships. Successful courtesans could also make money and obtain a degree of comfort and financial stability.

During the late Ming, when courtesans were most numerous and celebrated, they exerted a major impact on cultural life.[56] Although courtesans had been born poor, some received an extensive education akin to that of gentry ladies. The most refined performers were conversant in poetry and even had some knowledge of history and the ancient classics. Their clients expected elite courtesans to have mastered ten accomplishments: elegance, refinement, literature, art, singing, musical instruments, good taste, romantic charm, professional charm, and an aesthetic sense.[57] As these cultivated women socialized with important men, they influenced their clients' ideas about painting, poetry, food, and other refined pursuits.

Some courtesans gained fame for painting and calligraphy.[58] Although most Ming female painters were from literati families, a surprising number came from relatively low backgrounds. Most were courtesans or concubines. Courtesans often took up painting so that they would have more in common with literati clients. Courtesans exchanged paintings and other tasteful gifts with talented men to build up a cultured social network. Their literati customers were amateur painters, so these men liked to chat with courtesans about art. A talented courtesan painter could find herself in high demand as a companion.

Because literati took the artistic opinions of courtesans seriously, these lowborn women ended up having a significant impact on the conventions of painting. For example, at this time, it became popular for courtesans to paint long-leaf Chinese orchids. Women had previously avoided this subject matter, as it was a serious genre identified with literati. Courtesans took up orchid painting so that they could discuss it with their customers. These women justified their appropriation of a stereotypically masculine theme by redefining its symbolic implications. Although literati had traditionally considered the orchid a symbol of moral purity, courtesans used it to represent the boudoir. Redefining the orchid as a symbol of the female realm made it acceptable for them to paint it. Literati clients were amused by the novel interpretations that courtesan painters gave to this stock artistic theme and enjoyed exchanging views with them regarding their shared genre.

The exceptionally talented Ma Shouzhen (1548–1604) exemplifies the courtesan painter.[59] She lived in Nanjing during the late Ming era. At that time, the city had a large pleasure quarter famed for its particularly refined atmosphere. Although Ma was an accomplished writer who composed poetry and wrote the scripts of stage dramas, she gained lasting fame for her paintings. Ma Shouzhen was not an artistic innovator. She confined herself to conventional techniques and themes that her male contacts would readily appreciate. Yet in spite of her conservative style of painting, she used her talent to imbue conformist artworks with a sense of freshness.

Courtesans also engaged in literary activities. As professional singers, they became intimately familiar with song lyrics.[60] Since the Song dynasty, lyrics had been considered an important type of poetry. People enjoyed reading lyrics silently or chanting them out loud, enjoying them as they would other forms of poetry. Because courtesans had to keep up with the latest lyrics, publishers put out illustrated songbooks aimed specifically at this market. Song lyrics were usually formulaic, using stock images and phrases, so it was easy for courtesans to impress their customers by improvising witty lines while singing.

Some courtesans wholeheartedly embraced literati culture and managed to insinuate themselves into the world of cultured men. As with creative literati, talented courtesans gained attention by skillfully mixing together different artforms.[61] Xue Susu (fl. 1575–before 1652) garnered praise for mastering both poetry and painting. She cleverly displayed literati sensibilities regarding these arts in order to gain approval from her educated patrons. For example, Xue once wrote a poem on a painted fan expressing her desire to withdraw from worldly affairs. This theme might seem odd for a courtesan, as she had nothing to do with public life. However, by writing the sort of poem that an educated man might write and displaying it to her clientele, she demonstrated her cultural solidarity with them. Male customers appreciated her imitations of male poetry and art, and their enthusiastic praise made her famous.

Educated men turned to the demimonde to escape the frustrations and disappointments of public life. During times of bad government, upright men traditionally renounced the decadent world. The stereotypical hermit lived in a thatched hut on a scenic mountaintop. During the Ming dynasty, however, many so-called recluses consorted with courtesans as a form of withdrawal. Art documents the changing views of eremitism. Song and Yuan painters had depicted recluses as residing in remote wild places. They distanced themselves from humanity to symbolize renunciation. In contrast, a Ming-era painting of the Song dynasty polymath Su Dongpo (1037–1101) depicts him in an urban setting surrounded by courtesans.[62] Modern viewers will likely misinterpret this scene as a portrait of a bon vivant, but Ming literati understood it as a portrayal of principled reclusion. Rejecting government service to engage with refined courtesans became a new style of eremitism. While some men declared themselves recluses simply as an excuse for irresponsible dissipation, many considered this a respectable way of expressing their political position. Even a few women took these ideas very seriously. When the Ming dynasty fell, the talented courtesan painter Fan Jue declared herself a loyalist to the previous dynasty and withdrew from the world. She put aside her beautiful clothes and luxuries and refused to meet with outsiders, devoting the rest of her life to tea appreciation and spiritual pursuits.

As courtesans and literati interacted, some developed intense emotional bonds.[63] Late Ming writers became fascinated with sentiment (*qing*) and praised it as a positive aspect of humanity's psychological makeup. They saw emotional authenticity as an antidote to sterile Confucian platitudes and cynical political posturing. Discourse about sentiment affected how people regarded the interactions between courtesans and their clients. These women may have been allowed to participate in literati activities, but educated men did certainly not regard them as equals. Courtesans' customers considered them desirable women and engaged with them in emotional and even romantic ways. The titillating presence of attractive courtesans in literati circles helps account for the increasing discussion of emotionalism in late Ming fiction.

The popular author Feng Menglong (1574–1646) wrote about romances between courtesans and scholars.[64] These stories constituted a variation on the traditional scholar-and-beauty genre, in which a student falls in love with an attractive woman. Because courtesans had such a high profile in the late Ming, writers sometimes replaced the stock romantic beauty with an alluring courtesan. However, student and courtesans came from opposite ends of the social scale, so authors had to defend the propriety of this sort of romance. According to Feng, people of such different backgrounds could find common ground by sharing an intense emotional bond. He portrayed sentiment (*qing*) as the focal point of their unconventional rapport.

Feng wrote about courtesans in fairly positive terms. In fact, the courtesans in his stories often seem far more sincere and perceptive than the men who love them. The growing popularity of this genre likely emerged in response to widespread dissatisfaction with conjugal life. Because parents arranged their children's marriages for pragmatic gain, husbands did not necessarily have any feelings for their wives. It was common for men to look elsewhere for emotional fulfilment. Late Ming literature idealized courtesans and made them icons of romantic desire. In this way, they became fantasy material for emotionally frustrated men. Because courtesans lived outside of established social bonds, they could be elevated into ideal women who represented both refinement and passion, hence suitable subjects for the daydreams of discontent literati.

Chapter 4

Education

Over time, the education of women in elite families became increasingly common and rigorous. By the Ming era, it was expected that a woman of good birth would be familiar with literature and ethics. Overall, however, the general educational level of women remained low. Few could read anything more difficult than rudimentary texts, and most remained illiterate. Even among gentry families, women rarely achieved a high level of learning. In 1372 the Hongwu emperor tried to recruit educated women to serve as teachers in the harem. Out of forty-four candidates, only fourteen could pass a written examination.[1]

The education that women received varied considerably according to region and background.[2] Peasant women in the countryside had no use for poetry and the ancient classics, and they were almost always unlettered.[3] But in prosperous towns and cities, both sexes had higher than average literacy rates. Literati families throughout China maintained high cultural standards and educated their daughters to prove their commitment to learning. They also wanted to educate young women so that they could eventually teach their own children. Ever since the Song dynasty, elite families had realized that literate mothers who began teaching their sons at an early age gave them a valuable head start in their studies. Men often attributed their success in large part to early maternal instruction and encouragement. For this reason, the Ming state honored the mothers of officials. Yet even in the most cultured families, women almost never received the extensive classical education expected of their brothers. Since they could not participate in public life, serve in the bureaucracy, or write academic texts, studying the classics could seem like a waste of time. Women and men studied different curricula, and an education gap divided the sexes.

Authors and publishers aimed certain kinds of literature at a female reader-ship. Women enjoyed simple novels with stock plots, as even readers with a low level of education could understand them. Because novels and short stories had a large female readership, they often featured female protagonists and plots of interest to women. Publishers produced inexpensive imprints of popular novels for the mass market and lavish deluxe editions for sale to women in rich families. Women of all backgrounds also enjoyed oral litera-ture such as ballads and religious stories, which were entertaining and easily comprehended.

Because men and women had different levels of learning, they tended to perceive the world in dissimilar ways. Male literati had a comprehensive understanding of the classical tradition and orthodox literary canon, and these sophisticated ideas influenced their worldview. In contrast, few women mastered this sort of rarified learning, so their thinking tended to be shaped by popular culture. High and low culture embodied distinct value systems, so the sexes tended to understand things differently and pursue divergent goals. Educated men were likely to sympathize with classical values while women responded to popular ideals.

Even though female education had become common among the gentry, leading thinkers debated whether women should even be literate.[4] Some con-servatives believed that education and talent corroded female virtue. They argued women should be kept ignorant to safeguard their naïve good nature. Yet in spite of these qualms, the practical benefits of female education led the gentry to embrace it.

People had different ideas about what women should learn and how they ought to study it, and during the late Ming era female learning became a topic of contention.[5] Due to the influence of Neo-Confucianism, many authorities promoted education as a useful means to raise women's moral standards. Confucians did not view learning as the mere accumulation of knowledge. More importantly, they believed that education should encourage moral self-cultivation and mold impressionable young women into chaste wives and model mothers.

The unconventional Neo-Confucian thinker Lü Kun (1536–1618) wrote at length on the propriety of female education.[6] He had a positive view of learning, seeing it as highly beneficial for either sex. Lü considered women capable of substantial cultivation and achievement, and he believed that they should receive an education to bring out their inner potential. However, he did not consider every type of instruction equally useful. In particular, he criticized the prevailing emphasis on poetry in the female curriculum. Tra-ditionally many women had received a literary education aimed at enabling them to appreciate and write poetry. Lü worried that the contents of literature were not always morally elevating. Immersion in literature might even tempt women to imitate romantic protagonists and behave in untoward ways.

To avoid these problems, Lü argued that female students should focus on serious ethical works. However, he admitted that this sort of learning was not always easy. Some of the standard texts for female education, such as *Biographies of Women* (*Lienü zhuan*) by the Han dynasty scholar Liu Xiang (77–6 BCE), were difficult to understand. Liu wrote in archaic language and often expressed his ideas obliquely through subtle poetic allusion, so students could find it challenging to comprehend his ideas. Lü considered these sorts of challenging old texts to be a barrier to learning. He wanted to simplify female education so that it could become more widespread. Lü believed that girls should be taught using easily understood texts written in straightforward language. This sort of material would allow them to effectively grasp the finer points of female ethics.

Lü Kun put his theories into practice by writing a textbook for female students called *Exemplars for the Women's Quarters* (*Guifan*).[7] He intended this book to be a study aid for female readers with rudimentary learning. Although Lü was extremely erudite and could have written in an elaborate style, he chose to employ simple wording and illustrations to help readers understand the contents and keep them engaged. He also tried to empathize with his readers and examined matters from a female point of view. In consequence, Lü adopted a moderate tone that women found inviting. Whereas radical Neo-Confucians praised women who committed suicide or mutilated themselves for the sake of virtue, Lü condemned self-harm. Instead, he stressed the importance of female wisdom. A woman did not have to injure her body to prove a commitment to virtue. She just had to behave prudently and hold herself to high ethical standards. These sorts of works facilitated the spread of female learning by simplifying educational materials.

Women also expressed enthusiasm for education. In a poem to her son, Zou Saizhen enjoined him, "Trace things to their roots and know the value of study."[8] The fact that she was able to couch her teachings in a refined poetic medium attested to her own learning. Her elegant diction has as much impact as the substance of her remark. Perhaps the most influential statement by a Ming woman regarding the value of education was *Instructions for the Inner Quarters* (*Nei xun*) by Empress Xu (1362–1407), wife of the Yongle emperor. She prefaced her book with an eloquent defense of female learning.[9] Xu took the standard Confucian approach to the issue and argued that education gives women the opportunity to study ethics in detail, elevating their moral standards.

Women occasionally took a more strident tone in defending female education. Gu Ruopu (1592–ca. 1681) wrote a poem declaring that she would not
allow herself to be silenced by male reactionaries.[10]

> But if we fail to practice poetry and prose,
>   how shall we display our natural gifts?
> An elder woman scolded me for this:
>   "You don't pursue the true and wifely way,
> Engaging teachers to instruct the girls
>   as if they sought to win the world's regard.
> They put aside our normal woman's work
>   and waste their efforts to recite and learn."
> I listened well to what she said
>   but it left me unimpressed.
> In human society sexes segregate
>   and yet preserving chastity is hard;
> How can we in women's quarters
>   fail to take the ancients as our teachers?
>   . . .
> Not treating moral training seriously
>   will visit shame upon the family name.

Gu cleverly employs rhetoric likely to appeal to the sort of conservatives who
criticized female writers. She does not defend female talent or achievement as
an end in itself. Instead she embraces the Confucian argument that education
allows women to engage with complex ethical texts, elevating their character.

Female learning had support at the highest levels of society. The Ming
emperors made sure that their daughters and consorts received a decent education, in line with the conventions of previous dynasties. Traditionally, the
emperors saw the education of palace ladies as a way to impose order, raise
the cultural level of palace life, and discourage harem women from misbehav-
ing. Ming emperors also valued educated women as interesting companions.
They often favored learned consorts, as they found the company of these
women stimulating.

When the dynasty began, the Hongwu emperor feared that consort kinsmen would eventually gain power and destabilize the government, as had
often happened in the past. He saw the moral education of palace ladies as a
way to curb their ambitions and those of their kinsmen.[11] For this reason, the
palace education system relied heavily on ethical texts. Literate women could
serve in the palace bureaucracy, so ambitious concubines received training to
enable them to carry out administrative tasks. During the early Ming, female
palace officials served as teachers in the harem. In the mid-fifteenth century,

educated eunuchs took over teaching responsibilities. There were between three and six eunuch teachers at any time.

The palace schools used various texts.[12] Female students started with elementary textbooks that taught basic literacy then moved on to ethical works. Numerous books dedicated to female ethics were in circulation by that time, so palace schools had ample classroom material. The most ambitious students went on to study classical texts such as the *Analects* (*Lunyu*) of Confucius. Women also received detailed instruction in court ritual, as they had to periodically carry out complex ceremonies. Yet in spite of this educational infrastructure, the general level of learning in the Ming palace was not very high. Overall, the cultural level of the Ming palace fell below the standards set in the Song dynasty. Moreover, harem women lived in isolation and did not have contact with erudite role models, so they did not pursue learning with the enthusiasm of women from literati backgrounds.

A woman's social position influenced what she knew, how she learned it, and what she did with this knowledge.[13] Gentry women generally received the most comprehensive educations. The intensely competitive civil service examination system fostered a culture of learning among the landed elite. The gentry put great emphasis on the education of their sons, as an official degree would earn tangible rewards. The atmosphere of learning and high culture in these households affected women as well. The education of gentry women focused on ethics and poetry. In addition, they might study painting and other arts. Parents and teachers also socialized women to accept the norms and values that would allow them to carry out the key life roles of daughter, wife, and mother. Girls were also taught practical skills such as domestic management, needlework, and proper dress and deportment.

Unlike male students, girls could not attend regular schools.[14] Parents usually taught their daughters at home. The educational level of a girl's parents thus usually determined the potential extent of her education. In the late Ming, it became common for professional teachers to enter the homes of wealthy families to teach their daughters. Both men and women worked as home tutors, but it seems that most were men. However, the rising demand for quality female education inspired more women to take up the teaching profession, so the presence of female teachers in the homes of the wealthy became increasingly common. Although these women went into the inner quarters of strangers' homes, they were nonetheless treated with respect due to their learning and good background.

Textbooks targeted at female students introduced ethical principles appropriate to women's roles in life. Ancient works on female propriety by the Han authorities Liu Xiang and Ban Zhao remained very popular. Some widely circulated works had been written during the medieval era. There were also newer texts by Ming authors who sought to make Confucian ethics relevant to the circumstances facing contemporary women. Female students might study basic moral texts of interest to men as well, in particular the *Classic of Filial Piety* (*Xiaojing*).[15]

During the Ming dynasty, women's textbooks underwent standardization for the first time. It became common for female students to study the so-called *Four Books for Women* (*Nü sishu*).[16] The editor Wang Xiang selected four books, added basic annotations to make them more accessible, and published them as a set in 1624. He intended families to use this set of books as the main teaching material for their daughters, as they provided a comprehensive moral curriculum. Notably, women wrote all four works. The quartet included two texts from earlier periods. The Han dynasty *Admonitions for Women* (*Nü jie*) by Ban Zhao had long been a cornerstone of female education. The more easily understood *Women's Analects* (*Nü lunyu*) was attributed to two sisters who lived during the Tang dynasty, Song Ruoxin and Song Ruozhao. The book had been subsequently edited to simplify the style and structure, and its readability made it very popular.[17] Wang added two Ming-era works, *Instructions for the Inner Quarters* (*Neixun*) by Empress Xu and *Records of Achievements of Female Exemplars* (*Nüfang jielu*) by Madame Liu, his own mother. He deliberately chose four works to make this a female counterpart to the canonical four books of Confucianism promoted by Zhu Xi. The *Four Books* had an immense impact on female education. This quartet not only became standard teaching material in China but was also widely used in Korea and Japan.

Of these four books, Empress Xu's *Instructions for the Inner Quarters* had a particularly large impact. It stands out as perhaps the most significant statement on female ethics produced during the Ming.[18] Many women studied this book very carefully in their youth, so it influenced female perspectives toward gender norms. Empress Xu wrote this work at a time when Neo-Confucianism had become the dominant intellectual framework. This school of thought put great stress on classical orthodoxy, and adherents argued for stringent restrictions on female behavior. Empress Xu released this book early in the dynasty, when Hongwu's dictates still carried great authority. When Hongwu founded the Ming system, he was very careful to institute safeguards to prevent imperious empresses dowager from usurping control. The moral education of palace women was a central feature of these plans, and Empress Xu seems to have seen herself as carrying this project to fruition. She subjected palace women to a restrictive ethical regime to limit their political influence.

Empress Xu had received a good education and wrote in a clear and persuasive style. She had carefully studied previous works on female propriety and sums up their most important views in comprehensible language. The work's twenty chapters describe conduct appropriate for the kinship roles of daughter, wife, and mother that structured a woman's life. Empress Xu argues that women should practice restraint to avoid transgressing moral boundaries. Overall, however, she counseled moderation. Even though chastity rhetoric was on the rise, she mentions widow fidelity but does not give it much attention. In later centuries, widow chastity would eventually become symbolic of female rectitude in general, but during the early, Ming this shift had not yet occurred.

Although people of the time did not stress the importance of novels as a tool for learning, popular literature seems to have been a particularly important way for women to learn about the wider world at this time. During the Ming dynasty, long-format fiction became extremely popular. Elite women had copious leisure time, and they became enthusiastic novel readers.[19] The authors of popular fiction wrote in simple language and spun amusing plots that kept the reader engaged. To cloistered women, these books were far more than just entertainment. Popular narratives also conveyed highly detailed information about society, geography, history, moral principles, religion, and many other useful facts. Reading light fiction was one of the most important ways that women used to understand what was happening beyond the walls of their homes.

☞━━◆━━☜

Not only was the number of literate women increasing, but they also wrote more than before. According to one study of surviving women's writings from the entire imperial era, about 10 percent date to the Ming.[20] The number of female writers rose significantly toward the end of the dynasty. At this time, the publishing industry expanded, and editors aggressively searched for books with commercial potential. Female readers often favored books written by women, so publishers were open to female talent as never before.[21] The growth of commercial publishing in the late Ming gave female authors unprecedented exposure. Previously, women had usually circulated their writings in manuscript editions. Most handwritten texts were only seen by a small number of people and disappeared after the author's death. In contrast, the booming publishing industry allowed women to publish their writings in inexpensive printed editions that were professionally produced and marketed.[22] Particularly in the south, every city had communities of literate women who published their writings and discussed the output of their female peers. The large number of female readers made these books profitable, so male publishers and editors put out women's writings for commercial gain.[23]

Due to technological innovations and efficient commercial networks, published works were disseminated widely, allowing female authors to rapidly reach a large and diverse readership. Publishers used the latest equipment to print huge numbers of inexpensive books. Illustrations also became common. The late Ming was the highpoint of woodcut printing. Publishers ornamented new titles with attractive woodblock prints as a way to attract attention and increase sales. They also reprinted classic books, such as Liu Xiang's *Biographies of Women*, in lavishly illustrated editions to attract new readers. Readers came to expect woodblock illustrations, and it was difficult to market books that lacked them. The increasing importance of illustrations affected the contents of published works. Artists preferred to depict beautiful scenes or dramatic events rather than profound ideas. Authors reacted by making their works increasingly vivid so that they could have engaging illustrations.

The tastes of Ming readers differed from those of previous eras. People were less interested in abstract ideas and books written in difficult language. They preferred entertaining and practical works, preferably with lively illustrations. To cater to the demand for simple texts, publishers edited books about female role models into new formats. Traditionally, these narratives had followed Liu Xiang in classifying female paragons according to the virtues they represented. Each chapter described women who exemplified the same sort of virtue. Ming editors organized the material from older didactic works into more engaging formats. They arranged narratives chronologically or according to the kinship role of the protagonist, rewrote them in a more entertaining manner, and added illustrations.

A book needed to have skillful storytelling if it was to sell well. Commercial pressure led publishers to present female role models in more dramatic ways. They downplayed women renowned for staid characteristics such as intellect, wisdom, or argumentation. Instead they highlighted theatrical actions such as suicide or self-mutilation. Commercialization of ethical texts thus encouraged editors and writers to present female virtue in increasingly extreme ways.

Changing ideas about good literature helped legitimize women's writings.[24] In earlier eras, critics tended to prize stiff rhetoric and adherence to classical orthodoxy. Changes in the intellectual world undermined this sort of pedantry. Followers of the iconoclastic thinker Wang Yangming (1472–1529) promoted a more subjective type of Confucianism. They criticized rigid formalism and slavish devotion to ancient ideas. This critique encouraged new ways of thinking and writing. Readers increasingly valued psychological authenticity and emotionalism. They also wanted stories about ideas and behaviors that ran contrary to traditional verities. This open milieu encouraged female creativity and fostered popular demand for women's writings.

Some female readers applied what they read to their daily lives, putting into practice these new ideas about gender.[25] Lively writing also provided women with persuasive ways of speaking. Poetry and other prestigious literary formats disseminated language that people considered particularly convincing. Women could draw on this reservoir of poetic words and phrases to justify their behavior.

As more women became writers, they began to think about themselves in new ways. Gentry women adopted a female version of the literati identity, potentially elevating themselves in the eyes of those around them. As for male reactions to female authorship, reactions shifted over the course of the dynasty.[26] During the early Ming, many educated men still considered literary talent inconsistent with female virtue. Some even praised a woman's lack of talent, as this seemed to imply a commitment to integrity. Although conservatives might accept talent in a courtesan, they thought of talented gentry women as unattractive, unfeminine, and asexual. By the late Ming, however, views had decisively shifted. Elite men became far more accepting of female talent and even considered it necessary to be a good mother. As a result of these changes, it became much easier for talented gentry women to publish their writings.

Some women from cultured families took the female literati identity to an extreme. Like some courtesans, they portrayed themselves as hermits who had retired from the world.[27] Of course, since women were confined to the home and barred from participating in public life, announcing that one had become a recluse made little sense. A woman was already secluded in the home, so she had little to renounce. Even so, a gentry woman occasionally took on the image of the Daoist recluse. Adopting the persona of an other-worldly hermit elevated a woman's necessary seclusion by associating it with virtue and mystical cultivation, increasing her moral authority, and increasing the importance of her literary output.

Women wrote in a wider range of genres than before. In previous eras, they had mostly confined themselves to poetry, but during the Ming, numerous women wrote prose works ranging from essays to eulogies.[28] Readers responded enthusiastically to new types of writing. There are several reasons for the increase in prose works by women at this time. Most importantly, prose became more common overall. Men wrote far more prose than before, and this shift in literary taste drew the attention of women. Moreover, more women were attaining a high level of education. Erudition made them confident about their literary abilities, so they dared to venture beyond stereotypical feminine poetry and write prose. Women also founded literary societies that facilitated the circulation and publication of their prose works. Writing new genres allowed women to expose a different side of themselves to the world. Whereas poetry highlighted the author's emotions, prose tended to be more factual and grounded in social experiences, revealing women's views on practical matters.

As before, women frequently wrote letters. During the medieval era, it had already become common for literate women to write letters, particularly in response to major life events such as funerals, but it seems that letter writing became far more common in the Ming.[29] Writing a letter was not a simple matter, as daunting rules and conventions regulated the composition of a proper epistle. Books of model letters from the time include many examples of female-authored letters. When women tended to follow these models, they often wrote in a stiff impersonal style. For this reason, women continued to write letters in poetic form, as it allowed them to express their innermost thoughts and feelings.

To secluded women, epistolary culture was particularly important. Writing letters allowed women to keep in touch with relatives living in other homes and even develop friendships with like-minded counterparts in distant places whom they would never have a chance to meet in person. Cultured women also wrote letters to accompany gifts of paintings and poetry. These letters allowed isolated women to encourage one another to persevere in their efforts. A cloistered woman would have welcomed encouragement from a kindred spirit, particularly if she did not dare to circulate her works to the wider public.

Female authors were also extremely interested in performance literature. Women who spent most of their lives confined to the home took great pleasure in singing, storytelling, and stage plays. Performances offered a welcome break in their daily routine and also gave them a valuable window on the wider world. Also, because performances were popular artforms, scripts were easy to understand. Even women with minimal learning could follow these accessible works.

Tanci became popular in southern China during the Ming dynasty.[30] In this style of performance, a performer sang narrative lyrics while accompanying herself on a stringed instrument. *Tanci* lyrics consisted of ballads written in lines of ten syllables. Women eagerly embraced this genre, and many lyricists were female. *Tanci* allowed women to publicly address matters of heartfelt concern. Lyrics often expressed dissatisfaction with unfair gender norms. Ballad writers called for greater equality between the sexes, parity between spouses, protection of women's dowries and inheritance rights, an end to concubinage, and even female participation in government.

Unlike a simple *tanci* performance, which required just a single singer and a musical instrument, stage plays required sets, costumes, and a cast. The expense of staging a play made it hard for female authors to see their scripts performed, and only a handful of women ever wrote for stage dramas.[31] Nine drama scripts written by five Ming dynasty female authors are known. These writers were mostly born into families of performers, so writing scripts was part of their family profession. Playwrights not only wrote lines for female performers but also for male roles. Writing drama scripts thus gave a small number of women the rare opportunity to imitate the male voice and have their own sentiments mouthed by men.

As before, when women wrote, they usually wrote poetry. Even though men wrote the most poems by far, poetry was the most important realm of female cultural endeavor. The critic Lu Qingzi (fl. 1600) even claimed poetry as a predominantly female form of literature. In the preface to an early seventeenth-century poetry collection she declared, "Poetry is definitely not the calling of men; it is really what belongs by right to us women."[32] Poetry writing did not encounter much opposition, even from conservative Neo-Confucians, as it had been so closely associated with women for so long. As a cultured activity, poetry suited the refined atmosphere of a literati household. Skill at poetry writing even raised a woman's marriage prospects, as a competent female poet could confer a measure of prestige on her husband's family.[33]

By the late imperial era, women's poetry had a long and fruitful history. Reflection on this rich legacy made Ming women extremely sophisticated and self-conscious as both writers and readers. This era saw the emergence of methodical literary criticism of the female canon.[34] Women were publishing increasing quantities of poetry, so critics felt obliged to establish clear standards of judgment. Literary criticism appeared in various forms ranging from formal verse to casual observations in letters. Some works of criticism were widely read, sparking considerable discussion of the proper criteria for evaluating women's poetry.

Most women were tethered to the home and socialized among kin. When a woman wrote a poem, usually only family members would read it.[35] Sisters had comparable educations and background, so they usually had similar taste in literature. Women often found their sisters to be their most sympathetic readers. Even after a woman married, it was not uncommon for her to exchange poems with her sisters as a way to keep in touch. Exchanging poetry among family members allowed women to stay connected to siblings and other relatives even after they disappeared into seclusion in their husbands' homes. The family bond was so important to women's creative production that many female poets came to regard all of their literary companions as surrogate sisters.[36]

Educated women also exchanged poems with their spouses. Particularly when a man was away from home, a couple could use poetry to declare their enduring affection and keep one another informed of recent occurrences. Poetry could be extremely emotive, so it could be far more expressive than a formal letter. Some poems exchanged between spouses had surprising content. Traditionally, women wrote poems to express worries and loneliness to a distant spouse. But a poem by Lu Qingzi to her husband, a soldier serving on a faraway frontier, voices her ardent desire for victory at any cost.[37] Although she adopts a stereotypically masculine tone, appropriate for discussing war, she also expresses wifely concern that her husband succeed in his important undertaking.

> Don't dwell upon the joy
>   we had here, hand in hand,
> Just swear to meet your death
>   there on the field of battle.
> When a young man's body
>   is promised to his country,
> Should his wife have any cause
>   to feel the wound of grief?

Some women directed their poems to a wider audience. One way to gain a wide readership was to write a poem on a wall in a public place. Wall writing became popular during the Tang dynasty, when male travelers wrote poems about their journey on the walls of inns. Women also took up this type of public poetry, but their wall poems had distinct content.[38] Whereas men usually complained about the arduousness of their journey, women often took advantage of the public forum to write about personal matters. Occasionally someone copied down one of these poems and published it, preserving this ephemera for posterity. Female wall poems attracted so much attention that some men took on a female literary persona and wrote poems in this genre. In fact, male imitation of this genre of female poetry was surprisingly common. Because so much wall poetry was anonymous, it is often unclear whether a feminine poem was written by a woman or by a man who had assumed the female voice.

Female poets also circulated their poems among family members, friends, and acquaintances through the intricate network of gift giving that permeated domestic life. Ming novels describe women in large households constantly exchanging little gifts such as ornaments, clothing, hand-embroidered shoes,

and food.[39] This custom had many uses. Gift giving strengthened social relationships. A present from superior to inferior within the household expressed
benevolence and also reminded everyone of their relative ranks. Women also
presented gifts to solicit cooperation or support. People living in different
households could exchange gifts to forge new bonds and extend their network
of acquaintances. Literate women used this gift-giving network to garner
sympathetic new audiences for their writings. They would send poems, paintings, and calligraphy to women in other households, extending their audience
while remaining demurely cloistered within the home.

Some women met in person to discuss literature and compose poems
together. In the late Ming, it became common for literary women to found
poetry clubs.[40] These groups took various forms. The women of a large
household might establish a club in their home so that they could participate
in organized cultural activities while remaining secluded. There were also
local poetry clubs within the wider community, giving women from different
families an excuse to leave their homes and meet to share a common love of
literature. It seems that these groups were extremely common in urban areas.
Women usually organized poetry groups themselves, although sometimes a
literatus served as patron. Some men hosted groups of courtesans while others presided over a club attended by women of high birth.

There were also formal channels that allowed women to disseminate their
works. Ming publishers put out numerous anthologies of women's poetry.[41]
Poems by men and women rarely appeared in the same collection, as each sex
usually wrote about different themes and used distinct styles. Female poets
had their works published in dedicated anthologies. The increasing popularity of poetry collections stimulated women's literature. Poets had a reason to
raise their art to the highest level, as an outstanding work might be published
and widely read.

Male literati collated most collections of women's poetry. Ambitious men
edited these anthologies to garner prestige by publicly associating themselves
with a respectable cultured activity. Literati who failed to obtain office often
turned to literature to confirm their elite status. Although some men edited
anthologies of women's poetry for the sake of self-promotion, many were
genuinely enthusiastic about female authors and actively promoted them.
Whatever their motives, male editors helped shape a canon of women's poetry. They also helped construct a body of appropriate literary criticism. In
deciding which poems to include in the compilations, editors had to ponder
the standards appropriate for judging women's poetry. They realized that
these criteria had to be different from those used of men's poetry, as the sexes
usually wrote differently. Editors often used prefaces to express their views
toward the nature of women's literature.

Women's poetry traditionally differed from the literary mainstream, which was dominated by men.[42] Because elite women were confined to the home, much of their poetry dealt with domestic life. They depicted the inner quarters as not just a physical space but also an idea. The outpouring of women's poetry in this era helped construct the standard image of the inner quarters (*gui*). Early medieval poetry had stereotypically depicted the boudoir as a sexually charged space. But to women who spent much of their time in their bedroom, it seemed like a mundane place, so their poetry de-eroticized it. To them, the interior spaces of the home were neither mysterious nor sensual, nor were the inhabitants necessarily beautiful. They described the inner recesses of the home in a straightforward manner as a mundane realm that happened to be occupied by women. Instead of a heartbroken beauty pining for an absent beloved, they enumerated the wide range of activities that took place within gendered female space. Poems describe women doing needlework, chatting, reading and writing, painting, conducting religious activities, playing board games, playing and listening to music, having dinner parties, interacting with children and other women, or simply resting. The overall impression is distinctly positive. Ming poetry makes the domestic realm seem like a cheerful and cultured place. In fact, compared with the lives of men plagued by professional pressures, the female world seems almost utopian. The alluring atmosphere of female society was a major attraction of women's poetry. Even so, women chafed at their confinement within a constricted space. Awareness of these constraints often imbued descriptions of boudoir life with a tinge of gentle pathos.

During the Ming, many women thought very deeply about the fundamental nature of their art. The poet Meng Shuqing (fl. 1476), also an incisive literary critic, demanded that women abandon stale poetic conventions and embrace fresh themes.[43]

> Buddhist verses not reeking of incense and paper money, feminine themes not overwhelmed with cosmetics and rouge, humble scholar poems not imbued with shabbiness and misery, Daoist poems not steeped in life-prolonging quackery, or mountain hermits' poems mired in seclusion and misery.

These sorts of bold declarations help expand the scope of women's poetry and infuse it with unprecedented vigor. Particularly toward the end of the dynasty, when fundamental institutions had fallen into alarming decay, female poets expressed concern about the problems plaguing their society and government.[44] In doing so, they put aside the stereotypical feminine style of writing, which employed delicate language and studied decorum. Instead they took on the so-called masculine voice to write directly and forcefully. Fang Weiyi (1585–1668) wrote of the travails she endured during the dynasty's collapse. Yet in spite of her suffering (or perhaps because of it), she espouses strong patriotic sentiments.[45]

> Left home for an outpost ten thousand miles away
> Where the mountain roads are severed by wind and smoke.
> Too many taxes, no extra victuals,
> The frontier is barren—no planting of fields.
> Foot soldiers ever mindful of death,
> A grasping official still demanding his sum—
> Relying on the bounty of our lord and king,
> When will we sing out: Victory!—and home!

Her poems document the collapse of the Ming into chaos and suffering. She wrote another poem in an uncertain tone, expressing worry that she might never see the end of her travails.[46]

> In my declining years, I run into troubled times,
> When will I return to my native land?
> Bandits invade the southern townships,
> Military orders are dispatched to the northern passes.
> Human horror is at its height:
> Layers of blood coat our swords to the hilt.

Besides writing about current issues, female poets also took on past events. Male literati were well versed in history, as they considered it a repository of useful wisdom that could help prepare them for service in the bureaucracy. Some educated women absorbed the tastes of the men around them and read historical works.[47] However, the sexes came to the study of history with different outlooks. While elite men read history to prepare for a civil service career, for women it had no practical purpose. They simply saw it as interesting leisure reading. But even though women read history for enjoyment, it ultimately had a tangible impact on their art. Engaging with these weighty texts gave them the confidence to compose poetry about historical themes and past personages. They often used poetry about historical events to obliquely express their own ideas and values, a time-tested literary technique. Historical poetry allowed women to widen their artistic palette, impressing readers and drawing the attention of demanding male critics.

Besides poetry and other forms of writing, some talented women also expressed themselves through the visual arts. In the late Ming, it even became fashionable for literati to admire paintings by women.[48] Because women could not take the official examinations or serve in government, people assumed that their art expressed authentic sentiments. Largely due to this notion, interest in female painting grew through the course of the dynasty, reaching a highpoint in the early seventeenth century. Women's painting and calligraphy became more respected than ever, allowing talented female artists to display their works with confidence and enjoy public praise.

Some courtesans had considerable artistic ability.[49] Cultivating artistic talent earned the respect of educated men and helped a courtesan attract a cultured clientele. Men also valued talented concubines skilled at painting.[50] Some concubines received extensive training in the arts, and they worked hard to improve their technique. A talented concubine could raise her social status, as men found an artistic woman more interesting than just a pretty face. Many gentry women also pursued the arts. Their works were considered far more respectable due to their high background.[51] In gentry families, parents encouraged their daughters to develop nascent artistic talent, as it increased their marriage prospects. Literati valued a talented wife who could pass on her knowledge of artistic technique to their children. Both men and women learned painting from their mothers. Because male and female gentry painters lived under the same roof, they frequently exchanged ideas and techniques. This interaction inspired some women to go beyond stereotypical female subjects, such as pretty flowers, and explore new themes. Some even followed the lead of daring and eccentric male painters.[52] Women may have been confined to the inner quarters, but this did not mean that their art was naïve or provincial. In fact, literati homes were the center of China's cultural life, as most artistic activities took place within the mansions of the elite. Creative women from elite families often used their privileged position to their advantage. In spite of their physical isolation, they could use the visual arts to express themselves, make contacts with the wider world, and win public admiration.

Chapter 5

Religion

Because men dominated most public institutions and activities, women frequently turned to religion in search of opportunity. They could use spiritual beliefs to justify leaving the domestic sphere, avoiding marriage and childbirth, living in an autonomous female community, and studying profound philosophy. The most talented believers could even become respected leaders of a religious organizations.

By the Ming dynasty, religion had a far more modest place in Chinese society than before. During the medieval era, people had little confidence in weak secular institutions, so they directed their energies toward religious activities. People from all rungs of society spent heavily on religious patronage, which consumed a large proportion of society's resources. During the Tang dynasty, many of the brightest minds pondered religious issues, elevating both Buddhist and Daoist thought to a pinnacle of refinement. Subsequently, however, religion went into decline. Teachings were simplified, many ceremonies became perfunctory, and the reputation of clerics declined. Given the many openings that religion offered to women, its decay had significant consequences for their position in society.

Temples and shrines still dotted the landscape, and almost everyone participated in some kind of religious practice. However, economic development had produced new opportunities and amusements that diverted attentions away from religion, causing the number of fervent believers to decline considerably. The Confucian revival positioned secular learning as the primary focus of intellectual inquiry. Also, centuries of experience dealing with meddlesome monks had made officialdom extremely wary of empowering religious institutions. Instead of revering religious figures as wise and saintly, the government saw them as ignorant troublemakers.

At the grassroots of society, people still worshipped myriad deities. Many gods were venerated in only one locality, and religious beliefs and practices varied by region. The religious lives of Hakka women exemplified the fragmentation of popular religion. Hakkas usually worshipped local deities and showed little interest in the major organized religions.[1] In contrast with Buddhism and Daoism, which taught abstract metaphysical concepts, people looked to folk gods for practical aid and benefits. Hakka women appealed to familiar local deities for help with tangible problems, such as curing illness or allowing them to bear a son. They worshipped these gods in little shrines in village temples or at home.

The profusion of popular deities discomfited literati. They abhorred the sight of peasants in the thrall of such an untidy belief system. To make matters worse, these gods had unclear powers and nebulous identities. Some seemed strange and potentially malevolent.[2] The educated elite decided to subject religion to a clear organizational scheme. They sought to establish a standard national pantheon consisting of a small number of beneficent gods with well-defined characteristics. Magistrates and the gentry encouraged people to abandon local deities and turn their attentions to major gods. This movement was extremely successful, and the number of gods worshipped in China declined considerably.

As before, some of the most important popular deities were female. New Year prints and paintings often depicted the goddess Nü Wa (Nü Gua), attesting to her wide following. By the Ming era, Nü Wa's identity had merged with that of Queen Mother of the West (Xiwangmu). Worshippers called both goddesses Niangniang, a respectful term of address used for empresses. In ancient mythology, Nü Wa and Xiwangmu had distinct identities, but by the Ming era, they had melded together, and their worship had been simplified into a fertility cult.[3]

The goddess Mazu, also known as Tianhou, was also extremely popular. This deity originated as a local goddess of the sea, and her cult became widespread in Fujian during the Tang dynasty.[4] During the thirteenth century, long-lasting warfare and banditry disrupted the economy of north China, giving rise to serious food shortages. Huge amounts of grain had to be shipped in from the south to feed impoverished northerners, so the number of sailors traveling from south to north surged. Southern sailors established shrines to Mazu all along China's coast, spreading her worship across a large area. The Mongols also favored this deity, so her popularity increased during the Yuan dynasty. As Mazu gained more followers, her identity expanded, and they worshipped her as a benevolent maternal deity.

In addition to these major goddesses, there were dozens of lesser female deities.[5] Believers identified many goddesses with maternal qualities such as creation, fertility, motherly love, and compassion. Some female deities were considered the mothers or wives of holy figures, such as Houtu Laomu (Venerable Mother of Houtu). Others became detached from the Daoist or Buddhist pantheon and became an object of popular devotion divorced from their original context. For example, the goddess Cundī (Fomu) originated in esoteric Buddhism but became a popular maternal goddess. Although these deities had various origins, identities, and powers, they tended to personify stereotypical female roles and virtues, such as motherhood and kindness.

The adherents of novel heterodox religious movements also worshipped goddesses. During the late imperial era, many new religious movements emerged, and some became prominent for a time. The authorities always regarded new religions with suspicion, as rebels often utilized heterodox beliefs as political ideologies. Most famously, devotees of the widespread White Lotus (Bailian) sect, which emerged in the sixteenth century, worshipped a goddess called the Eternal Venerable Mother (Wusheng Laomu), whom they credited with creating humanity and the cosmos.[6] They believed that this goddess loved humanity as her own children and sent bodhisattvas down to earth to aid mortals. Adherents obeyed the teachings of her self-proclaimed emissaries as a path to salvation.

While most new religions consisted only of beliefs and rites, the White Lotus sect stands out for founding comprehensive institutions as well. Religious leaders organized their followers into an orderly community that provided them with both spiritual and material support. The activist spirit of the White Lotus religion made it attractive to people living on the margins of society, such as the poor, elderly, and childless. While this religion did not require celibacy, believers considered abstinence as a way to express divine purity. They established residence halls for unmarried and widowed women who wanted to remain chaste. By creating such a wide range of useful institutions, the White Lotus sect provided female believers with many opportunities. They could live within a supportive community, avoid marriage and childbirth, gain a degree of independence, pursue an education, and even become local leaders.

○═╋═○

Although Daoism had declined in influence over the centuries, it remained a significant cultural force. The Hongwu emperor initially hoped that his new dynasty would be an earthly Daoist paradise.[7] However, his harsh and invasive policies violated the free and easy spirit of Daoism, and he soon put aside his utopian ambitions. Subsequent Ming rulers showed little interest in the religion. They tolerated Daoism but did not pay it much heed. Likewise, few Ming palace women embraced the faith. During the early Tang dynasty, many princesses had been ordained as Daoist nuns. Strong links bound Daoist nunneries closely to the palace, and there was a great deal of back-and-forth between palace and monastery. In contrast, during the Ming, only one imperial consort, the formidable Empress Zhang, is known to have become a Daoist cleric.[8] It seems that Zhang had a political rationale for adopting a religious persona. Portraying herself as a holy woman established a virtuous identity independent of her husband and helped justify her political power. A painting of her ordination ceremony depicts Empress Zhang surrounded by an array of supernatural figures. However, the emperor is notably absent from the scene. This depiction implied that her authority came from heavenly deities, not the titular ruler. Taking on the identity of a Daoist nun allowed Zhang to claim supreme power while still managing to appear benign.

The general lack of enthusiasm for Daoism among the imperial establishment reflected the religion's deteriorating reputation in society at large.[9] Yuan stage dramas had portrayed Daoist nunneries as hothouses of sexual abandon. The nuns in these plays misbehave in shocking ways and feel no shame for their wanton conduct. Even elderly Daoist nuns had a dubious reputation. Many people believed that these women remained licentious even into old age. As long-format prose literature gained popularity, authors disseminated prevailing negative stereotypes more widely. The concupiscent Daoist nun became a stock character in Ming novels and short stories.

Daoism may have been in decline, but it still had many adherents. The religion's dogma and rituals also continued to develop at this time. During the early Ming, sectarian groups circulated a new genre of religious text called "precious scrolls" (*baojuan*).[10] Although devout Daoists wrote these works, they targeted a popular audience, so these texts used straightforward language to expound topics of interest to average people. Instead of discussing profound philosophical ideas, the authors told engaging stories and explained rituals believed to evoke miraculous powers, such as healing, divination, and exorcism. These ideas were integrated into ballads and oral storytelling, giving them a wide audience.

Many precious scrolls taught that both sexes have equal spiritual potential. The authors often put great emphasis on female deities. In addition to appropriating the Eternal Venerable Mother (of the White Lotus sect) and giving her a central place in the Daoist pantheon, precious scrolls assimilated Buddhist elements as well. One text relates the myth of Princess Miaoshan, who had become associated with the bodhisattva Guanyin in the early twelfth century.[11] According to these legends, Miaoshan's father tried to force her to marry against her will, but she steadfastly refused to wed and became a nun instead. He was so enraged by her defiance that he had her executed. After the gods resurrected her, she donated her eyes and arms as ingredients needed to compound a miraculous medicine capable of curing his terminal illness. This compassionate self-sacrifice caused her to become the bodhisattva Guanyin.

The strange story of Miaoshan/Guanyin conflicts with the orthodox depictions of female virtue in secular writings. Literati composed narratives in which daughters demonstrate virtue through filial obedience and adherence to wifely duty. In contrast, Miaoshan attained enlightenment by defying her father and refusing to marry for the sake of a higher goal. The contradictions between religious teachings and secular ethics help explain the enduring popularity of Daoism among female believers. Because this faith offered alternate ideas about gender and female duty, women often turned to Daoism in search of personal liberation.

Although the authors of precious scrolls stated that they were writing for both female and male readers, in fact they often aimed them specifically at women. The plots of some stories encourage women to be brave and act in their own best interests. Strong women who defy social conventions are portrayed as heroic. Although these unusual female role models suffer for their insubordination, they nevertheless willingly forgive their persecutors. Given the gender egalitarianism of precious scroll texts, it is not surprising that this new genre of literature, and the popular performances that they inspired, sparked the interest of many women and helped ensure the continuation of Daoist worship among the female faithful.

Daoism went far beyond specific religious beliefs and organized worship. This school of thought also influenced the development of culture. During the Ming era, the cultural influence of Daoism probably had much more impact on women than did its overtly religious aspects. Many poems reveal how Daoist ideas and values affected the mindset of female poets. In one work, Zhang Jing'an (fl. 1450) expresses a conventional Daoist worldview.[12]

> Vast river, falling leaves, eagles' sorrowful cries,
> Frost dyes crimson maples, all plants wither.
> Not knowing itself a dream, a butterfly
> Flits toward a cold twig in this autumn scene.

This poem follows the standard convention of projecting the poet's own feelings onto the natural world. Zhang sets the poem in a melancholy winter landscape that seems to imply the ultimately futility of human achievements. The butterfly is a stock image attributed to the ancient Daoist sage Zhuangzi. He told the story of a man who dreamed he was a butterfly. When he woke up, he was not sure if he was a man who dreamed he was a butterfly, or a butterfly dreaming he was a man. Likewise, the butterfly in this poem contemplates the dreamlike uncertainty of our existence.

Ye Wanwan (1610–1632) wrote a poem that similarly expresses ancient Daoist teachings about the unreliability of our perceptions.[13]

> Floating life is nothing but a dream,
> Ambitious people are pitiable creatures.

These lines also allude to the teachings of Zhuangzi. As a solution to the ontological quandary of living amid deceptive reality, Ye counsels aimlessness as the best response. But while these sentiments would have been unsurprising coming from a male Daoist, they seem odd coming from a woman excluded from public life and most professions. The pressing problem that women faced was not the danger posed by excessive ambition, but rather the lack of opportunity to pursue their aspirations.

To women and men, an otherworldly Daoist pose had different psychological functions. Men used it to cope with professional failures and pressures, but for women it served as a way to accept lifelong reclusion and thin prospects. Rather than admitting that she was being unambitious out of necessity, Ye Wanwan elevated her constricted circumstances into a profound philosophical position. She assumed an air of superiority even as she accepted the restrictions she faced. These sorts of sentiments gave rise to the phenomenon of cultured women taking on the guise of a Daoist recluse who had renounced the world in favor of spiritual pursuits. Courtesans often adopted this persona to interact more smoothly with literati clients. The principled hermit was traditionally a male identity. By taking on this role, women could deal with men in a manner that they understood and respected. Gentry women also declared themselves recluses.[14] Because this type of renunciation was called "boudoir reclusion" (*guiyin*), female recluses sometimes used the written character for recluse (*yin*) in their pen names.

Women originally took part in Daoist reclusion by being the wife of a hermit and participating in her husband's withdrawal. When a man decided to become a recluse, his wife would have no choice but to adopt his lifestyle. Sharing a husband's austerities could bring a woman honor, as it allowed her to share in this respectable social role. During the late Ming, sometimes a woman would adopt the role of renunciant and styled herself a "mountain person" (*shanren*), a standard appellation for hermits. However, society usually did not let women adopt a full-fledged hermit lifestyle. Leaving the family and living alone in a thatched hut in a remote place would have been morally ambiguous and potentially dangerous for a woman. Instead, they became renunciants in a psychological sense by rejecting ordinary social constraints. Elevating herself above secular society might allow a woman to achieve a degree of liberation from the strictures of Neo-Confucian ethics. The phenomenon of female hermits was unique to the late Ming.

⌀━✦━⌀

Although Buddhism had declined in prestige, popularity, and substance since its acme in the medieval era, it remained the most important religion in China. When the Ming dynasty began, Hongwu singled out the Three Teachings of Confucianism, Buddhism, and Daoism as orthodox beliefs. Of the three, he was most familiar with Buddhism. In his youth, Hongwu had spent time as a monk, albeit of a very lowly sort. He took the tonsure out of desperation rather than piety, as the monastic life offered the poor young man a degree of social advancement and economic security. Although Hongwu had an uncertain grasp of Buddhist doctrine, he nevertheless viewed it favorably. However, he understood the political problems that had arisen in previous eras when the clergy gained too many privileges, so he avoided elevating Buddhism into state ideology.

As Hongwu's reign progressed, his view of Buddhism began to change. He started to view the religion in a negative light, suspecting the clergy of disloyalty and immorality. The emperor seems to have absorbed the prejudices of the Confucian officials around him. Whereas the medieval elite had held Buddhism in high regard, many Ming literati were strongly anti-clerical.[15] They looked down on clerics as lazy and greedy troublemakers. The gentry were particularly suspicious of nuns. Many of these women were of low birth, and elite men felt uncomfortable allowing such base people to mingle with their female relatives. They feared that the crude habits and dissolute values of lowborn women might bring down the moral standards of a respectable household. Some wealthy men forbade nuns from entering their mansions and prohibited their wives and daughters from visiting abbeys.

The Song dynasty Neo-Confucian thinker Zhu Xi had a poor opinion of nuns. Because Buddhist nuns refused to marry and left their families to live in a monastery, their lifestyle directly violated the classical rites. Moreover, Zhu feared that women who failed to bear children would end up feeling lonely and unfulfilled. While he did not absolutely prohibit women from taking the tonsure, he strongly discouraged it. The rise of Zhu Xi's ideas to canonical status during the Ming gave his prejudices great weight. But even though educated men tended to view nuns with suspicion, their women enjoyed meeting with female clerics who could regale them with interesting religious stories, render advice, and share the latest gossip. Contact with nuns helped cloistered gentry ladies glimpse the world beyond the walls of their home.

Hongwu eventually became alarmed about the extent of Buddhist influence on society. He promulgated harsh measures intended to uphold the Confucian rites, weaken the clergy, decrease the numbers of unproductive monks and nuns, and prevent clerics from causing trouble. In 1391 he initiated a persecution movement. Within a few months, the government closed down most monasteries and consolidated resident clerics in a few major temples in each region. New regulations raised the age at which a woman could become a nun. Previously, many women had become nuns when young, but under Hongwu, only women age fifty or older could enter a monastery.

The government forbade the clergy from mingling freely with laypeople. In particular, officials sought to discourage laywomen from participating in Buddhist activities, as the religion had been officially singled out as a potential threat to female morals.[16] They discouraged women from visiting temples and going on pilgrimages to distant religious sites, as they feared that religious activities would break down separation of the sexes, allow people of different social classes to mix freely, and expose women to assault by dissolute monks. The law also forbade Buddhist nuns from entering private homes, lest they exert an immoral influence on women of good family. Clerics were to stay inside their temples, adopt an otherworldly mindset, and devote themselves fully to spiritual pursuits.

When Hongwu died, the government lifted these onerous restrictions. Nevertheless, the religion had already suffered immense losses, and many monasteries never reopened. This persecution movement may have been relatively brief, but it had immense consequences. Buddhism was never again as important as before. The intellectual tenor of Buddhism also decayed. Meditation and scholarship declined, and most clerics spent their days performing funerals. Compared with earlier eras, there were very few prominent nuns during Ming.[17] It seems that the remaining nuns were also less educated and talented than before, reflecting the declining standards of Buddhism in general.

In 1537, the state once again briefly persecuted Buddhism, this time directing its attentions specifically to nuns.[18] Minister of Rites Huo Tao (1487–1549) sent a memorial to the emperor accusing nuns in the city of Nanjing of licentiousness, fretting that the alleged misconduct of female clerics might affect the morals of the region's laywomen. The Jiajing emperor heeded these warnings and expropriated seventy-eight convents, turning them into schools and shrines dedicated to paragons of virtue, and forcefully laicized the residents. Nuns over the age of fifty had to return home. Those under that age had three months to find a husband. Otherwise they would be married off to soldiers.

In spite of official antipathy toward Buddhism, a few high-placed women nevertheless showed great devotion to the faith. Palace ladies expressed their piety in the traditional ways, such as paying for the construction and renovation of temples, supporting religious communities, and commissioning sacred images. Copying sutras by hand had long been a way to express faith, and this practice also provided texts for the faithful to study, chant, and use in ceremonies. By the Ming, printed texts had become extremely inexpensive, so instead of promoting hand copying, several empresses and consorts aimed their patronage at the publication and distribution of sutras.[19] Their support helped make printed sutras more readily available than ever before.

Empress Li (1544–1614), wife of the Longqing emperor and mother of Wanli, stands out for her lavish patronage of Buddhism.[20] Wanli raised the tax rate and did not hesitate to employ heavy-handed methods to collect as much money as possible from his subjects. The resulting windfall allowed the pious Empress Dowager Li to build and renovate many temples. She also funded many charitable enterprises. This enormously costly spending spree drained state coffers. Li also tried to reinsert Buddhism into court life. She backed important Buddhist figures, and they used their influence to participate in the relentless intrigues that plagued the Wanli era. Largely due to the enthusiastic support of Empress Li, the reign of the Wanli emperor stands out as the highpoint of Ming dynasty Buddhism.

Beyond the palace, many members of the gentry still practiced the religion. As before, pious mothers and wives often convinced the men around them to become more devout. Particularly during the late Ming, landowners in south China actively patronized Buddhist activities. Some were genuinely pious, but many others pragmatically used Buddhist events and charities to become local leaders. As the government became increasingly corrupt, gentry participated in Buddhist organizations as a way to exercise leadership over local society while holding themselves aloof from tainted state institutions. Some literati also continued to appreciate Buddhist ideas and culture, and they integrated the most refined aspects of the religion into their own writings.

Overall, the Ming elite backed away from Buddhism. As the religion lost its most learned believers, intellectual standards declined. During the Tang dynasty, Buddhist thinkers had pondered profound schools of Indian philosophy such as Madhyamaka, which theorized on the nature of emptiness. But as religious education languished, few Buddhists studied these sorts of heady abstractions. Instead of intricate intellectual systems, they preferred simple beliefs, concrete rituals, and practical wisdom. For example, some nuns and monks studied medicine and became practicing physicians to express Buddhist compassion in a useful manner.[21] The most educated nuns learned about healing by studying standard medical textbooks. However, the faithful often placed more value on curative rituals. At this time, many believers began to see Buddhism largely as a technique of mystical healing.

Detailed records document life in the Nunnery of Unimpeded Filiality and Righteousness (Xiaoyi Wuai An), constructed in Hangzhou at the end of the sixteenth century.[22] The prominent monk Lianchi Zhuhong (1535–1615) conducted fundraising to build the nunnery and wrote two texts setting down rules for resident nuns to follow. Although ancient *vinaya* texts on monastic conduct had been translated from Sanskrit centuries earlier, Chinese Buddhists found them difficult to comprehend. Moreover, because conditions in Ming China were so different from those in ancient India, these foreign rules were often irrelevant or impossible to implement. The leaders of Chinese monasteries thus sometimes wrote codes of clerical conduct specific to a particular institution to keep order.

Zhuhong designed regulations that would keep the nuns isolated and otherworldly. He forbade large groups of laywomen from attending regular sutra recitations in the morning and evening. Nuns could not study funeral rites, as Zhuhong did not want them to frequently leave the monastery to attend funerals. He also forbade them from spinning, weaving, and embroidery. He wanted them to pray, not work. These stringent restrictions seem to have been a reaction to Buddhism's declining reputation. Zhuhong clearly hoped to restore the religion's prestige by holding nuns to the highest possible standards of conduct and isolating them from laypeople who might encourage undignified behavior.

Even as the overall vitality of Buddhism declined, new forms of popular devotion arose.[23] A violent movement with a female leader gained attention in Shandong. A peasant woman named Tang Sai'er (1399–after 1420) received martial arts training in her youth. At first she joined the White Lotus sect and became a local leader. Over time, she began to aggrandize herself, proclaiming herself Mother of the Buddha and claiming the ability to predict the future. Tang also declared that she had magical powers, saying that she could even turn paper cutouts of men and horses into a real army. Angered by the oppressive government, she led her followers to rebel in 1420. They won some victories and captured several towns, but eventually the army quelled this uprising. Rumor had it that Tang Sai'er had escaped and become a Buddhist or Daoist nun, but officials searching nearby monasteries never found her, and she lived out the rest of her life in obscurity. After Tang's mysterious disappearance, she took on a legendary stature. Although most historians consider her little more than a bandit, her reputation fared much better in popular fiction. Ming authors reimagined her as a righteous heroine who used her magical powers to strike a blow at tyranny.

Although fanatics periodically led rebellions against the state, popular religion was usually peaceful. In this era, mainstream Buddhism amalgamated with Daoism and Confucianism. The resulting belief system may have been shallow, but it gained wide support. This syncretizing trend allowed Buddhist ideas to influence secular culture, but also vulgarized Buddhist ideas and practice. Simplified popular Buddhism supplanted many traditional religious expressions. Luo Menghong (1442–1527) founded a new type of mystical Buddhism known as the Luo Teaching. He enjoined his followers to worship symbols that signified emptiness, an important concept in both Buddhism and Daoism. In the seventeenth century, believers used the goddess Eternal Venerable Mother (Wusheng Laomu) to personify this sacred principle. They practiced meditation to seek salvation and reach the Buddhist Pure Land. This sect began in Shandong but was spread by pious boatmen to towns and cities along the length of the Grand Canal.[24] The Luo Teaching is notable for its egalitarianism. Female believers were drawn to this religion as an escape from the restraints of Neo-Confucian ethics.

During the late imperial era, religion became increasingly worldly.[25] Because secularized Buddhism had absorbed Neo-Confucian ideals, women could learn about conventional female ethics without studying difficult texts. Oral Buddhist teachings exposed even the illiterate to secular views of female conduct. Sermons aimed at women sometimes highlighted Confucian virtues such as filial piety and maternal love, presenting them as religious duties. People also turned to religion to obtain practical benefits, seeing it as little more than magic. Female believers were especially interested in rites that promised useful results. Many carried out Buddhist devotions to implore the gods for a son, and they treated the bodhisattva Guanyin as a fertility deity.

The profusion of printed books enriched the literary dimension of Buddhism. To many people, religion had become something that they encountered by reading entertaining stories rather than worshipping in temples or studying sutras. Nuns frequently appeared as characters in popular tales.[26] Sometimes the protagonist of a love story was a nun. Readers appreciated love stories between a young man and an alluring nun as a fresh variation on the traditional scholar-and-beauty tales that had circulated for centuries. Other than the religious identity of the female protagonist, there was not much difference between previous stories and this new variant. Sometimes the author even describes the nun as akin to a Daoist immortal, as this supernatural identity increased her appeal. These stories usually depict nuns as respectable, sincerely pious, and dedicated to their faith. Sometimes the parents of these characters had even put their daughter in a nunnery to safeguard her virginity during a time of upheaval.

The rise of Neo-Confucianism challenged the propriety of female participation in public religious activities. It had traditionally been common for women to undertake pilgrimages to famous temples and other holy sites. At this time, however, men increasingly looked on female pilgrims with suspicion and criticized their behavior.[27] Also, a female traveler had to be accompanied by a man to ensure her safety. As the restrictions on female movement multiplied, men increasingly regarded this obligation as a nuisance. Nevertheless, the growth of the commercial economy gave more women the financial means to travel, especially in the prosperous southern regions, so many women still managed to make religious journeys.

Closer to home, many women attended local temple festivals.[28] Cities and towns in every region held festivities to celebrate religious holidays. These lively events combined spiritual ceremonies with secular amusements. Hawkers and itinerant entertainers catered to the crowd of celebrants. Everyone looked forward to these events, which provided an excuse to celebrate and have fun. Women showed particular enthusiasm for temple festivals, especially those dedicated to female deities. It was customary for both sexes to attend these rites, and women of all ages participated. Even as Neo-Confucian strictures kept women more firmly secluded on a daily basis, temple festivals provided precious opportunities for women to leave the home and see the wider world. Ostensibly they left the home to worship, but the secular trappings of these events provided a major draw.

Overall, female believers often turned to Buddhism and other religions in search of self-empowerment. A poem by a Ming dynasty nun nicknamed One Eyed Diamond (Dumu Jinggang), written during the early seventeenth century, sums up the appeal of religion to female devotees. This nun received her odd nickname because she supposedly read the *Diamond Sutra* (*Jingang jing*) for so long that she became blind in one eye. One of her poems employs religious ideas to interrogate the validity of gender stereotypes.[29]

> Male or female: why should one need to
>   distinguish false and true?
> What is the shape in which Guanyin would
>   finally take form?
> Peeling away the bodhisattva's skin would be of
>   no use whatsoever
> Were someone to ask if it were the body of a
>   woman or that of a man.

Women could harness the powers of goddesses or their mastery of sacred wisdom to claim an equal footing with men. Even as society demanded that women observe strictures that blocked their free movement, religion still provided ways for women to justify sexual equality, gain authority and prestige, and exercise their creativity.

Chapter 6

Virtue

Toward the end of the Ming dynasty, society developed a decadent fin de siècle atmosphere that led many writers to lament the dissolution that surrounded them. The unparalleled culture of the late Ming, effervescent yet raucous, aroused moral panic. In response, female ethics became a subject of lively debate. A topic often becomes widely discussed not because it is common, but out of concern for its absence. Thinkers focused on female ethics out of fear that society's moral fiber had frayed, giving rise to a surge in blatant immorality.

Anxiety over an alleged decline in propriety can be attributed to the explosion of popular literature at the time. Traditional genres of provocative writing circulated far more widely than before. For example, many epigones wrote imitations of the controversial fifth-century compendium *A New Account of Tales of the World* (*Shishuo xinyu*), titillating readers with depictions of eccentric and provocative female behavior.[1] Instead of promoting Confucian propriety, these authors praised women for their clever wit and repartee. Sometimes a woman gained acclaim for publicly humiliating a male rival. Although these sorts of texts had been available for centuries, mass-market publishing brought them to the attention of a large readership.

New types of writing were even more sensationalistic. Literature had traditionally been composed and read by proud literati obsessed with their public reputations. They wanted to project an air of dignified propriety, so they usually limited themselves to orthodox compositions. However, the authors of commercial mass-market fiction had no such qualms. They wrote to make money, so they took on sordid and titillating themes to attract lowbrow readers. Publishers relied on shock value to sell new novels and short stories. Moreover, as the dynasty declined, the political system became obscenely corrupt and people sensed that they were living in a time of decay. Rapid

economic and cultural change further exacerbated the collective disorienta-
tion. In response to these confusing circumstances, late Ming fiction took on
a disconcerting tone. Publishers bombarded readers with numerous tales of
louche and depraved women, giving them the impression that female morals
had degenerated to the point of crisis.

Some changes in literature might seem fairly subtle but nevertheless challenged traditional norms and stereotypes. Tang Xianzu's wildly popular play
The Peony Pavilion (*Mudan ting*) of 1598 gained attention by presenting
female emotions in a novel manner.[2] Traditionally, the female characters
in romantic stories had usually been fairly passive. This play surprised
audiences by showing women who forthrightly seek love. They behave so
confidently because they have a sense of their own worth, and are also more
self-conscious than the female characters of previous eras.

Many other works featured promiscuous women who felt completely un-
constrained by traditional morals. Readers felt both fascinated and revolted
by images of the "wanton woman" (*yinfu*) who blithely transgressed the rules
of decency.[3] By seeking sexual gratification outside of marriage, these female
characters acted like men. People had extremely different expectations for
each sex, so when a woman acted like a male philanderer, readers experienced both frisson and alarm.

Some Ming fiction even tried to stun the reader with blatant decadence.
Lu Tiancheng (1580–1618), author of the extravagantly grotesque vernacular
novel *The Wild History of the Embroidered Couch* (*Xiuta yeshi*) of 1597,
used foul language to describe a sequence of rapes and orgies.[4] This sort of
lurid pornography appealed to a small niche market. Authors could attract far
more readers by expressing risqué themes in a subtler manner. For example,
they might describe music in a way that gave it suggestive overtones, then
use this musical background to envelop female characters with a sexually
charged aura.[5]

Fiction authors also created female characters who disturbed readers by
contravening social norms. Stories about jealous women were not new, but
the rise of mass-market vernacular fiction exposed a broad readership to
traditional stereotypes of violent and hysterical shrews.[6] Stories of jealous
women fascinated readers because they knew that this was not just fiction.
Jealousy was a genuine social issue. Female possessiveness grew out of the
inequity of the Chinese marriage system. Husbands demanded absolute fidelity from their wives but felt free to seek sexual partners elsewhere. Wives
also envied their husbands' money and opportunities.[7] Female insecurity
generated mistrustfulness, which could give rise to complaints and threats.
Concerns about jealous wives made the shrew into a common character in
mass-market fiction.

Authors liked writing about shrews because these characters had great dramatic and comic potential. Prose fiction was written by men, and of course male authors uniformly portrayed viragos in a very negative light. These characters seem domineering, confused, unruly, and threatening. Many fictional shrews have other negative traits as well, making them seem even worse. They might be ugly, gluttonous, or lazy. And even though shrew characters are jealous of their husbands' liaisons, they are sometimes sexually immoral themselves. In this case, the author can explain away a woman's jealousy as mere lustfulness. She demands her husband's full sexual attentions to satisfy her voracious libido.

During the sixteenth and seventeenth centuries, many male authors wrote essays bemoaning the unhappy fate of the man married to a shrew. Husbands feared that a jealous wife might make a scene in public and cause them to lose face. The threat of humiliation gave wives considerable ammunition to attack an unfaithful spouse. Essayists did not counsel husbands to be faithful to their wives and treat them as equals. Instead they warned husbands to maintain firm control over their spouses, lest they cause trouble.

Writers discussed various possible cures for female jealousy.[8] Some counseled the henpecked man to lash out with violence, cowing his wife and forcing her to submit to his will. A gentler Buddhist approach was to remind the shrew of the bad karma she was accumulating, threatening her with perdition. Confucians stressed the value of education. They believed that proper ethical training would inculcate conventional values and lead her to see the error of her ways. Another school of thought viewed female jealousy as a medical disorder and advised that it could be treated with medicine or a change in diet.

Ming readers also enjoyed stories about violent women. This type of fictional character attracted attention by transgressing fundamental female virtues such as reclusion, gentleness, and obedience. However, as these characters employed violence to achieve a moral goal, it was difficult for conservative thinkers to find fault with them. In previous eras, women had occasionally harmed or killed others in an act of revenge. During the Han dynasty, this sort of righteous vengeance had been common and widely accepted, in spite of the many problems that it caused.[9] Although retribution was usually undertaken by men, sometimes a woman would seek revenge on behalf of a wronged family member if she lacked a father or brother to carry out the act. A number of records of female vengeance also date from the chaotic medieval era.[10] Due to the weakness of institutions at that time, people often took justice into their own hands. Women of the time occasionally sought revenge for wrongs as well. However, as society stabilized and pacific Confucian teachings gained more influence, violent vengeance became marginalized.

Ming literature associates righteous vengeance most closely with outlaws, such as the characters in the rough-and-tumble world depicted in the famous fourteenth-century novel *Water Margin* (*Shuihu zhuan*). Sometimes a woman imitated these sorts of ragtag heroes, taking on the identity of a female knight-errant (*nüxia*) who gained respect for exacting revenge, enforcing justice, and protecting the weak. In other stories, an ordinary woman feels compelled to seek vengeance. Sometimes a righteous woman would attack someone simply because he had wronged a stranger, even though the matter had nothing to do with her. More commonly, a female character exacted revenge on behalf of a murdered father or brother. They also took revenge in response to injustices that they had suffered personally.[11] In earlier times, stories about female retribution had usually been confined to works of history and biography aimed at an educated readership. But during the late Ming, the vengeful woman became a common character in popular fiction, exposing far more people to tales of female violence. Readers were intrigued by the moral ambiguity of women who broke the ordinary rules of female virtue in the name of Confucian righteousness.

The martial woman was another transgressive stock type that became popular at this time. Although real women very rarely took up arms or set foot on the battlefield, readers nevertheless enjoyed stories about tough female characters using martial arts to vanquish their foes. In response to this demand, authors concocted imaginative plots that featured female warriors.[12] Madame Zhurong, a character in the fourteenth-century masterpiece *Romance of the Three Kingdoms* (*Sanguo yanyi*), stands out as one of the most famous martial women of Chinese literature. The novel describes her as the wife of a chieftain who ruled a kingdom of the southern Man people, and she fights alongside her husband to defend her tribe against incursions from an invading Chinese army. Zhurong was named after the god of fire, from whom she claimed descent. This supernatural lineage intensifies her fierce image and also helps account for her martial prowess. Not only does Zhurong lead troops, but she also engages in combat personally, throwing daggers at the enemy with deadly accuracy. The author depicts her as a successful warrior who initially manages to defeat the Chinese invaders. Nevertheless, Zhurong herself is eventually captured. In the end, she and her husband accept Chinese domination, and he continues to rule his people as a compliant chieftain.

Notably, the character Zhurong is not ethnic Chinese. Her foreign heritage, which Ming readers would have considered barbaric, constitutes an important detail, as it justifies her martial behavior. As a foreigner, she simply has no interest in Chinese female ethics. The novel features this warrior woman as a way to emphasize her tribe's alien culture. In the eyes of the novel's readers, her people are not merely different but inferior, as they lack even the most basic Chinese morals. Although the author depicts Zhurong as a powerful and successful female warrior, he stresses her transgressive nature. She is certainly not depicted as a role model for other women to emulate. To the contrary, she represents the savagery and chaos of a society devoid of the civilizing influence of the Chinese rites.

∘━━✦━━∘

Of course, not all literary representations of women were so negative. In addition to depictions of louche wives and depraved beauties, writers portrayed many women notable for their integrity. Many stage plays featured female paragons of Confucian virtue, portraying them as chaste, filial, and righteous.[13] Even so, the profusion of disturbing images and ideas that permeated late Ming popular literature stimulated thinkers to ponder their society's ethical priorities.[14] Some took a critical approach and cast doubt on traditional ethics. This era's freethinking atmosphere made them suspicious of arid platitudes. They felt uncomfortable mouthing conventional banalities about virtue and condemning those who failed to live up to these arbitrary standards. As an alternative, they explored ways to harmonize ethical priorities with contemporary standards of conduct.

The Neo-Confucian reformer Wang Yangming (1472–1529) stands out as the most influential of these original thinkers. Unlike Song dynasty Confucians such as Zhu Xi, who considered ethics an objective reflection of the cosmic order, Wang took a more subjective approach to moral questions. He believed that we must use our minds to engage directly with the world to such a degree that the mind unites with what it perceives. Only in this way can we fully understand both society and the natural world. Once people achieve clear understanding in this manner, they can use their insights to improve themselves and their community. Wang's mystical ideas offered a welcome alternative to the rigid doctrines of Song Neo-Confucianism. He justified this subjective attitude as a way to reassess social norms and perhaps recalibrate gender ethics.

Although advanced thinkers embraced daring new ideas, most people continued to rely on traditional ethics. Girls were educated to accept standard Confucian virtues.[15] These teachings socialized young women by enjoining them to be gentle, kind, and content with their place in life. Overall, families put immense importance on their daughters' moral development. They believed that for a woman to become fully mature, she had to understand and accept the norms of female behavior.[16] They took the position that women are made, not born.

The Roman historian Tacitus famously commented on the incongruous link between civilization and servitude, an observation that might readily be applied to Ming women.[17] To be considered refined and moral, women had to accept a submissive place in the prevailing social hierarchy. Yet this moral training also had practical advantages. By understanding how society worked and what was expected of each kind of person, a young woman attained sociological competence.[18] Understanding social expectations allowed her to form and keep relationships, win approval for her actions, and gain acceptance.

Women had access to numerous books on ethical matters, many of them far more inviting and attractive than before. The rise of illustrated books in particular gave women new perspectives on ethical questions. Previously, they had often learned about Confucian doctrines by reading texts or hearing them explained. The profusion of illustrated books put out during the Ming transformed virtue into something tangible that they could see. People expected women to replicate these visual scenes in their own lives.[19] Woodblock prints depicted virtuous women acting out virtue physically. These illustrations not only made virtue seem visual and concrete but also emphasized the connection between morality and the physical. In the late imperial era, women increasingly personified virtue by manipulating their bodies, sometimes in extreme ways. The increasing visuality of female ethics gave impetus to this trend.

New books basically repeated moral themes set down by Liu Xiang during the Han dynasty. However, priorities had changed.[20] Liu depicted a wide range of positive female role models whose qualities ranged from wisdom to self-sacrifice. In Ming writings, some of these virtues, such as intelligence and talent, receded in importance. Unlike the Han, authors wrote few stories of women chastising immoral men. Nor did they put as much emphasis on the effects of good and bad palace women on the dynastic cycle.[21] During the Ming dynasty, palace women were politically marginalized, so this discourse had become less relevant. In place of those waning themes, the authors of moral works put far more emphasis on the relationship between husband and wife. The wife became the central social role for women. If a woman wanted to be considered good, she had to carry out her conjugal role in a way that conformed to the rites.

Among the spectrum of female virtues, reclusion became increasingly important. Girls and boys of elite families could play together until seven or eight years of age.[22] Then they were separated, and girls could no longer mingle freely with boys from other families. With the exception of rare outings, girls of high birth remained isolated at home for the remainder of their lives. Footbinding made it impossible for women to walk very far without enduring terrible pain, further limiting their movements.

Since antiquity, Chinese thinkers had classified space as the male outer (*wai*) realm and female inner (*nei*) realm. These terms referred to physical places inside and outside the home. Significantly, this conceptual model associated each realm with gender. The outer region, which offered opportunities and the possibility of public accomplishments, became a strictly male preserve. However, because educated men spent much of their time at home, they also had to inhabit the feminine inner zone.[23] Women's authority over inner spaces of the home allowed them to exercise some power over male interlopers.

Even within the inner recesses of a wealthy family's home, space was further subdivided into male and female zones of activity. Proper domestic architecture translated Neo-Confucian moral priorities into tangible spaces.[24] A house was not just a place where people lived. The imaginary architecture of the home also physically expressed the family's dedication to propriety. An ancestral shrine marked the center of domestic space. Surrounding areas were considered either individual or common places. Bedrooms (*gui*) were relatively private while the larger halls and other rooms (*tang*) were used for collective activities.

Women considered the bedroom their personal space. Female poets set innumerable poems in the boudoir, and these creative works helped construct popular perceptions regarding these inner spaces.[25] In the early medieval era, male poets described the boudoir as mysterious, erotic, and forbidden. According to men's poems, the inhabitant of the boudoir spends her time preening her beautiful body and thinking about an absent male lover. The loneliness and isolation of the bedroom give this feminine space an air of pathos. Female poets had a very different view of the boudoir. To them, it was an ordinary place where women spent much of their day. There they engaged in numerous activities, few of them related to love or sex. Women's poems describe the bedroom's quotidian features. They depict the inhabitants doing needlework, playing board games, caring for children, and socializing with other women. In direct contrast with the decadent poetry written by men, women often portray the isolated bedroom as an especially moral space. Instead of restraining the inhabitant, the sheltered boudoir protects her from evil influences outside, allowing her to uphold high standards of virtue.

Having a dedicated female space within the home provided women with precious opportunities for self-empowerment. When a bride entered her husband's family, she found herself isolated among potentially hostile strangers. In particular, her new mother-in-law might well resent the young wife, seeing her as a rival for her son's attention. A bride would want to bear children as quickly as possible so that she could raise her position in her new family.

Once she bore a child, a mother could then manipulate the domestic feminine space to construct a protective circle of close kin within the confines of her husband's larger patrilineal family.[26] Anthropologists refer this arrangement as a "uterine family." To gain allies, a mother would strive to make her children loyal to her above all others. She would often try to alienate them from their father and paternal grandmother. Creating a tight kinship unit around herself raised her standing in the household, helping to insulate her from hostile in-laws. However, the uterine family was fundamentally unstable. When children came of age, daughters left to marry into other families, and sons brought in a wife. The new daughter-in-law threatened a son's tie to his mother. In response to this menace, a woman might imitate her own mother-in-law and react with jealousy and spite. While uterine families may have been temporary, this contrivance nevertheless provided invaluable support for young wives at the most vulnerable point in their lives.

Women who lived a cloistered life saw outings as important events. Literature shows that women yearned for freedom of movement. Attending a temple festival or accompanying a husband on a journey seem like a dream come true. Economic growth had made travel more convenient and interesting than before.[27] Women toured the gardens of local mansions and took part in entertainments and cultured activities held within garden precincts. They took day trips to scenic spots not far from home. Groups visited temples and sometimes undertook pilgrimages to more distant sacred sites. Sometimes they took pleasure cruises to scenic spots on rivers and lakes. Women might also travel out of necessity, such as when they married a husband in a distant place or accompanied a spouse to a distant posting.

In an era when transportation consisted of wooden boats, palanquins, horses, and carriages on bumpy roads, travel was uncomfortable. Even so, poetry makes it clear that women usually enjoyed their journeys. Those venturing out into the wider world, perhaps accompanying a father or husband to a distant official posting, considered it a precious opportunity. The strange landscapes and unfamiliar customs that they encountered along the way expanded their horizons and stimulated poetic creativity. Where men usually dreaded the discomforts of obligatory travel, poetry shows that women often greeted it with excitement. With the female sense of space so constricted, events that men regarded as mundane seemed like a thrilling adventure to a sheltered wife. Numerous women wrote books, essays, and poems about their journeys, and female readers hoped to follow in their footsteps. Women's travel literature did not just describe alien landscapes and customs. It also imbued unfamiliar surroundings with emotional consequence. Leaving the familiar confines of the home and experiencing new places could seem extremely meaningful and charged with emotion. It gave women a rare opportunity to temporarily transgress ethical norms, break out of seclusion, move around the outer realm of male spaces, and interact with the wider world.

c⇥⃘

During the late Ming, the widespread reassessment of a quality called *qing*, translated into English as emotion, sentiment, or passion, had a profound effect on the realms of ideas and culture.[28] An encyclopedic compendium on the subject titled *Typology of the History of Emotion* (*Qingshi leilüe*), published around 1630 and traditionally attributed to the accomplished writer Feng Menglong (1574–1646), consists of more than eight hundred narratives classified into twenty-four categories that organize and describe the spectrum of human emotion.[29] The fact that Feng felt obliged to put together such a huge compilation on the subject attests to its prominence in both the academic realm and popular culture.

Ming literati had an ambivalent attitude toward *qing*. While they found emotional authenticity liberating, its unpredictability troubled them. They realized that following the emotions could easily lead a person to violate ethical norms and act immorally. Although the rising importance of emotion might seem like an outgrowth of the subjectivism of Wang Yangming's philosophy, early Ming literature shows that interest in the emotional side of humanity dates farther back, to the beginning of the dynasty.[30] Many educated people had been chafing under the yoke of rigid Neo-Confucian dogma, and they saw the advent of a new dynasty as an opportunity to explore subjective and emotive alternatives to oppressive orthodoxy.

For generations, Neo-Confucians had dismissed emotion as a largely negative force that can easily inspire us to commit evil acts. Neo-Confucian thinking on the matter developed out of teachings of the ancient sage Xunzi, who emphasized psychological control as a major goal of personal cultivation.[31] Xunzi believed that because the individual's emotions are potentially destructive, society must institute rules, norms, and rites to keep people's behavior in check. In contrast, the ancient thinker Mencius declared human nature to be fundamentally good, so he optimistically saw emotion as a largely positive force. Mencius believed that our good inner nature often gives rise to feelings of compassion and instills us with a desire to be virtuous.[32]

Song Neo-Confucian thinkers favored Xunzi's position on the matter, so they assumed that unrestrained feelings tend to give rise to selfish and covetous desires.[33] To counter this threat, the Neo-Confucian project encouraged suppression of the emotions. However, this approach made many people uncomfortable. They did not consider it right to systematically subdue feelings that well up naturally within us. Dissatisfaction with the Song Neo-Confucian position led them to seek a more openminded and positive view of the human condition, sparking intense discussions of nature of emotion.[34] Some thinkers turned to Daoism and Buddhism for inspiration, while others embraced Wang Yangming's Confucian subjectivism.

More broadly, Ming thought also reassessed the basic composition of the human being.[35] Neo-Confucians had previously downplayed the importance of the body and instead stressed the supremacy of the mind. They understood the individual not as flesh and blood, but in psychological terms. Initially, they interpreted people's actions as mostly motivated by conscious and thoughtful decisions. However, during the late Ming era, thinkers began to recognize the passions as a major motivation of human behavior. Even when we do not understand the source of our feelings or accept them as the normal state of affairs, they nevertheless exert an immense impact on our behavior. As Ming thinkers explored the non-rational side of human nature, they began to appreciate its power and richness.

The controversial writer Li Zhi (1527–1602) issued influential opinions on the subject.[36] Li regarded the thought of Zhu Xi as too inflexible and prescriptive to act as a workable template for real life. To circumvent the stifling legacy of Song Neo-Confucian orthodoxy, Li turned took a subjective approach to moral and intellectual issues. In search of inspiration, he perused the mystical writings of Xuanxue (Dark Learning or Neo-Daoism) that had been popular during the Six Dynasties era from the third to sixth century. That school of thought had probed psychology and epistemology, making it a useful vehicle to explore emotion. Li controversially rejected Zhu Xi's belief that the rites constitute the social glue that binds people together. Instead he declared that shared feelings create the most important interpersonal bonds. Although Li Zhi lacked sufficient intellectual discipline to bring his various ideas together into an organized body of thought, readers nevertheless found his opinions fresh and intriguing, and his works were widely read.

Whereas Neo-Confucian thinkers regarded emotion with suspicion, the literary world took a different approach.[37] Ming writers and critics embraced the emotional side of humanity, seeing it as authentic, important, and generally positive. They also realized that emotional content made narratives dramatic and compelling, thereby attracting more readers. Many Ming literati turned to literature for fulfillment, particularly those who had failed at an official career, and their love of fiction made them sympathetic to emotionalism. They regarded the stern suppression of emotion among Neo-Confucian pedants as hypocritical and artificial, and came to detest the suppression of natural desires.

As a result of this reassessment, views toward emotion became extremely diverse.[38] Lü Kun believed that the feelings could be extremely positive as long they remained moderate and non-erotic. Nevertheless, he feared that un-restrained emotion could easily break down the barriers separating the sexes and lead to debauchery. Fiction writers tended to have fewer qualms. Like Mencius, Feng Menglong realized that benevolent feelings spur us to treat others well, making them a prime motivation of virtue. Imbuing literature with strong emotional content not only made it more moving but could also increase its aesthetic value. Critics realized that authentic emotions could make a female character seem more attractive, so they began to emphasize emotionalism as a major component of literary aesthetics. In addition, people began to connect *qing* with physical desire, linking it to both romance and eroticism.[39]

Women were seen as more forthright than men in expressing their feel-ings, so the dialogue about emotion influenced views toward gender. From an early age, young people were socialized to view emotion as largely femi-nine. Although parents supposedly valued boys more than girls, in fact they often lavished more affection on their daughters, perhaps to compensate for the paucity of opportunities that girls faced in a patriarchal society.[40] Parents tended to encourage girls to express their feelings. Forthright female emo-tionalism affected women's views of married life. Many young women hoped to avoid an arid marriage based on ritual formality and instead wed a husband who loved them. The rising emphasis on emotion also affected the relative standing of wives and concubines in the household.[41] A beloved concubine might gain a higher status simply in recognition of her close emotional bond with the master of the house. *Qing* thus diminished the importance of the rites and family background, altering the dynamics of family life.

A rising appreciation of emotion led more men to empathize with women. Overall, men became far more interested in female voices. Women had traditionally used poetry to express themselves, and they sometimes articu-lated strong feelings in verse. Rather than dismissing this sort of writing as embarrassing or inappropriate, male readers were increasingly intrigued. The growing respect for *qing* gave women a more persuasive public voice. Some influential male figures supported them. Although Lü Kun came out of the Confucian tradition, he nevertheless showed considerable sensitivity to the difficult circumstances that women often faced.[42] Lü's awareness of emotion also made him more mindful of women's feelings, and he reassessed female ethics from the standpoint of the feelings they aroused. Lü Kun recognized the lack of security that women felt in their lives, as they depended so heavily on men. He also understood the emotional trauma that women experienced when they were unfairly forced to choose among conflicting values.

Emotionalism had an immense impact on Ming literature. Writers began to describe the world through a filter of intense feelings. Emotionally charged literature seemed authentic, elevating it into a significant mode of social discourse. The rising emotional content of literature resulted from a contradiction. As the economy expanded the opportunities for female self-expression, orthodox thought had become increasingly conservative. Fiction writers were the most creative expositors of new gender ethics. Unlike Neo-Confucian thinkers, authors took a generally positive view of *qing*, emphasizing its positive aspects such as benevolence and love.[43] They crafted narratives that described the range of human feelings in great detail. Many writers dissected the emotional life of wives and husbands as a way to explore this theme.[44] Rather than just parroting traditional platitudes and depicting marriage in static terms, they showed how the conjugal relationship affected the feelings of the spouses involved and how these emotions altered the mechanics of their relationship. Injecting emotionalism into tales of marriage transformed the ways that male writers depicted women, and how women thought about their own lives.

Readers were not just fascinated with emotion. They also respected it.[45] In this era, aesthetics became untethered from politics and history. Readers wanted to engage directly with moving literature, unmediated by serious ideas and ideologies. Emotion provided the obvious means for readers to straightforwardly relate to narratives. In influential Ming masterworks such as *The Peony Pavilion*, the impact of emotion on people's lives constitutes a major theme. Talented authors used their powers of description to create a particular mood that seemed to influence their characters' emotions. Readers felt drawn to literature centered on *qing* because they recognized how much influence this quality had on their own lives. Emotion brought the contents of fiction closer to real life, making these stories far more relevant. Shared feelings even seemed to forge an emotional community between writer, reader, and fictional characters. Female readers were particularly enthusiastic about stories that explored the passions, and writers responded by imbuing literature aimed at women with greater emotional depth.

Emotionalism influenced serious writing as well. Lü Kun criticized the dullness and difficulty of ethics textbooks and considered their forbidding style an impediment to moral cultivation. He realized that emotional writing could convey weighty ideas in an engaging manner, serving as a valuable medium of communication. Li Zhi took an even more radical approach. He tried to bypass Confucian texts entirely and use fiction to foster moral improvement. Li promoted popular literature such as *Water Margin* as useful texts for moral instruction.[46]

Much fiction did indeed disseminate ideas and imagery concerning virtue. The emergence of the chaste courtesan as a stock character exemplifies this trend.[47] Some novels describe a courtesan character firmly devoted to one man. Although she cannot possibly marry him, she remains steadfastly faithful to her beloved. In fact, the couple's inability to marry elevates their relationship. Whereas the classical rites bind spouses together, love unites the courtesan and her lover. This sort of story demonstrated how emotion could even give rise to fidelity.

Of course, not all Ming fiction showed female emotion in a positive light. People also understood the link between feelings and physical passion, and Ming authors churned out reams of erotic literature.[48] Although romance had long been a popular literary theme, authors had traditionally avoided explicit descriptions of physical intimacy. Out of modesty, they presented love as something psychological and perhaps almost spiritual. But because Ming readers felt far more at ease with strong emotions, writers began to describe physical desire more forthrightly. As stories showed the emotions affecting body as well as mind, late Ming romance became increasingly sensual.

Other kinds of innovative writings expressed unfamiliar views of female emotion. Ling Mengchu (1580–1644) wrote two collections of stories that captivated readers by taking a relatively open-minded attitude toward female emotion.[49] Ling had obviously been influenced by the freethinking Li Zhi, who took a relatively egalitarian view toward the sexes. Some of Ling's stories describe women's romantic sentiments and sexual desire in ways that make them seem completely reasonable. Nevertheless, there were limits to his tolerance. When a female character seems particularly strong, he diminishes her somewhat by depicting her as unfeminine or threatening. In this way he shows that although the permissible bounds of female emotion ought to be expanded, there should be limits to female autonomy.

Emotional writings also affected depictions of real people. The authors of history and biography make a subject's life "readable" by interpreting it through standard narrative models that associated events with particular feelings.[50] Highlighting the emotional content of a subject's life made narratives more meaningful and interesting, eliciting a positive response from readers. As subjective rhetorical techniques rose in importance, nonfiction writings took on an increasingly sentimental tone. Eulogies of wives and mothers became much more emotional than before.[51] Readers no longer considered it sufficient to simply describe the merits of the deceased in an objective manner. They also wanted to see the writer's subjective reaction to a person's life. The fact that the deceased could evoke an emotional reaction in the eulogy's writer and readers stood as an implicit testament to her importance.

The ascent of emotional literature had a major impact on female writers. At this time, women tended to write in new ways. They had always used their poetry to express concealed feelings. However, the shift in prevailing priorities toward emotionalism freed female poets from previous constraints, so their works manifested passions and desires much more forthrightly.[52] The range of emotions and their many effects became major themes of women's literature.

Although the passions became more prominent in women's writings, they still faced limits in how they could publicly express themselves.[53] Most female authors came from educated gentry families. Men usually edited collections of women's poetry, saw these anthologies through to publication, and arranged their dissemination. Most often, a male patron was the relative of at least one of the female authors represented in the collection. Although literati appreciated women who wrote cutting-edge emotional poetry, they did not want their female family members to create a scandal. Male editors served as a moral filter, ensuring that female poets expressed themselves in ways that did not depart from baseline propriety.

As the emotional content of literature became increasingly vivid, women adopted a far more critical tone. In retrospect, the emotions expressed in earlier women's poetry began to seem naïve and one-dimensional. Instead of just writing guilelessly about love and other strong feelings, the most skilled writers used their poems to analyze these emotions. A poem by Shen Yixiu demonstrates this sort of inquisitive approach to the romantic feelings.[54]

> In ancient times the poet Yu Xuanji
> Without sufficient reason discussed feelings thus:
> "It is easy to seek a priceless treasure,
>   but hard to find a man with a heart"—
> How greatly mistaken was her statement!
> When is the world ever short of passions?
> But all in all these are not genuine feelings;
> One party may harbor intense passions
> While the other's feeling is thinner than paper;
> The impassioned one cannot forget the remote other,
> And pursues daily her obsession in vain.

Shen takes on standard poetic conventions, implying that many of the feelings that poets express, and that people mouth in their daily lives, are in fact lies. She realizes that the stock emotions expressed in literature are often nothing more than an expedient pose. As these alleged feelings underwent more scrutiny, critical female writers realized that they were often shallow or insincere.

This is not to suggest that the emotions expressed in women's poetry were always contrived. The content of many poems ring true, and some can still move readers many centuries after they were written. The sixteenth-century poet Wang Jialuan hanged herself after her lover married another woman.

Before her death, she wrote the long and impassioned "Song of Everlasting Resentment" in which she lamented her lover's behavior and justified her decision to commit suicide. A small excerpt is sufficient to convey the magnitude of her explosive passions.[55]

> A long white silken sash will hang me from high rafters;
> And drifting, lost in a sleep, my soul will then disperse.
> As soon as it's reported that Jiaoluan has died,
> The whole town will laugh to scorn the Lin'an Wangs.
>
> Oh, how ashamed I am that I was not a good girl!
> I dared to take too lightly the conduct of the women's chambers.
> My debt of love is now paid—I will return to the springs below;
> Down below in those springs I still will not forgive you.
>
> The way you loved me at first is not the way you now behave.
> And the fury that I have for you is as deep as the sea.
> I know that my intentions were kind, upright as well—
> Not knowing that your heart was no different than a beast's.
>
> So again I take a length of the finest silk
> And send it sincerely off to where you are.
> Alas! That my rise and fall should be due to this!
> Murder may be forgiven, but never the death of feeling.

This was precisely the sort of occurrence that Neo-Confucians wanted to avoid. They considered women inherently more emotional than men and feared that unchecked female passions would often have adverse consequences. In this instance, society had encouraged a woman to vent her feelings. Ultimately, these uncontrolled passions led to her self-destruction. While many creative minds reveled in the era's emotional liberation, moralists felt compelled to impose clear restrictions on women's feelings to prevent them from spiraling out of control. Both female poets and ordinary women had to navigate this confusing clash between the desire for psychological autonomy and moral constraints.

Chapter 7

Chastity

Specialists in Chinese women's history often look to the treatment of widows to judge the overall standing of women in a particular period. Significantly, notions about widowhood changed considerably during the Ming dynasty. In part, these shifts resulted from a repudiation of certain policies promoted by the previous regime. The Mongol occupation had confronted the Chinese with disconcerting alien ideas about marriage and kinship. Whereas Han families had traditionally given widows leeway to decide what to do after a husband's death, Mongol custom mandated that a widow should immediately engage in a levirate marriage and wed one of her deceased husband's close kinsmen.[1]

Mongol priorities seem to have been shaped by their customs regarding marriage finance. Mongols put immense stress on bridewealth, making marriage very costly for grooms and their families. Having paid out a large sum to acquire a bride, the groom's family assumed that she had been effectively purchased, so they should have permanent control of her labor and childbearing capacity. They expected a wife to remain with her husband's family permanently, even after his death. Mongol views of widowhood affected official policies during the Yuan, which fluctuated over the course of the dynasty. Sometimes Yuan magistrates even tried to force ethnic Han widows to enter levirate marriages.[2]

According to traditional Chinese kinship concepts, for a woman to marry a husband's brother, father, uncle, or nephew constituted blatant incest. For this reason, Ming law prohibited levirate. Even so, the practice did not immediately disappear. Many Chinese men had realized the utility of reducing women to property and keeping widows in the family. Commoditizing wives might not have benefited women, but it could serve the interests of their in-laws. Because some people found levirate useful, even though Ming laws were strict in theory, enforcement remained lax.[3]

Society had very different expectations for each sex regarding conjugal fidelity. When a wife died, a man could remarry without embarrassment if he considered it convenient. In fact, if he did not yet have an heir, remarriage was expected.[4] Wives faced entirely different circumstances. During the Ming dynasty, widow chastity attracted increasing attention, putting women under increasing pressure to decline remarriage if possible.

Since antiquity, moralists had praised widow chastity. Initially, however, it was a marginal virtue. The Han dynasty scholar Liu Xiang did not put great stress on chastity in his influential collection of female biographies. By the Ming, however, records and stories of chaste women had become extremely common. Both the state and private individuals issued numerous books on this theme. *Ming History* (*Mingshi*), the standard account of the dynasty, lauds 307 exemplary women for their chastity. *Veritable Records of the Ming* (*Ming shi lu*), an official account of government matters, records 4,909 chaste women.[5] And *Complete Collection of Illustrations and Writings from the Earliest to Current Times* (*Gujin tushu jicheng*), a massive encyclopedia completed in 1725, devotes more than three hundred chapters to the lives of exemplary women throughout Chinese history. Of the chaste widows de-scribed, 72.91 percent lived in the Ming era. In contrast, only 0.06 percent dated to the Song dynasty, a vast discrepancy.[6]

The authors of fictional works also devised characters who personified this virtue. Ming popular literature disseminated ideas regarding widow chastity to a wide audience. Interest in highly charged emotions made this a common theme in vernacular novellas (*huaben*).[7] But in contrast to serious works on the subject, fiction portrayed chastity as less important than other moral prin-ciples. In fact, writers showed increasing empathy toward women who lost their chastity. Rather than looking at the matter from the standpoint of Confu-cian virtue, they tended to see it from the perspective of fallible individuals who had to contend with complex and often ambiguous circumstances.

The majority of chastity stories appeared in gazetteers (*fangzhi*) that de-scribed the history and conditions of particular localities. Early gazetteers differed widely depending on the interests of the compilers, but over time the contents became standardized. By the fifteenth century, almost every gazet-teer included commendations of female paragons, including chaste widows, written in a routine format.[8] Gazetteers were often edited by educated men who had failed at the civil service examinations.[9] Writing about the virtuous wives and mothers of the gentry helped them bond with other elite men, so it served as a kind of networking exercise. This activity could also earn an editor respect for his public embrace of state-sanctioned values.

The inclusion of so many biographies of exemplary women in gazetteers had a moral objective. Confucians had great faith in the power of education, which they often understood as the imitation of outstanding role models. The editors publicized the moral accomplishments of local women in the hope that others would take their examples to heart and conduct themselves in a similar fashion. These works describe various kinds of female virtue, filial piety in particular. The authors praise filial women for obeying parents in daily life, caring for them when sick, and conducting full mourning after their death.[10]

Gazetteers also single out chaste widows for praise. The frequency of chastity among widows varied according to locale. The largest number lived in coastal provinces. In areas where people held hardline views toward female ethics, such as Huizhou, a particularly large number of widows declined remarriage. The typical background of chaste widows also varied by region. Of the ninety-seven model women in a Ming dynasty gazetteer of Datong county in Shanxi, 32 percent belonged to military families and 47.4 percent were from ordinary civilian families.[11] The remainder were either related to officials or degree holders. Because the wives of soldiers were widowed at a higher rate than average, they accounted for an unusually large proportion of the chaste women in the northwest, as that region had considerably more soldiers than average.

A typical gazetteer from Ningde county in Fujian, published in 1538, records thirty exemplary women, twenty-three of whom were singled out for their chastity.[12] Most were widowed while they were still in their twenties, as a woman only received public recognition after several decades of widowhood. Some widows in the collection received additional praise for holding their families together, taking care of in-laws, educating their children, or being a kind stepmother. These biographies were often based on essays written by local literati to urge authorities to award a commendation to one of their female relatives. To make a woman seem worthy of official recognition, the authors of these applications often praised her to excess, which helps account for the overblown style of so many widow narratives.[13]

Authors of these accounts chose their language carefully, using words with moral and ideological implications that readers would readily understand.[14] They employed moral icons to represent a larger group, ignoring or explaining away any details that contravened the ideology they were promoting.[15] However, most of these virtues constituted ideals and norms, not requirements. Even if a woman considered a certain kind of behavior admirable, she did not necessarily conduct herself that way, as living up to the highest standards of virtue often entailed substantial personal sacrifice.

Each genre of writing came with implicit expectations and conventions that affected how authors wrote about women. While an epitaph tended to stress a woman's productivity, didactic biography often presented the female subject as a martyr.[16] Although Ming collections of women's biographies generally imitated the work of Liu Xiang, the priorities and style had diverged from early prototypes. Ming female biographical narratives had four stock plots: women who were virginal, filial, declined marriage, or resisted rape. Dramatic and violent narratives about forced marriage and rape attracted the attention of readers, so writers tended to favor them. These sorts of cases were also numerous. The Yuan dynasty underwent two decades of chaos before finally collapsing, and many women suffered rape and humiliation during that tumultuous era.[17] As Ming authors documented exemplary women from the previous era, they often ended up focusing on sexual violence. Rape narratives depicted a woman acting out her values. Many of the subjects committed suicide to safeguard their good names and the reputations of their families.

Although women's moral biography developed out of Han dynasty writings, newer literary currents had a major influence on these writings. Exposure to translations from Sanskrit had introduced Chinese to Indian ethics.[18] Chastity is a major theme in important Sanskrit works such as the *Ramayana*, which describes gods and monsters threatening a woman with rape. The ways that Indians handled these plots influenced Chinese authors. Supernatural elements and strange creatures seemed familiar to readers accustomed to the imaginative Indian tropes of Buddhist writings.

Popular fiction had a strong influence on Ming biographies of women.[19] Novels and short stories entertained readers by focusing on the strange and macabre. As biography adopted these conventions, descriptions of female virtue became increasingly dramatic and exaggerated. The female protagonists in new narratives were often young and attractive, introducing an undertone of masochistic eroticism as they acted out their virtues in radical and self-destructive ways. As in fiction, authors of biographies also frequently implied that the world has an implicit moral structure. In many of these narratives, a woman who behaved badly faced terrible retribution. If a widow remarried, her husband might become a ghost to seek vengeance.[20]

Most significantly, the authors of biographies implied that it was not sufficient for a woman to simply carry out basic moral duties. To be considered outstanding, she had to act out her goodness in a theatrical manner. Female virtue had become a dramatic ordeal, and those who attained it were martyrs. Instead of describing relatively ordinary women who did good deeds, Ming biographies of women lavished attention on horrifying incidents such as suicide, mutilation, and rape. Some of these role models seem heroic, but many others are merely pathetic.

❦

As marital fidelity gained prestige, increasing numbers of women declared themselves chaste widows. Sometimes even the fiancée of a man who had died prior to the wedding might refuse to marry another man, a new and far more stringent vision of widowhood. No one would fault such a woman for marrying someone else. For her to voluntarily take on the yoke of perpetual widowhood, even though she had never formally married, attests to society's high regard for this ideal.

Even though chaste widows presented themselves as self-sacrificing martyrs, they might enjoy certain privileges. It is often difficult to determine whether a woman decided to forgo remarriage out of principle or expediency. A widow could not inherit her deceased husband's property, but if she did not remarry she could manage it until a son came of age. If she lacked sons, she could maintain control of the estate until her death. The widow of a wealthy man could enjoy financial autonomy. A widow was expected to specify who would inherit the property, and the designated heir would receive it upon her death.[21] A widow could choose any of her husband's kinsmen as his posthumous heir. The son of a concubine or a nephew was an obvious candidate. Generally speaking, she would try to select the person least likely to cause her trouble. Some widows refused to appoint an heir because they feared that he might encroach on the estate while she was still alive. Occasionally, a widow would try to adopt an unrelated person as heir. Faced with this sort of unorthodox situation, her in-laws might try to expel the interloper, resulting in confusion and litigation.

Under the *Great Ming Code*, age often took priority over gender in determining seniority within the family. If a household lacked adult men, the senior female member (usually a widow) would assume authority over collective property and other matters, becoming the official family elder (*zunzhang*).[22] Even after her sons came of age, under Ming law they could not divide up the estate as long as their mother remained alive, so she could effectively serve as family matriarch for the rest of her life. The deference of adult children to a widowed mother was not just symbolic. Some surviving land sale contracts note that even though a man had carried out the transaction, his mother had approved it.[23] A strong-willed widow could retain control over her deceased husband's estate even after her sons had become adults.

Some women even managed to keep control over a deceased husband's estate after remarrying. A widow sometimes married again and brought the new spouse into her deceased husband's home, a variation of a matrilocal union.[24] This new husband could work in the fields and keep the family's lands productive. A widow could justify this arrangement as a way to carry out her duty to her first husband by keeping his household intact.

Although lifelong widowhood was considered virtuous, and could even have compensations, most widows did not voluntarily remain chaste. If possible, they would usually remarry. Everyone knew that widows confronted many hardships. Without a husband to protect her, a woman lacked a sense of security. And without an adult man to work or manage the land, she was financially vulnerable. Nor did those around her necessarily support her decision to remain unmarried. In-laws might bully her to try to force her to remarry so that they could reclaim their family property. Also, a chase widow had to remain absolutely faithful to her deceased husband. Any sexual encounter was considered adultery, and the community would despise a disreputable widow.[25] Some thinkers even believed that a widow who committed "adultery" should be forced to commit suicide.

People reimagined chaste widowhood by associating it with filial piety. Ming writings emphasized the importance of filiality and lauded extreme manifestations of the virtue. Gazetteers from this era give numerous accounts, apparently truthful, of people who spent years wandering through the countryside in search of lost parents.[26] Endless sojourning with scant hope of success demonstrated exceptional filial piety, and moral texts celebrated these martyrs who dedicated themselves to a hopeless task.

The scope of filial piety expanded over time. The ancients had originally defined this principle very narrowly as regulating the relations between sons and fathers.[27] Subsequently, it came to include mothers as well. In the medieval era, filial piety was extended even further to govern the relationship between wives and their parents-in-law.[28] Many Ming biographies emphasize women's exemplary filial behavior, which they could express in various ways.[29] Most frequently, a filial paragon would care for a sick or elderly parent. However, filiality might take unexpected forms. Among a sample of Ming biographies of filial women, 13.4 percent were widows who refused to remarry so that they could continue to look after their in-laws. People did not consider this a simple undertaking, as mothers-in-law had a reputation for being hard to satisfy. Some narratives even depict a monstrous mother-in-law who orders her son's widow to commit immoral acts.[30] Given the mother-in-law's bad image, for a widow to forgo her own interests for the sake of her deceased husband's parents constituted an impressive sacrifice.

Chastity rhetoric became much more radical and exaggerated over time. Compared to earlier collections of women's biographies, Ming editions had extremely violent content.[31] Although Liu Xiang's biographies had included a few tales of suicide and mutilation, these were marginal to his main themes. Starting in the Yuan dynasty, rhetoric about female virtue took a violent turn. Stories of women who harmed themselves in the name of virtue became increasingly common.

This violent rhetoric had various causes. The valorization of emotion tended to drive behavior to extremes. Many people had a positive view of the passions, so they accepted and even praised radical actions motivated by extreme emotions. In addition, the general coarsening of Chinese society encouraged violent manifestations of integrity. The Yuan dynasty left behind a legacy of trauma. The bloody Mongol conquest had caused untold millions of deaths. Thereafter, foreign overlords instituted a harsh system of administration to maintain their hold over a hostile populace. The Mongols even had wayward ministers beaten, a cruel custom that continued under the Ming.[32] And the collapse of the Yuan plunged China into chaos for more than two decades. Many women suffered from sexual violence, and numerous others committed suicide to avoid rape.[33]

Ming administration maintained many of the harsh aspects of the Mongol regime, fostering cruelty, tyranny, and chaos. Violent expressions of female virtue grew out of the general atmosphere of cruelty that became normalized during the Yuan. Brutality at the top of society set the overall tone for Ming culture, allowing and even encouraging people to engage in extreme behavior.[34] The atmosphere of violence seems to have spurred a rise in domestic violence. Under Yuan law, if a man caught his wife in the act of committing adultery, he could even kill her with impunity. The Ming maintained the same provision.[35]

The intensifying violence of chastity rhetoric can be seen most dramatically in the rising number of stories about self-mutilation. This was not a new theme. Tang dynasty writers had begun to portray female self-mutilation as an admirable expression of virtue.[36] A marginal medical practice inspired these stories. Pharmacological writings alleged that the ingestion of human flesh can cure certain illnesses. Of course, this strange ingredient could not be procured on the open market. Anyone who wanted to brew this medicine would have to cut some flesh from their own body. Tang writers described paragons of virtue who cut away flesh to brew medicine for a sick elder. Because of the pain and difficulty of self-mutilation, people began to consider it emblematic of filial devotion.

Initially self-mutilation narratives mainly described filial sons, but over time these stories began to focus primarily on women. Of a sample of 619 virtuous women in Ming records, 40 percent demonstrated filial virtue by allegedly cutting off flesh from their bodies. Among narratives of women recognized specifically for filiality, about 60 percent cut off flesh to brew

medicine for a sick elder.[37] As women's filial piety became redirected toward parents-in-law, these stories often described a model woman mutilating
herself to make a medicinal soup for one of her husband's parents. Although
some of these stories feature highly exaggerated details that mark them as
clearly fictional, many seem plausible. Self-mutilation was always considered extraordinary behavior, but it seems that at least a few women did indeed
carry it out.

Virtuous self-mutilation was especially popular in certain regions. Records
from northern Anhui describe a large number of women who undertook filial
mutilation.[38] About two-thirds or more of the filial female role models in local
gazetteers mutilated themselves. That region's particular circumstances help
account for the relative popularity of self-mutilation. Anhui was a relatively
poor and backward place plagued by frequent natural disasters. People who
could not afford herbal medicine often resorted to shamanism to treat the
sick. Traditional reliance on magical cures made people amenable to strange
potions with exotic ingredients, including human flesh. Moreover, Anhui was
particularly chaotic during the Ming due to periodic uprisings and endemic
banditry. Men were often away fighting, and a higher number than average
died an unnatural death. With so many men absent or dead, unusually large
numbers of women had to take on the primary burden of filial obligations.
It seems that some turned to self-mutilation to try to heal a sick parent or
parent-in-law.

The rising popularity of female self-mutilation disconcerted government
ministers.[39] Officials had received a Confucian education that emphasized the
importance of moderation. Although the most important Confucian thinkers
had occasionally praised extreme behavior in the name of virtue, they rarely
considered it a necessity. Educated men were also suspicious of the efficacy
of exotic drafts made with human flesh. Their skeptical attitude affected state
policy. Although the government did not outlaw self-mutilation, it was not
encouraged. Edicts of 1394 and 1426 forbade women who had practiced self-
mutilation from receiving official commendations for virtue. However, these
measures seem to have had no impact on popular attitudes.

Similarly, suicide for a righteous cause also became far more common.[40]
In fact, people increasingly considered suicide a standard way for women
to express exceptional virtue. Records of suicide steadily increased over the
course of the dynasty and reached a peak in the late Ming. Of the 35,829
Ming female paragons recorded in the *Complete Collection of Illustrations
and Writings from the Earliest to Current Times* (*Gujin tushu jicheng*), 8,688
either committed suicide or were killed.

Suicide for the sake of virtue might seem extreme, but in fact it grew out of
conventional moral principle. Confucian thinkers regarded morality as action,

not just good thoughts.[41] They believed that moral intentions have to be acted upon to become meaningful. Using the body to act out virtue is of course the most concrete way to express integrity. Some people used this line of reasoning to justify ethical suicide. Although earlier thinkers had not intended to encourage or even justify suicide, their arguments could be reinterpreted to provide convincing intellectual validation for this extreme behavior.

Virtuous suicide had many iterations.[42] Some widows killed themselves to express loyalty to a deceased spouse. Others were killed by rebels or bandits while resisting rape. Biographical writings include many accounts of suicide and murder. Among the biographies of exemplary women in *Ming History* (*Mingshi*), 78.5 percent died in order to preserve their integrity. About a third were killed resisting rape. Most of the remainder were widows who committed suicide to guarantee perpetual chastity.[43] Some unmarried women killed themselves after the death of their father to demonstrate filial piety. Sometimes women committed suicide out of lack of a good alternative. To widows facing impoverishment or mistreatment, suicide might have seemed like a reasonable option.[44] Suicide could also be deployed as a kind of moral weapon. A woman who felt shamed could name her attacker and then kill herself. By doing so, she publicly humiliated him and destroyed his reputation.[45]

As with self-mutilation, attitudes toward suicide varied by locale. Southern gazetteers record far more virtuous female suicides than those from the north. There were even significant regional differences within the south. Female suicide was far more common in Guangdong than Guangxi, and an unusually large number of women around the city of Huizhou killed themselves to preserve their integrity.[46] The methods of suicide also varied by place. In Fujian, women usually hanged themselves, and Shanxi women preferred drowning, while in Anhui, they would often fast to death. Some Fujian widows even committed suicide publicly, hanging themselves before an audience eager to witness their extraordinary self-sacrifice.

Whenever a woman contemplated suicide, she had to take into consideration contradictory factors and priorities.[47] Even if a woman killed herself for a noble cause, her loved ones would feel bereft. And a woman who attained martyrdom through suicide would have to receive an especially lavish funeral, imposing a financial burden on her family. Sometimes a woman expressed a desire to kill herself but did not go through with the act, as she had yet to fulfill important moral obligations. Most frequently, she might feel duty bound to remain alive to care for a parent, parent-in-law, or child. In most cases, only if a woman lacked pressing moral responsibilities would she consider committing suicide. Some waited for years until an elderly parent died or a child grew to maturity before belatedly killing themselves. Others attempted suicide and were rescued, so they vowed to simply remain chaste instead. Given the complicated circumstances enveloping suicide, some women left behind a poem to explain their motives.[48] However much they may have been influenced by prevailing ideas and values, they nevertheless saw self-destruction as their own decision and defended it as such.

Although suicide accounts elicit shock and revulsion in contemporary readers, at the time, the public regarded virtuous suicide as a moral victory.[49] They celebrated the fact that someone in their community had chosen to make the ultimate sacrifice in the name of virtue. Suicide narratives were not limited to history and biography. This theme also appears in many Ming dynasty novels, stories, and operas. The increasingly emotional content of literature made it easy for writers to integrate the theme of suicide. For centuries, audiences had enjoyed romantic tales. Female protagonists who killed themselves for the sake of love took the genre to a higher level of intensity. Literary representations spread these portrayals down into grassroots culture.

Female suicide was also related to the national renewal movement. A woman who killed herself attracted widespread attention, so she could readily serve as a dramatic symbol of the revival of cultural orthodoxy.[50] Literati encouraged women to publicly act out the moral ideals underpinning government and society. They imbued female martyrs with an almost sacred aura, lending widow chastity and related virtues the trappings of a religious cult.

The Ming state issued commendations (*jingbiao*) to women of exceptional virtue, mostly chaste widows. Official recognition of moral exemplars dated back to the Han dynasty.[51] Initially these awards were ad hoc. When the Tang revived this system, authorities made it regular and systematic, issuing awards for virtues such as benevolence, righteousness, loyalty, chastity, and integrity.[52] Most often, Tang authorities commended loyalty and filial piety. As society became more chaotic during the late Tang, the government put even more stress on the commendation system. Many officials attributed rising disorder to declining moral standards, so the government tried to use the commendation system to elevate moral standards and stabilize society. Although this scheme failed, the Song and Yuan nevertheless maintained the Tang system, seeing it as a force of order and goodness.

In 1368 Hongwu reestablished the commendation system. Whereas recipients in earlier dynasties had mostly been male, the number of female beneficiaries increased markedly at this time. The Ming government officially recognized the moral achievements of 27,141 chaste widows (*jiefu*) and 8,788 female martyrs (*lienü*) who died for the sake of virtue, with the number of annual awards rising over the course of the dynasty.[53] The government commendation encouraged widows to remain chaste in the hope that they might eventually receive prestigious recognition for their sacrifice. The standards used to determine commendation shifted according to prevailing views. At first the government issued kudos for filial self-mutilation, then announced that it would no longer reward this morally ambiguous act.[54] Even so, authorities continued to laud virtuous suicides and issued thousands of posthumous commendations for women who killed themselves.

As the commendation system expanded in scope, it developed into a two-tiered institution.[55] A woman could be nominated for commendation by either central or local authorities. National recognition had far more prestige, but the application process was complicated and rigorous. First, a candidate or her family would petition local officials, who investigated the claim and decided whether she qualified. If they thought that the petitioners had a strong case, they sent the file up to the prefectural level. The documents would then wend their way up through the provincial and national bureaucracy. The imperial court had final approval, so in theory, recognition came from the emperor, although of course actual decisions were taken by those around him. Applications were time-consuming and required applicants to meet very high standards of conduct. Many people preferred to simply apply for a commendation from their local government, as this was much faster. Minor local gentry cherished even local awards, so they actively discussed and recorded chastity cases. Lineage organizations also encouraged their widows to remain chaste, as they considered official commendation a collective honor.[56]

The embrace of widow chastity by the state made it symbolic of not only virtue but Chinese cultural identity as well. During the Ming dynasty, many ethnic Han soldiers, farmers, merchants, and exiles moved into border regions, spreading Confucian ethics to areas along China's margins. They introduced Chinese morals to regions along the empire's margins, presenting these values as emblematic of civilization.[57] Originally, the native peoples of Yunnan did not consider widow chastity a virtue, but Chinese migrants introduced this notion and urged them to adopt it. They had some success. The earliest Ming gazetteer for Yunnan lacks a section on biographies of virtuous women, but a similar work compiled in the middle of the dynasty includes these didactic narratives. Overall, Ming sources from Yunnan record 1,295 virtuous women. Of these, 635 were recognized for being filial and chaste. Sinicized concepts of female virtue were not limited to the Yunnan elite. Among these filial and chaste women, 77.6 percent came from neither families of officials nor literati. Conditions in Yunnan were often chaotic, so many women died defending themselves from rape. With the introduction of Chinese ideas about female virtue, these women came to be praised as martyrs. Some Yunnan women received government commendations for exceptional virtue, as the central government was pleased to encourage behavior that they associated with Chinese identity in the borderlands.

Likewise, the northwestern parts of Shaanxi and Gansu had very low population densities, and the inhabitants belonged to various ethnicities.[58] The government mistrusted the loyalty of non-Han communities. To strengthen the northwest border, the government encouraged ethnic Han to settle there. Officials established border towns to house Han officials, troops, and their dependents. In addition to buttressing defense, it was hoped that these Han settlements would also influence the surrounding inhabitants and convince them to adopt mainstream Chinese customs. Because this colonization movement was aimed at Sinicizing the surrounding region, Han migrant women were expected to safeguard their chastity and set a positive example for native peoples to imitate. Gazetteers from the northwest border region record many cases of chastity. Nor was this merely a rhetorical project. As the border regions were inherently unstable, women faced frequent risks. Rape and murder were palpable threats, bolstering the importance of female physical integrity.

As more women expressed integrity through violent means, some observers began to feel uneasy. In many cases, self-sacrifice seemed completely unnecessary. Many women had no good reason to kill themselves. Moreover, suicide seemed morally troubling because it could prevent a woman from fulfilling her family duties as daughter, wife, and mother. Lü Kun thought that people should observe Confucian virtue in moderate ways, and he overtly denounced widows who committed suicide.[59] Although these women claimed that they were killing themselves for ethical reasons, he suspected that they were in fact motivated by unrestrained emotions and perhaps even sexual desire. He saw emotion (*qing*) as a dangerous force that was encouraging women to act in exaggerated and self-destructive ways. Lü believed that these suicides threatened the spirit of moderation that keeps society stable.

❦

Widow chastity had many manifestations, so its rising popularity cannot be attributed to a single cause. Numerous factors happened to come together during the Ming era, which bolstered existing values and made them more extreme. Chastity had various motivations and social functions, and each individual weighed them differently when deciding how to act. Widows who made great sacrifices, or even killed themselves, were not necessarily behaving irrationally by the standards of the time. While most widows were temperate, some took extreme measures.

Changing social conditions help account for the radicalization of female virtue at this time. The previous era of Mongol rule had been unusually cruel, coarsening Chinese society and legitimizing violence. Moreover, endemic banditry and periodic rebellions plagued Ming China.[60] Many men died in battle, leaving their widows exposed to violence and exploitation. In many places, pervasive banditry was the norm, posing a constant threat. Coastal piracy exemplifies this trend. Japanese pirates ravaged seaside regions, and their incursions were often particularly cruel. Ming stories of the women caught up in these attacks portray some as heroes and others as pathetic victims. A few female warriors bravely fought pirate foes. People admired these strong women for taking on stereotypical masculine roles in a time of crisis and fighting to defend their community. More frequently, however, documents describe women being raped or killed, or else committing suicide to preserve their honor. Similar chaotic conditions exposed women to danger in places across China. With so many women threatened with rape and murder, people put increasing stress on the integrity and purity of the female body. As chaste widows and suicidal martyrs garnered increasing respect, more women followed their examples.

Widow chastity and related behaviors varied by region, so local factors also had an impact on ideas and actions.[61] Most people accepted widow remarriage as the norm. But in some regions, such as Huizhou, the community held remarried widows in contempt. Places where widow chastity became especially common tended to have unusually high population densities. A surfeit of people and shortage of land gave rise to widespread hardship that put pressure on local society. As conditions became dire, people became more amenable to extreme value systems.

Elite men also developed a different mentality that influenced their views of female virtue. As the number of students taking the civil service exams increased, the possibility of passing became extremely remote, so fewer educated men achieved professional success. Repeated failures frustrated and humiliated them. In response, many literati expressed dissatisfaction with the overall state of society. They had received an extensive Confucian education, so they looked to these teachings for answers. To rectify the problems around them, they demanded that members of the community hold themselves to exacting Confucian moral standards. In transmitting these values to their daughters and wives, they encouraged them to act out ethics in extreme ways.

The rising influence of Neo-Confucian teachings also affected women's values and behavior. Ming literati wanted to purge Chinese culture of Mongol influence and revive previous norms, leading them to embrace Song dynasty values. Many of them embraced Song Neo-Confucianism, a previously marginal school, as representing orthodox Chinese culture in general. Hardline Neo-Confucianism thus became political and social orthodoxy.[62] This school of thought justified extreme manifestations of female propriety.

A few outliers in the Neo-Confucian movement, such as Cheng Yi (1033–1107), had advocated violence in the name of female ethics. Cheng believed that a woman had a duty to commit suicide to preserve her integrity if necessary.[63] Although Cheng's alarming views have received considerable attention from historians, in fact they represented a very marginal position and had little impact outside of a small academic circle. Even so, mainstream Neo-Confucianism promoted extremely stringent ethical teachings. Zhu Xi was no fanatic, yet even he demanded considerable sacrifices from women. His steadily increasing stature lent these ideas considerable weight, affecting the values and behavior of Ming women.

Educated men frequently drew parallels between the chaste wife and loyal official. Ever since antiquity, writers had likened the roles of wife and government minister.[64] Although people today might consider these two social types to be extremely different, moralists pointed out that wives and officials share closely related ethical obligations. Under a monarchical system, members of many families served the state generation after generation. Family and government became closely intertwined, so the elite saw the two realms as comparable. Both wife and official should be absolutely faithful to a man, whether husband or lord. Although they exhibit loyalty differently, the underlying virtue is similar. The unending crisis and factionalism of the Ming government made thinkers emphasize male loyalty. Female chastity, its gendered moral counterpart, grew in importance by association.[65]

Alterations to the kinship system also help account for the intensification of chastity during the Ming dynasty. Changes to ritual practices and the law tied a woman more closely to her husband's family and lineage, transferring her allegiance to his relations.[66] The redirection of women's filial sentiments from parents to parents-in-law increased the moral import of marriage.[67] When a bride married, she did not just enter into a righteous bond with her husband. She also undertook an obligation to serve his parents. As filiality interpenetrated marriage, people came to associate widow chastity with filial piety. A widow who refused to remarry, ostensibly so that she could continue to care for her parents-in-law, displayed exemplary filial devotion. About 60 percent of the stories of filial Ming women describe a widow or wife caring for a sick parent-in-law. Half of these paragons cut off a piece of their own flesh to brew medicine to treat the illness. Burgeoning popular literature, such as stage plays, embraced the theme of filial piety, exposing audiences to innovative ideas on the topic.[68]

The rise in widow chastity was part of a much wider movement to promote Confucian ethics. The early fifteenth century saw a sudden spike in the construction of shrines dedicated to male paragons of virtue.[69] Likewise, people began paying more attention to women's morals. Numerous books on female ethics were in circulation at the time. Many had been edited or rewritten to conform with Neo-Confucian ideals, exposing female students to a stringent vision of ethics. An increasingly effective system of female education integrated these beliefs, influencing growing numbers of women. The rising number of chaste widows and virtuous suicides attests to the effectiveness of moral education. Shang Jinglan (1604–ca. 1680) wrote of her deceased husband, "Though the living and the dead walk on different roads, / My chastity complements your integrity."[70]

Emotionalism also influenced the popular perceptions of female ethics.[71] Women who undertook terrible sacrifices for the sake of a moral ideal were often driven by powerful feelings. Authorities had traditionally been suspicious of acts of passion, but many Ming writers cherished the authenticity of strong emotions. A woman who behaved virtuously by following her feelings was not just mechanically carrying out a moral duty. She had a genuine desire to behave in an exemplary manner, making her sacrifice seem far more meaningful. Some writers even claimed that moral acts could only be considered valid if they had an emotional motivation. Strong feelings both explained and legitimized the female martyr's sacrifices. Readers were fascinated with stories of women who undertook sacrifices due to strong passions. A widow who remained chaste for decades or committed suicide might perhaps have acted out of love rather than duty, allowing readers to reimagine earlier accounts as tales of stirring romance. Writers began to concoct stories of beautiful young widows dying from grief over the death of a spouse, emphasizing the intensity of wifely passions.

Women who committed extreme acts exhibited agency. A model woman received many influences from various sources, but in the end, she decided how to respond to her particular circumstances. Each widow's situation varied, and she had to balance different factors when deciding on a course of action. She had to weigh her available resources and options against family responsibilities and a desire for respect and status. Her financial prospects, family circumstances, and whether or not she had children all contributed to her decision.[72] The fact that women who faced similar challenges reacted in different ways attests to the power of the human will. People were moved by extraordinary acts of suicide or self-mutilation because they recognized it as an expression of extraordinary resolve.

Most fundamentally, in order to resist remarriage, a widow needed sufficient resources to survive without a husband's support. If a man left behind a sufficient estate, chastity was a feasible option. However, most widows had few resources. When their husband died, they had no choice but to quickly remarry. Because most widows remarried out of financial necessity, chastity became a status symbol. Wealthy families encouraged their widows to remain chaste as a way to flaunt their affluence.[73] The growing use of chastity as a sign of conspicuous consumption helps account for its increasing popularity among the gentry.

Under Ming law, a widow who remarried could not take her dowry into a new marriage. She had to forfeit it to her first husband's in-laws. This constituted an immense blow, as a wife without a dowry lacked a sense of security. If she remarried, she would be at the mercy of in-laws who would likely look down on her for entering their home empty-handed. The intensification of chastity rhetoric had already cast suspicion on the morals of remarried women. When compounded by poverty, a remarried widow would likely assume a depressed status in her new husband's family. Because a woman lost property and status when she remarried, she would think carefully before deciding to take this step.[74]

Not only did remarriage have increasingly negative connotations, but chastity also gained more prestige. History is filled with examples of people who undertook arduous feats in order to gain respect and raise their social status. The early Christian martyrs, who often came from the bottom of society, raised their social standing by publicly suffering for the sake of principle.[75] Likewise, Chinese widow chastity served as a strategy for social advancement. During the Ming and Qing dynasties, a rising number of lower gentry and commoners encouraged their family's widows to remain chaste. By adopting the ethical standards of a higher social class, they could raise their status in the eyes of others.[76]

In sum, a widow took complex and contradictory factors into consideration when deciding how to respond to her predicament. Poetry confirms the strength of conviction that some widows felt. They did not always follow the easiest possible path. A growing number decided to sacrifice themselves for the sake of a moral ideal. Sometimes a woman used a poem about a departed husband to ruminate on the importance of marital fidelity. A sixteenth-century poem by a Madame Wen exemplifies this sort of sentiment.[77]

> With devotion I read over the writings of women past,
> After nine detours I grasp and extend their lessons.
> Others may envy, in their blindness, a woman's delicate beauty,
> But I adopt purity, heaven's own virtue.
> When I recall my departed husband's fine manner
> My heart sways to and fro as if I were drunk.
> My hair is uncombed and tangled like a mourner's;
> Though I have planted forget-all-care, I cannot sleep.
> Whoso holds pure chastity in the square inch of her heart
> Flies on wings of fame to be honored in Heaven's court.

Distraught by her husband's death, Wen vowed to remain chaste. She did not consider this a difficult decision. Works about female ethics had taught her the propriety of widow chastity, making her determined to carry out these injunctions to the letter. This poem employs strikingly passionate language. Widow Wen made her decision by taking into account various factors. She was not just motivated by moral teachings, but also out of intense affection for her departed husband.

○══✦══○

Anthropologists have noted that many cultures link wifely fidelity with premarital virginity. Sometimes these paired virtues are promoted in tandem as a deliberate social strategy. Early Christians encouraged both virginity and widow chastity as a way to lessen women's reliance on men.[78] If a woman held herself aloof from men, she could become more independent. And if she exercised control over her own body and sexuality, she gained more autonomy. Promoting these practices as virtues advanced emancipation under the guise of ethics.

Other cultures prohibit women from engaging in premarital sex to reinforce the patriarchal order. Male control of women's bodies subjugates them. Some societies go to extraordinary measures to safeguard the virginity of young women prior to marriage. Tongan chiefs would even tie their daughters' legs together each night to prevent them from being sexually active.[79] Because chiefs married off their daughters to build useful alliances with other powerful men, they had to keep them virginal to obtain an optimal match. In this sort of situation, enforcing virginity ended up reducing female autonomy.

These examples serve to show that the causes, uses, and expressions of virginity and chastity vary widely. Some cultures allow premarital sex but condemn adultery. Others demand virginity before marriage but allow wives to have extramarital affairs. During the Ming dynasty, as in most historic societies, women tended to marry young, so virginity applied mostly to adolescent girls. The emphasis on virginity grew out of the custom of sending off a bride with a generous dowry. The ancient Chinese emphasized the betrothal gift from the family of the groom to that of the bride as necessary for a proper wedding.[80] Although families also provided a trousseau and perhaps a dowry, this was not required. Dowries rose considerably in value during the Song dynasty, and this custom continued into the Ming. As success in the civil service examinations became the standard path for a prestigious career as a government official, families offered large dowries to attract a son-in-law with good prospects.[81]

The dowry marriage system made it important for a girl's family to preserve her virginity. Because parents paid out a large dowry when their daughter wed, they went to great pains to avoid inappropriate marriages. If their unmarried daughter entered into a sexual relationship with a low-status man, became pregnant, and ended up having to marry down, the dowry would be completely wasted. A significant amount of wealth would leave the family with nothing to show for it but an embarrassing connection with the wrong in-laws. Every ambitious young man knew that impregnating an unmarried woman from a higher background could earn him social advancement, however much his accidental in-laws might resent him for ruining their daughter. A teenage girl and her male relatives had different priorities, so they could not leave this decision to her. Parents took measures to shield their daughter from potential seducers until they had selected an appropriate spouse.

To discourage girls from engaging in premarital sexual relations, society made virginity an important virtue. Valorizing virginity served the interests of elite families. Some young women would have rebelled if told that they had to stay virginal for the sake of their family's wealth and status, so families enveloped virginity with the air of propriety. A girl hoped to be a virgin bride so that she could enter her husband's home with head held high. Although this arrangement made practical sense for wealthy families who could offer large dowries, framing virginity as a virtue made women of humble backgrounds value it as well. Even peasants could demand respect for safeguarding their daughter's maidenhood. Making virginity a status symbol spread this virtue down to affect every level of society.

As a side effect, the emphasis on virginity may have bolstered conjugal fidelity and wifely chastity as well. Because families put such great stress on the chastity of their unwed daughters, people began to use it as a reference point for understanding female sexual morals in general. If it is unethical for a woman to have intercourse before marriage, it can easily begin to seem as if all sex outside of marriage is equally wrong. According to this social logic, it seemed reasonable to demand that wives avoid extramarital affairs. The emphasis on virginity could even make widow chastity seem more virtuous.

The particular conditions of each time and place affect how ethics are formed and manifested. The cult of virginity led people to admire women such as nuns who renounced sex entirely. However, secular Chinese ethics had very different priorities. Of the four hundred exemplary female role models described in *Ming History*, 3.25 percent earned recognition for preserving their virginity in the face of difficulty.[82] This might be a small proportion of the total, but it suggests a stronger emphasis on virginity than before. It was the norm for women of elite families to remain virginal until marriage, so no one considered this behavior exemplary. Writers mentioned it far less frequently than suicide, self-mutilation, or even widow chastity, which were all exceptional acts. To receive attention for virginity, a woman had to express this virtue in an unusually stringent manner.

During the latter half of the Ming, people began to laud so-called faithful maidens (*zhennü*). These women had been betrothed, but their fiancés died before the marriage was concluded.[83] They considered themselves akin to widows, even though they had never been married, and declined to marry out of fidelity to their would-be husband. This sort of sacrifice was never considered mandatory or even customary, so the decision to remain a lifelong virgin expressed extraordinary resolve. Because women entered this state at such a young age, their sacrifice usually lasted longer than that of chaste widows, making them seem more virtuous in comparison. A few of these young women even committed suicide to follow their fiancé to the grave.

The rise of the faithful maiden cult had various inspirations. In the seventeenth century, popular literature dramatically depicted hardline Neo-Confucian ideas, inspiring some young women to live up to these high standards. However, some faithful maidens were probably behaving pragmatically. As a de facto widow, a maiden could seize control of her deceased fiancé's property, allowing her to live independently and avoid the restrictions that came with married life. Others may have sought respect and fame. They could be confident of eventually receiving an official commendation from the state, bringing honor to themselves and their families. Some women may have wanted to avoid marriage and childbirth altogether, and permanent maidenhood gave them an excuse to forgo an unwanted way of life.

People had mixed feelings about faithful maidens. Some admired their extraordinary commitment to both chastity and virginity, while others criticized them as fanatics. Such a great and unnecessary sacrifice violated the spirit of Confucian moderation and went far beyond what the classical marriage rites required. Moreover, records describe some faithful maidens entering into a state of permanent virginity against the wishes of their parents. In doing so, they violated the dictates of filial piety. These maidens accomplished one virtue by breaking another, making their actions seem morally ambiguous. Nor did the family of their deceased fiancé necessarily want to receive them. Faithful maidens expected to live with the family of their would-be in-laws, as they were akin to widows. However, the parents of deceased fiancés were usually unenthusiastic about the unusual and awkward presence of an unmarried woman from another family in their home. They often considered these faithful maidens to be interlopers and accepted them only grudgingly.

Even though no one demanded that faithful maidens pledge lifelong virginity, and most of those around them likely opposed their decision, some of these women nevertheless managed to remain lifelong virgins. They were usually only teenagers when they declared themselves faithful maidens, making their tenacity particularly striking. Some women decided to live as faithful maidens because they sought prestige within a patriarchal society. The fact that they managed to live out their lives as virgins attests to the power of female agency.

Chapter 8

Image

The Ming dynasty was a particularly dynamic era in Chinese history. As the economy, society, and culture changed, standard images of womanhood shifted in response. Most visibly, Ming writers and artists showed a renewed interest in the nature of the female body. This was not a new concern. Ancient thinkers considered men and women fundamentally different and demanded that the sexes be clearly distinguished and kept separate to a degree. Ethical dictates often sought to control the female body, which male moralists considered a potential source of trouble.

The explosion of popular literature and other forms of mass culture during the Ming era generated even more interest in female physicality. At this time, rather than simply reading about women in dry tomes, people encountered numerous descriptions in emotionally charged stories and visual images in woodblock prints. To make female characters seem more compelling, writers and artists put great emphasis on their appearance. They depicted women using their bodies to act out their beliefs or inner character, whether through suicide, chastity, or sex. More than ever before, a woman's body was considered to represent her personhood.

Changing medical notions also affected the ways that women were understood. In the late imperial era, the practice of medicine underwent a fundamental change, as numerous students who had failed the civil service examinations put their literacy to use by turning to medicine.[1] This new breed of erudite physicians differed from traditional healers. They had received extensive training in the ancient classics, so they combined literati notions with medical practice. As medical theory integrated Confucian moral ideas, doctors began to perceive women in new ways. In many respects, the result was positive. Partly due to the influence of classical teachings, the new breed of physicians considered female and male bodies to be fundamentally different, so they paid more attention to female ailments than in the past. Ming physicians were also more likely than before to offer different treatments to each sex. This mindset stimulated detailed investigations of gynecology, obstetrics, and other aspects of medicine targeted specifically at women. For example, diseases of the female breast received far more attention than before, resulting in better treatments.[2]

Not all developments were so positive. Mass-market literature disseminated extremely negative images of women, which had a major impact on popular assumptions. To catch the attention of the reading public, publishers offered increasingly dramatic and strange tales. Authors inserted repellant female characters into stories, promulgating unappealing female stereotypes.[3] In Ming fiction, the evil female character is often ugly, bestial, or even demonic. Exaggerated popular fiction encouraged readers to associate unpleasant female appearance with base morals. Occasionally, however, Ming literature portrayed a virtuous woman as ugly. In these cases, an author used a woman's plain appearance to convey the hardships that she had endured. Readers pitied these characters for having suffered terrible privations, intense anxiety, or illness. These sorts of ugly women were objects of pity, not scorn.

Other characters attracted attention for gender ambiguity or fluidity. Chinese thinkers traditionally linked gender to metaphysical ideals such as yin and yang. Although binary, these cosmic features were believed to be in constant flux. Linking personhood to these fluid qualities implied that gender identity might change. Ming popular literature and even factual accounts describe androgynous people, individuals who change their gender, and women with stereotypically male characteristics.[4] Although readers viewed these occurrences as a natural outcome of metaphysical dynamics, they nevertheless considered gender inversion strange. During the late Ming, readers became fascinated with unusual people and events, so gender ambiguity became a prominent topic. Rather than accentuating the physical aspects of androgyny and sex change, writers tended to focus on the awkward social ramifications of gender mutability.

In this era, more writers openly discussed menstruation. Popular medical texts and fictional works popularized the idea that menstrual discharge pollutes the female body, posing a grave threat to men. Menstrual taboos were not unique to China. In many cultures around the world, menstruating women suffer discrimination. Various societies use women's alleged pollution as an excuse to exclude them from public activities, religious rites, and even ordinary social interactions.[5] In China, the belief that menstrual fluids pollute the body persisted into the twentieth century.[6] Even so, menstruation also gave women a kind of power. The invisible nature of this pollution seemed mysterious and almost magical, imbuing women with an imposing aura. Men considered the polluted female body as potentially dangerous, so women could use their physical attributes to threaten men and provoke fear.

Popular literature embraced the view that womanhood is both dangerous and powerful. Long before, during the early medieval era, authors had begun writing narratives about malicious foxes. These sorts of stories became extremely popular during the Ming. The technical sophistication of Ming prose allowed writers to describe foxes in far greater detail than before, simultaneously terrifying and entertaining their readers. Authors depicted fox spirits as harmful creatures who sometimes took on female form to seduce unsuspecting male victims. A man who realized that he had been in a sexual relationship with a fox reacted with horror. The fox spirit embodied the contradictory view of woman's inner nature as both polluting and powerful, serving as a physical representation of menstruation.[7] By turning menstruation into a type of literary character, writers could explore how this polluting power affected men and also the terrified reaction of male victims. The enduring allure of the fox genre speaks to men's alarmed fascination with women's physical nature.

The authors of lowbrow mass-market literature often tinged their stories with erotic undertones. An increasing number of works were even blatantly pornographic. For the first time, it became easy for people to procure books that dealt forthrightly with sexual themes, affecting popular attitudes.[8] Ming fiction described sex from different perspectives, giving readers a panoramic view of the topic. The boom in erotic literature emerged due to the general commercialization of sex. As the economy developed, merchants catered to every aspect of popular demand, so erotic goods became readily available on the open market. Shops offered a range of commercial aids to boost sexual performance or increase pleasure, including drugs to be ingested for various purposes.

Books about sex became widespread, and the subject came out into the open. Daoist mystics and physicians had long written about sexual acts in religious and medical works, but these specialized writings had a small audience. As a result of the Ming publishing boom, ideas about sex that had been discussed by specialists for centuries became fodder for mass-market fiction, pushing them into the popular consciousness and affecting the thinking of ordinary people. Detailed descriptions of sexual encounters often ran contrary to the romantic view of physical affection, which was also popular in the late Ming. In fact, erotic and romantic fiction offered contradictory views of sex. Some ancient books on sexual technique had portrayed intercourse as a struggle for dominance between the participants, and fiction authors took on this theme. According to this view, each side tried to use the encounter to vanquish the other. While the man was traditionally considered sexually dominant, a woman also had considerable physical power, as she could deploy the polluting aura that men regarded with awe.

The Chinese have always regarded sex as healthy, natural, and even necessary. Technical works on the subject usually stressed the functional aspects of intercourse. People did not see sexual relations merely as pleasure or procreation. Medical and religious authorities taught that if the sexual act were performed in a certain way, it could act as a potent kind of physical cultivation that harmonized the elements of the body, strengthened the physique, and aided health. Some even believed that certain sexual techniques could induce longevity. The functional utility of sex made it seem good in moderation. The scandalous reputation of erotic literature such as *Jin Ping Mei* came not from the description of the sexual act per se, but from detailed portrayals of dissipation.

The functional view of sex is often apparent in Ming erotic literature. Even in *Jin Ping Mei*, kissing is not just a form of carnal pleasure. More importantly, it could be employed as a technique for physical cultivation. The author sometimes describes a couple deliberately swallowing one another's saliva. According to certain Daoist texts, ingesting saliva during the sexual act strengthens the body and increases longevity. By integrating this sort of previously arcane sexual lore into popular fiction, novelists exposed the general reading public to functional views of sexuality and the human body, raising awareness of the physical aspects of womanhood.

In every era, women ornamented, manipulated, and altered their bodies for various reasons. The explosion of material culture during the late Ming gave people far more opportunities to manage their appearance and use it to gain respect. They utilized various material goods to pursue social strategies. Women selected clothing, jewelry, makeup, and other items to construct a visible social identity. They also associated themselves with particular objects, such as fans and mirrors, which they employed as props during social performances. Many items such as clothing and jewels became associated with particular manifestations of female identity.[9] Materializing the feminine transformed womanhood into a standardized institution that encompassed set rules of appearance and behavior. Even so, each individual still maintained a degree of agency. She could decide whether she wanted to use a particular object, and how and when she would deploy it. Constant give and take between institutionalized femininity and individual agency allowed women to express a degree of autonomy while remaining within the bounds of acceptability.

People today often describe the clothing of Ming women as particularly graceful.[10] It was less flamboyant than medieval fashions, which seem colorful and exaggerated in comparison. Beginning in the Song dynasty, women began to take a more restrained approach to clothing and makeup. The Confucian revival encouraged moderation and unpretentiousness, and Ming women continued to observe these ethical principles. The clothing of wealthy women had several collars and narrow sleeves. Skirts often had pleats, which made the wearer's movements seem light and supple. Embroidered capes, sometimes with intricate designs, were also popular. Colors were relatively muted, giving upper-class women a far more modest appearance than their medieval counterparts. Ming women used understated fashion to construct a social identity that emphasized virtue instead of sensuality. When a high-status person deliberately adopts relatively simple attire, this can have the paradoxical effect of accentuating her rank.[11] The Ming ideal of female beauty expressed moral superiority by exhibiting a reserved appearance.

Most radically, bound feet became extremely common at this time, making the gross malformation of the body an integral aspect of female beauty. This cruel practice already had a long history.[12] At first, footbinding was extremely rare and marginal, so its exact origins will probably never be pinpointed. By the late Tang and Five Dynasties, dancers from central Asia tied bindings around their feet to make them look dainty, and audiences found these abnormally small feet attractive. Some people then began to mutilate the female foot by breaking bones, folding it over, and tightly wrapping it in bandages so that the bones would fuse into a much smaller configuration. Footbinding seems to have been common at the imperial court during the Tang dynasty, lending it official imprimatur and bringing it to the attention of the elite.

Whereas people originally sat on mats on the floor, chairs became commonplace during the Song era. When chairs replaced mats, women no longer had to take off their shoes when they entered the home, and they no longer had to stand up from a seated position on the floor. This change in interior design made footbinding practical for the first time. Song dynasty books and paintings began to depict bound feet as elegant and attractive, showing the penetration of this practice into the upper reaches of society. In the Yuan era, more people embraced footbinding, and it spread throughout China.

Although footbinding did not begin during the Ming dynasty, this is when it became extremely common. As seen in erotic literature such as *Jin Ping Mei*, men had begun to regard bound feet as a requisite aspect of female beauty. Because husbands wanted attractive wives, parents bound the feet of their young daughters so that they could marry well. At first, only the elite bound their daughters' feet. By the end of the dynasty, footbinding had spread down to the lower reaches of society, making it difficult for women to work outside of the home.

Even as footbinding became common, some groups resisted it. Deforming the feet prevented a woman from walking normally and sentenced her to a lifetime of throbbing pain. Some social groups could not accept the disabling of women. Hakka women were known for undertaking even the most difficult types of agricultural labor. Because they were expected to work in the fields alongside men, they could not have bound feet. Hakkas rejected footbinding out of economic necessity.[13] Other ethnic minorities along China's border-lands refused to adopt this practice as well. Because certain groups enthusias-tically embraced footbiding while others demurred, mutilation of the female foot became a physical marker of ethnic and national identity.

For girls, having their feet broken and bound in tight bandages was per-haps the most important feature of their childhood. Male family members usually had little to do with the process, as mothers oversaw the painful ordeal. Mothers did not view their actions as abusive. To the contrary, they regarded binding a daughter's feet as an expression of maternal love and concern. If a woman from a good family did not have sufficiently small feet, she would be unable to find a good husband, reducing opportunities in life. A responsible mother felt obliged to see that her daughter's feet were prop-erly bound, regardless of pain and suffering.[14] The loving mother guided her daughter through this excruciatingly painful process. The concern that moth-ers showed for their daughters at this vulnerable time often brought the pair closer together, making the binding process an intense bonding ritual. Moth-ers and daughters also spent many hours together sewing and embroidering gorgeously ornate shoes that would highlight a girls' newly formed stumps.

Hobbling around on bound feet is difficult for people today to even imag-ine. Many Ming dynasty women endured terrible foot pain for their entire adult lives. The degree of discomfort differed according to how much a woman walked. If she spent most of her time sitting, she would likely have to contend with a dull throb. But if she walked too much, the pain would have been excruciating. The unending discomfort of mutilated feet constituted a basic feature of female life at the time. Foot pain conditioned how women felt, moved, and acted.

Since antiquity, normative female identity had been associated with beauty. Yet ideas about conventional beauty shifted over time. Various writ-ers had previously posited aspects of a woman's beauty as comprising virtue, intelligence, and talent as inner traits. Although footbinding had many moti-vations and affects, most fundamentally it was an erotic practice that catered to male carnal appetites. Women had to endure terrible pain as the price of beauty and sex appeal.

When footbinding became the norm, it was seen as more than just attractive. Small feet were necessary to become a fully realized woman. The ancient rites emphasized the need to visibly distinguish the sexes. Bound feet displayed female identity in a highly visible manner, serving as an unambiguous gender difference that highlighted a woman's identity. Associating normative womanhood with foot mutilation helped shift the focus of female identity to the body. The feminine was not just an idea. It was a physical state that had been achieved through mutilation of the body and the endurance of constant pain.

Because men and women had different degrees of mobility, they developed different impressions of space. To women, the world seemed like a much smaller place. Physical disability confined them to a constricted zone of potential activity. Most spent their lives sitting down within the inner quarters of the home. There is a reason why women wrote so much poetry about their bedrooms. Footbinding had reduced the scope of possible interaction with the wider world. It is not because they slept more than men or were eagerly waiting to have sex. Their bedroom was the center of a small area where they could move about without experiencing unendurable agony.

◦══╪══◦

As advances in publishing made books inexpensive and common, visual images of women proliferated. The managers of commercial presses knew that readers liked illustrations. To sell more books, they made woodblock prints a standard feature of the publishing industry. Illustrations became so common that readers came to expect them, and it was difficult to sell a mass-market book that lacked pictures. Female characters featured prominently in popular literature, so many woodblock illustrations depicted women. Because of these developments, ordinary people were exposed to numerous pictures of women for the first time. This explosion of imagery challenged prevailing conceptions of womanhood. Previously, female identity had been something that people learned about by interacting with actual women, or by reading and hearing about how women ought to be. Changes in the printing industry made feminine imagery highly visual. Woodblock prints in books became an important medium for disseminating concepts of normative female behavior.

The visual portrayal of women changed significantly over the centuries.[15] Ancient art featured very few human figures, so when artists finally became interested in depicting people, they could not look to traditional artworks for guidance. Out of necessity, they turned to literature to find out how women ought to be portrayed. The ancient *Classic of Poetry* (*Shijing*) thus became an important template of representations of the ideal woman.[16] Artists following the conventions of ancient poetry tried to express the high character of female role models. Didactic Han dynasty paintings portrayed each female figure as the representation of a particular social type, such as an empress or servant. These characters lacked individuality. Artists of the time did not portray female figures as dynamic or unique. They intended them to serve as static depictions of abstract ideals, whether moral or social.

The Tang era saw the emergence of very different female imagery. Whereas Han dynasty visual depictions had depicted idealistic female archetypes, late-medieval artists began to portray ordinary female subjects and their lives. Their works often showed women in informal, ordinary settings, such as chasing butterflies or enjoying a banquet. Artists also became intrigued by the theme of female beauty. They began to depict women who were neither overtly virtuous nor representations of a social type, but who stood out for their beauty alone. Genre paintings of female beauties, called shinü, became very popular.

Song dynasty painters were heavily influenced by descriptions of beautiful women that they read in the sixth-century poetry collection *New Songs from a Jade Terrace* (*Yutai xinyong*). Early medieval poems described female protagonists as ravishingly beautiful and clad in elaborate garments. The ideal woman in these imaginative works reposes in luxurious surroundings that complement her flamboyantly gorgeous appearance. Although many critics later dismissed this sort of poetry as decadent, it nevertheless had a major impact on ideas about the ideal women. These poems inspired artists to amplify the portrayal of female beauty, so they painted stunningly beautiful female subjects. In doing so, they depicted the ideal woman as an object that existed for the enjoyment of the male viewer. The rise of *shinü* painting posed a quandary for critics, who felt torn between conflicting standards of appreciation. They debated whether it was sufficient for a painting to depict women as mere beauties for the delectation of male viewers, or whether artists ought to penetrate beyond externals and display the female subject's inner character.

With the revival of Confucianism, educated men questioned the propriety of appreciating paintings of beautiful women. To avoid overtly blatant erotic overtones in their works, painters began to rely on symbolic items that provided clues about a figure's identity in a tastefully indirect manner. Sophisticated viewers understood this visual language, so when they saw apricot blossoms, they interpreted the image as an invocation of a female figure's beauty, while the plantain tree represented her delicate fragility. The addition of flora and other symbols led artists to alter their portrayals of women. Whereas painters had traditionally placed female subjects against a blank background or within an architectural setting, they began to position them in natural environments such as a garden. The interaction between a woman and the surrounding symbolic plants imbued the picture with more meaning and avoided potential misunderstandings. Consequently, artists often relegated the female subject to a minor element in a much larger landscape composition, reducing her importance. She had been assimilated into the wider landscape and objectified as part of the natural world. Focusing on the background landscape made this sort of composition suitable for literati painting and allowed educated men to paint women in a respectable manner. Literati used these paintings to flaunt their own skill and creativity. They usually gave little thought to the identity of the women who served as an ornament for their landscape compositions.

Ming woodblock images of women had a much larger audience than painting, exerting an even greater impact on ideas about ideal female appearance and identity. Woodblock prints placed women in a wide range of situations, reminding readers of the variety of female roles and the diversity of their experiences.[17] Novels frequently featured images of historic women, both real and imagined, thus changing the ways that people thought about past women. Although previous readers had to use their imaginations to envision historic women, commercial illustrations set down tangible images. These images guided popular perceptions of important historic women and fictional characters.

Woodblock prints suited collections of biographical narratives, so Ming publishers put out newly illustrated editions of classic texts such as Liu Xiang's *Biographies of Women* as well as more recent collections.[18] In addition, wealthy families known for their adherence to Confucian virtue, such as the Huizhou magnates, published lavishly illustrated private editions of works on female ethics.[19] Ming illustrations of moralistic narratives depicted ancient women anachronistically wearing contemporary clothing and moving among current styles of architecture and furniture. Transposing old stories into modern visual settings imbued these tales with a sense of immediacy, increasing their impact on readers. Many prints of model women resemble the illustrations used to ornament popular novels and plays. Publishers often reused stock images, presenting a fictional character as a paragon of virtue and vice versa. As a result, the conventions of illustration in popular literature influenced portrayals of virtuous women. Depicting virtuous women with vivid pictures aimed at the mass market made ethical injunctions seem concrete and compelling. Fine woodblock prints emphasized the importance of books on female ethics by making them appear physically attractive and even luxurious.

The rising commercial importance of illustrations affected the content of works about women. Early narratives of female virtue described moderate behavior, such as prudence and wisdom. Artists often had no choice but to portray these sorts of female paragons in static poses that viewers found monotonous. To sell illustrated works, artists sought ways to make images of virtuous women more visually exciting. For example, the popular play *The Story of Shang Lu Who Won Three Zhuangyuan* (*Shang Lu san yuan ji*) recounts the story of Shang Lu (1414–1486), a high official under the Ming.[20] He gained fame as the only person to win the highest grade on all three levels of the civil service examinations during the dynasty. A late Ming edition of the script includes a woodblock print of Shang's mother seated at a loom. She is cutting off the end of her woven cloth, deliberately destroying her work to demonstrate the waste that resulted when her son failed to complete his studies. This incident was directly copied from a famous episode in the life of the ancient sage Mencius. Liu Xiang alleged that the mother of Mencius did the same thing.[21] In this Ming image of this story, the artist clearly tries to make a fairly stationary scene seem more dramatic. Although Shang's mother is sitting, her son dramatically kneels before her to apologize for his laziness. To avoid ambiguity, a caption at the top explains what is taking place. By manipulating images in this manner, the visualization of virtue became increasingly dramatic.

Ming woodblock artists had a commercial mindset, so they preferred to titillate readers with dramatic moments in the lives of female martyrs. A woman cutting off her nose or throwing herself into a burning building was far more visually arresting than a sensible wife giving her husband good advice. The rising violence of chastity rhetoric in the Ming gave woodblock artists ample material to create theatrical pictures. These graphic images may have shocked and horrified readers, but also convinced them to buy the book. The commercial pressures of the publishing business led printers to disseminate increasingly radical and dramatic depictions of female virtue.

Overall, perceptions of the female body changed significantly during the Ming dynasty. The abundance of published illustrations made the variety of female types seem concrete and immediate. People no longer had to use their imaginations to conjure up images of virtuous women or historical beauties. Instead they could look at a picture and let the artist's interpretation guide their imaginings of different kinds of women. In addition, shifting ethical priorities turned attention away from a woman's mind to focus on her physical integrity. Women who wanted to prove their dedication to virtue increasingly engaged in radical forms of behavior that involved physical harm, such as self-mutilation or suicide. Damaging the body constituted a sacrifice that could definitively substantiate a woman's commitment to integrity. At the same time, large numbers of women were binding their feet to blatantly eroticize their bodies. Although the various kinds of self-harm might seem different, they all grew out of an intensified objectification of the female body. Whatever a woman's goal, she was increasingly likely to manipulate her body to achieve it.

Conclusion

Every era of history is a time of both change and continuity. Likewise, during the Ming dynasty, in spite of the emergence of many novelties, the general circumstances affecting women remained consistent with earlier norms in key respects. The most basic concepts of Chinese gender relations, such as separation of the sexes, monogamous marriage, and concubinage, had been set down long ago. The ancients codified fundamental values as the classical rites, a highly prestigious and conservative format that guaranteed enduring influence. During the Ming, these concepts remained touchstones for gendered behavior.

In other ways, however, Ming gender relations stand out from what came before and after. Rapid economic growth in the latter part of the dynasty manifestly altered the ways that people lived and how they thought. More families could afford to send a daughter into marriage with a generous dowry, making wives confident and allowing widows to decline remarriage. Houses contained more furniture, and women wore clothing of better quality. Wealthy ladies had access to a far wider range of goods, rendering their lives increasingly refined, comfortable, and interesting. They could afford books, painting materials, finely crafted board games, and other items that helped them cope with seclusion within the home. The boom in commerce also raised the price of fine needlework, giving women new economic opportunities. Prosperous families purchased large amounts of finely embroidered fabrics for clothing, shoes, and bedding. This demand provided cloistered women with new opportunities to generate income. Capable embroiderers could earn good money while remaining demurely hidden in the inner quarters.

As the commercial economy developed, people found themselves surrounded by an unprecedented variety of manufactured goods. Previously, the items that most people used had been simple and functional, but as material culture flourished, consumers could choose from among a wide range of items. They selected their purchases to convey information about themselves to onlookers. Consumers associated many objects with either men or women, so they employed material goods to express information about their gender identity.[1] Men worried that they might mistakenly use feminine goods or decorations, calling their manhood into question. And women used certain consumer goods to reinforce an image of normative femininity. Because so many consumer goods had gender associations, items intended for female use often had ornamental emblems denoting a desired female trait, such as fertility. The popular "Hundred Boys" motif exemplifies this sort of gendered consumer object.

An atmosphere of affluence at the top of society gave rise to a new mindset that affected mainstream thinking on many matters. The late Ming stands out as an astounding era of cultural effervescence when creative people remade literature and invented new ways of living. Many people became much more open minded and individualistic. Sometimes this attitude devolved into liber-tinism, moving people to become denizens of the demimonde. The search for diversion propelled the floating world of courtesans and entertainers to reach a zenith of sophistication. Others applied this new mindset more positively, thinking critically and speaking out against deleterious customs and ideas. They reimagined ethics and advocated new views of history, poetry, and art.

Even though the economy boomed, women could not take full advantage of the resulting developments. Tightening standards of propriety excluded them from most jobs outside the home. Moreover, footbinding limited them to traversing a small area where they painfully hobbled about on mutilated stumps. Reduced mobility shut women off from many of the developments taking place outside. While men ate in restaurants and squeezed into crowded performance venues, their wives and daughters remained at home, keeping house and engaging in textile work.

∘━╪━∘

Over time, female literacy steadily had become more widespread, allowing increasing numbers of women to engage with written works. Many of them read Confucian texts that conceptualized women though the primary kin-ship roles of daughter, wife, and mother. However, they read provocative medieval works as well. The gossipy fifth-century *New Account of Tales of the World* (*Shishuo xinyu*) and the decadent boudoir poetry of the Liang dy-nasty described women in ways that contradicted Confucian ethics. Medieval authors often described particular women as unique individuals rather than representative social types. Reading these sorts of works tended to make educated women assured and self-consciousness. The canon of women's literature fostered women's psychological liberation, even as the society around them imposed rigid directives in the name of morality. Historical consciousness allowed women to position their works within a far larger temporal context, and this expansive point of view informed their creative efforts.

Women also put forward their own views on gender matters. Increasing numbers of women wrote poetry, and more of them dared to have their works printed and circulated among strangers. In previous centuries, few women had published their poems, so female literary culture remained largely hidden from view. Ming female poets dared to come out into the open. As women's literature gained visibility, more people discussed and analyzed these works. Women looked back to the poems of previous dynasties and positioned their own efforts within a lengthy tradition of female creativity that stretched back to antiquity. Critics of both sexes debated the qualities of women's poetry and discussed how it ought to be evaluated.

The rising educational level affected general attitudes toward women. Over the centuries, learning had become increasingly widespread. Confucian thinkers had always promoted education, and the intense examination culture elevated the prestige of reading and studying. The printing industry made great strides during the Ming. As books became inexpensive and ubiquitous, many ideas that had been locked away in rare handwritten texts became widely accessible for the first time. These technological changes ended up intensifying the effect of certain ideas. The initial impact of Neo-Confucianism had been limited in part because few people had access to books written by this school's adherents. By the Ming, bookstores were filled with inexpensive imprints of texts by conservative thinkers such as Zhu Xi, propelling Neo-Confucianism to the forefront of intellectual discourse. Similarly, works on female ethics from the Han and Tang dynasties had initially circulated in a limited number of manuscripts, limiting their impact. Ming publishers printed these books in vast quantities, rendering them easily accessible.

The flood of cheap books did not just offer readers works on restrictive ethics and the classical rites. Far more people enjoyed popular fiction, which portrayed women in various ways. Whereas some readers wanted moral guidance, most were more interested in engaging plots and interesting characters. In the latter part of the Ming, publishers flooded the market with lowbrow fiction. The stock female characters in these works embodied a range of simplistic stereotypes, ranging from upright to louche. Yet fiction writers also explored the inner lives of particular women and highlighted their individuality.

Ideas regarding acceptable female values and behavior had always varied. The flourishing print culture of the Ming increased this diversity. At this time, a growing female readership had access to a wide range of books, exposing women to conflicting influences. They read about determined martyrs who had committed suicide for the sake of chastity, and also about free-spirited women who enjoyed extramarital affairs. Popular fiction did not present a singular picture of the ideal woman. Instead, readers encountered a profusion of images. Although this diversity could be confusing, it was also inspiring. Each reader could select from among these materials to create a version of womanhood that she found personally satisfying.

Although society at large engaged with a large number of various ideas, the Ming government promoted Neo-Confucianism as state orthodoxy. Although Neo-Confucianism had begun as a marginal school of thought, the Mongols had embraced it to lend their regime a patina of legitimacy and attract literati support. After the fall of the Yuan, even though Ming emperors spurned many Yuan practices, they maintained Neo-Confucianism as the basis for political order. This privileged school of thought encouraged mainstream thinkers to promote stringent views of gender relations that challenged the freewheeling individualism and emotionalism of popular culture.

The restructuring of society according to Neo-Confucian principles made the core values of the governing establishment increasingly patriarchal. Ming law enforced male domestic authority and sought to attach women and wealth firmly to the patrilineal family. Significantly, as during the previous dynasty, a woman who remarried could not take her dowry with her. She had to leave it behind with her former husband's family. This provision contravened traditional property customs. Since antiquity, it had been assumed that a wife's dowry was her personal property. Originally, parents dowered their daughters to provide them with some security in the event of widowhood or divorce. Yuan and Ming law upended centuries of precedent and effectively made dowry the property of the husband's family. A woman controlled this wealth only as long as she remained in her husband's home. Due to this legal shift, more widows stayed in the homes of their deceased husbands in order to keep control of their dowries. Not coincidentally, rhetoric about widow chastity intensified markedly at this time, as it reflected women's practical priorities.

In response to Confucian teachings, morals became more conservative overall. The intensification of rhetoric on women's ethics dates back to the Song. At that time, Neo-Confucians sought to cut through centuries of commentaries and engage with the ancient classics, which they saw as the definitive font of wisdom and moral guidance. They also invented novel metaphysical paradigms to justify ideological innovations. Neo-Confucians cast aside prevailing interpretations and advocated a far more demanding code of ethics. Although this new ethical vision affected both sexes, women faced far more demands than men. Neo-Confucians saw women as dutiful family members, not autonomous individuals. They expected daughters and wives to sacrifice their personal interests for the sake of their families. These moralists commanded women to cloister themselves in the home and content themselves with being good wives and mothers. Neo-Confucians also emphasized the importance of conjugal fidelity. Although they did not demand that a woman shun remarriage after her husband's death, they strongly encouraged widow chastity.

The spread of female literacy and the availability of inexpensive books disseminated these views to a wide audience. Textbooks on female ethics gained more readers, mostly impressionable girls who had yet to marry. Young readers were most likely to take these injunctions to heart and internalize stringent dictates regarding proper female conduct. The promotion of new ethical concepts was not just a rhetorical exercise. These hardline ideas affected actual behavior. Early writings on female ethics, such as Liu Xiang's Han dynasty biographies of exemplary women, had put the greatest stress on mild virtues such as prudence and responsible conduct. Liu believed that female integrity usually did not demand radical action. During the late imperial era, however, expectations became far more demanding. In part, this radicalization came in response to contemporary conditions. The Yuan began and ended in chaos, and rebellions and banditry continued to plague society during the Ming. Widespread lawlessness threatened women with sexual violence. Some committed suicide to avoid rape, or attackers killed them. People lauded women who sacrificed themselves to avoid defilement. The number of stories of women's suicide, murder, and mutilation increased significantly in Yuan and Ming records. Likewise, accounts of widows who declined to remarry rose steeply in tandem. Women resorted to extreme measures both in response to tumultuous circumstances and also to prove their devotion to virtue.

In spite of the transformations affecting Ming economy and society, earlier ideas continued to affect people's beliefs. Literati in particular had a profound historical consciousness, and they engaged intensively with the past. The educated elite did not regard historical studies as sterile antiquarianism. To the contrary, they believed that old books contained the teachings of sages, and were imbued with enduring relevance. Due to this attitude, the greatest minds of the day mined historical texts for practical wisdom. In studying the accounts of past eras, Ming scholars paid close attention to the mistakes of historic rulers and flaws in earlier systems. Their conclusions shaped assumptions regarding the influence of women on government. Literati then broadened their political views into generalities about the nature of human character, including the basic traits of male and female. In this way, musings about women in the past ended up guiding gender relations.

Historians convinced literati to associate female power with dynastic decline. This aversion was not new. Attitudes toward female power had been decisively molded by two events that occurred long before, during the Tang dynasty. First the indominable Wu Zetian seized control of the government, overthrew the dynasty, and declared herself emperor. Then the influential poet Bai Juyi made the imperial concubine Yang Guifei into a scapegoat for the catastrophic An Lushan rebellion. These episodes deeply traumatized the officialdom, who concluded that female participation in government would likely lead to disaster. Thereafter, they sought to ensure that a woman would never again determine policy.

Most late Tang emperors did not even appoint an empress for fear that consorts might leverage this grand title into tangible power.[2] Song rulers maintained the late Tang policy of methodically suppressing the ambitions of palace women.[3] The strong bureaucratic apparatus of the Song served as a further bulwark that blocked palace women from accruing power. Officials generally disliked powerful empresses dowager, as the two sides were locked in a zero sum game. Empresses gained power at the expense of the outer bureaucracy, and vice versa. Wary of losing ground to powerful women, bureaucrats restrained consorts and their kinsmen. The rise of the bureaucracy thus diminished female political power.

Although the Yuan empresses had relatively little influence on policy, Mongol women appeared openly at court and practiced martial skills such as archery and riding, which Chinese observers found disconcerting. The Ming repudiation of Yuan institutions therefore included a return to Song restrictions on palace women. Moreover, the Ming bureaucratic system resembled that of the Song in most respects, and officials worked to insulate the empresses from affairs of state.

When the Hongwu emperor set down the basic framework of administration for the new dynasty, he placed many constraints on imperial consorts. Most importantly, Hongwu prohibited women from serving as regents, depriving them of the most direct means for self-aggrandizement. Ming rulers also chose their empresses from unimportant families to ensure that these women's kinsmen would not accrue much power. Hongwu's decree that only the son of an empress should ascend the throne ensured that childless empresses would be deposed and replaced by a fertile successor. Moreover, the Ming emperors frequently divorced their wives, degrading the standing of empresses. These measures succeeded in blocking palace women from participating in important affairs for most of the Ming dynasty. Empresses, empresses dowager, and princesses were generally unimportant during the Ming. Palace women had only symbolic roles, and they mostly confined themselves to mundane palace administration, leisure activities, and religious ceremonies.

Efforts to reduce female power at the apex of the state affected the image of women in general. In response to concerns about female power, historians and fiction writers reinterpreted traditional stories to portray women as a threat to men. Mixing history with popular fiction, they depicted some of history's most important women as fox spirits disguised in female garb. Weird and malevolent, these creatures threatened to destroy any man who succumbed to their seductions. If they managed to entrance a ruler, they would encourage him to engage in decadent and irresponsible behavior. When Ming authors combined fox stories with historical legends, they created an entertaining synthesis. This new hybrid genre implied that women do not just threaten individual men but also pose a grave danger to the dynasty.

To reduce female influence on government, early Ming authorities set down institutions intended to lower the position of women in general. The effects of these measures reverberated throughout society. The *Great Ming Code* treated them as interchangeable daughters, wives, and mothers. Women had a legal obligation to adhere to the stereotypes associated with these kinship identities. Confucians had an ambivalent attitude toward law, as they preferred to use education and individual cultivation for social engineering. Even so, over time society had become increasingly legalistic, so officials used the law to force the populace to conform to their ethical ideals. Women became firmly attached to a family, either that of their father or husband. This project reduced the female subject by envisioning her not as an autonomous person, but simply as a subsidiary member of the patriarchal domestic unit.

○══╪══○

Changing views toward the female body stand out as another major development. Ming society increasingly emphasized the body as the locus of womanhood and icon of the nation. This perspective departed from earlier views. In early China, writers and artists put relatively little emphasis on female physicality. Early art had almost no figurative portrayals. When painters started representing the female form, they showed women as standardized social types, displaying set characteristics according to stereotypical roles. In other words, what mattered was not a woman's body but her place in society. Likewise, early written descriptions of women had little to say about their bodies. Writers rarely bothered to describe the appearance of even the most famous women. Instead they preferred to focus on thoughts and actions as the most meaningful expressions of female identity.

Over time, the body became an increasingly important component of womanhood. Painters dared to depict beautiful woman, emphasizing their outward appearance rather than their inner character or general social identity. Likewise, poets invited readers to ponder the beauty of the female form. Over the centuries, the turn toward objectification continued. During the Ming, the emphasis on the physicality of women intensified noticeably. The feminine became essentialized as a gendered body. Traditionally a woman had been considered attractive due to her outstanding virtue. But as footbinding became mainstream, people began to consider a woman beautiful because of a particular kind of physical mutilation. When the body came to be seen as the gendered female essence, women manipulated their physiques to produce a certain female identity.

Female virtue also became identified with manipulation of the body. Early ideas of women's probity had emphasized belief and behavior. Moralists saw the good woman as someone who held correct ideas about ethics and carried out expected obligations, as defined by her place in society. If she went beyond these basic responsibilities and undertook more stringent actions due to her morals, observers considered her behavior as exemplary. But during the Ming dynasty, people began to see female virtue in a new light. A woman who wanted to stand out as a paragon of chastity or filiality would often harm her body to demonstrate her resolve.

An appreciation of strong emotions together with the widespread diffusion of dramatic literature popularized extreme measures in the name of integrity. To qualify for inclusion in the pantheon of female role models, women resorted to theatrical measures, such as slicing off flesh or hanging themselves from the rafters. Strangely, when women saw the body as emblematic of their gendered essence, they became increasingly willing to damage it. According to this line of thought, the best possible woman was the one who harmed her body the most. But because she had been objectified and identified with her body, destroying it negated her own personhood. In other words, the greatest woman was the one who dared to disappear.

Glossary

An Lushan	安祿山
Bai Juyi	白居易
Bailian	白蓮
Ban Zhao	班昭
baojuan	寶卷
binü	婢女
Bo Shaojun	薄少君
Ciyou ju	慈幼局
Da Ming lü	大明律
Dadu	大都
Datong	大同
Dumu Jingang	獨目金剛
Fan Jue	范玨
Fang Weiyi	方維儀
fangzhi	方志
Feng Menglong	馮夢龍
Fengshen yanyi	封神演義
Fomu	佛母
fudao	婦道
furen	夫人
Gu Ruopu	顧若璞
Guanyin	觀音
gui	閨
Guifan	閨範
guiyin	閨隱
Gujin tushu jicheng	古今圖書集成
Hongwu	洪武

Houtu Laomu	后土老母
huaben	話本
huang guifei	皇貴妃
huang taihou	皇太后
Huang Yuanjie	黃媛介
huangdi	皇帝
huanghou	皇后
Huizhou	徽州
huzhu	戶主
Ji (empress)	紀
Jiajing	嘉靖
jian	賤
Jianwen	建文
Jingang jing	金剛經
Jinyin ji	金印記
jiefu	節婦
Jin Ping Mei	金瓶梅
jingbiao	旌表
Jingtai	景泰
juehu	絕戶
Kuaiji	會稽
Li (empress)	李
Li Tangmei	李唐妹
Li Zhi	李贄
Lianchi Zhuhong	蓮池袾宏
liang	良
lienü	烈女
Lienü zhuan	列女傳
Ling Mengchu	凌濛初
Liu (Madame)	劉
Liu Xiang	劉向
Longqing	隆慶
Lü Kun	呂坤
Lu Qingzi	陸卿子
Lu Tiancheng	呂天成
Lunyu	論語
Luo Menghong	羅夢鴻
Ma (empress)	馬
Ma Shouzhen	馬守真
Mazu	媽祖
Meng Shuqing	孟淑卿

Miaoshan	妙善
Mingshi	明史
Ming shi lu	明實錄
Mudan ting	牡丹亭
nei	內
Nei xun	內訓
Niangniang	娘娘
Ningde	寧德
Nü jie	女誡
Nü lunyu	女論語
Nü sishu	女四書
Nü Wa	女媧
nühu	女戶
nüxia	女俠
pipa	琵琶
qing	情
Sanguo yanyi	三國演義
Shang Jinglan	商景蘭
Shang Lu	商輅
Shang Lu san yuan ji	商輅三元記
shanren	山人
Shen Cheng	沈承
Shen Yixiu	沈宜修
Shijing	詩經
shinü	仕女
Shishuo xinyu	世說新語
Shuihu zhuan	水滸傳
Song Maocheng	宋懋澄
Song Ruoxin	宋若莘
Song Ruozhao	宋若昭
Su Dongpo	蘇東坡
Sun (empress)	孫
taihuang taihou	太皇太后
Taizu	太祖
tanci	彈詞
tang	堂
Tang Xianzu	湯顯祖
Tianhou	天后
Tianshun	天順
wai	外
Wang Xiang	王相

Wang Yangming	王陽明
Wanli	萬曆
Wen (madam)	文
Wen Shu	文俶
Wu Zetian	武則天
Wusheng Laomu	無生老母
Xiaojing	孝經
Xiaoyi Wuai An	孝義無礙庵
Xiwangmu	西王母
Xiuta yeshi	繡榻野史
Xu (empress)	徐
xuanxue	玄學
Xue Susu	薛素素
Xunzi	荀子
Yao	瑤
Yang Guifei	楊貴妃
Yang Wenli	楊文儷
Yang Yuhuan	楊玉環
Ye Wanwan	葉紈紈
yi	義
yifu	義父
yin	隱
yinfu	淫婦
Yingzong	英宗
Yongle	永樂
Yutai xinyong	玉臺新詠
Zhang (empress)	張
Zhang Jing'an	張靜庵
Zhang Tao	張濤
Zheng Ruying	鄭如英
Zhengde	正德
Zhengtong	正統
zhennü	貞女
Zhou Zhibiao	周之標
Zhu Yuanzhang	朱元璋
Zhurong	祝融
Zou Saizhen	鄒賽貞
zunzhang	尊長

Notes

EPIGRAPH

1. Kang-i Sun Chang and Haun Saussy, eds., *Women Writers of Traditional China: An Anthology of Poetry and Criticism* (Stanford: Stanford University Press, 1999), 252.

INTRODUCTION

1. For concise overviews of the Ming dynasty, see John W. Dardess, *Ming China 1368–1644: A Concise History of a Resilient Empire* (Lanham, MD: Rowman & Littlefield, 2012); Timothy Brook, *The Troubled Empire: China in the Yuan and Ming Dynasties* (Cambridge, MA: The Belknap Press of Harvard University Press, 2010).

2. For example, between 1207 and 1236, the registered population of Cizhou in Hebei decreased 85 percent, the registered population of Jinan decreased 82 percent, and the population of Yan'an in Shaanxi decreased 89 percent. Many other communities experienced similar depopulation. Liu Pujiang, "Jindai hukou yanjiu," *Zhongguoshi yanjiu* 2 (1994): 95. The population of China at the beginning of the Ming dynasty is unknown. It was probably somewhere between seventy and ninety million. Liang Fangzhong, ed., *Zhongguo lidai hukou: tiandi, tianfu tongji* (Shanghai: Shanghai renmin, 1980), 185, 203–4; Brook, *The Troubled Empire*, 27–28, 42–45, 95, 97–99, 162–63; He Bingdi, *Mingchu yijiang renkou ji qi xiangguan wenti 1368–1953* (Beijing: Sanlian shudian, 2000); Cao Shuji, *Zhongguo renkou shi*, vol. 4 (Shanghai: Fudan Daxue chubanshe, 2000).

3. Frederick Mote, "The Growth of Chinese Despotism: A Critique of Wittfogel's Theory of Oriental Despotism as Applied to China," *Oriens Extremus* 8 (1961): 18.

4. "Qingming Festival, 1646," *Women Writers of Traditional China*, Chang and Saussy, 359.

5. Brook, *The Confusions of Pleasure*, 86.

6. Noriko Kamachi, "Feudalism or Absolute Monarchism?: Japanese Discourse on the Nature of State and Society in Late Imperial China," *Modern China* 16, no. 3 (1990): 354; Dorothy Ko, *Teachers of the Inner Chambers: Women and Culture in Seventeenth-Century China* (Stanford: Stanford University Press, 1994), 31.

7. Kamachi, "Feudalism or Absolute Monarchism?," 339–43.

8. Tracy L. Sweely, "Introduction," in *Manifesting Power: Gender and the Interpretation of Power in Archaeology*, ed. Tracy L. Sweely (London: Routledge, 1999), 1.

9. Joan Wallach Scott, "Gender: A Useful Category of Historical Analysis," *American Historical Review* 91 (1986): 1053–75.

10. Keith Hazelton, "Patrilines and the Development of Localized Lineages: The Wu of Hsiu-ning City, Hui-chou, to 1528," in *Kinship Organization in Late Imperial China 1000–1940*, ed. Patricia Buckley Ebrey and James L. Watson (Berkeley and Los Angeles: University of California Press, 1986), 158–59. These kinship identities were codified into the law. Yonglin Jiang, "Legislating Hierarchical Yet Harmonious Gender Relations in the *Great Ming Code*," *Ming Studies* 69 (2014): 37–38. After a woman married, it was customary for people to refer to her by a kinship role rather than her name. Rubie S. Watson, "The Named and the Nameless: Gender and Person in Chinese Society," in *Gender in Cross Cultural Perspective*, ed. Caroline B. Brettell and Carolyn F. Sargent (Englewood Cliffs, NJ: Prentice Hall, 1993), 127.

11. Kong Min, "Tangdai xiaoshuo nüxing xingxiang dui Ming Qing wenxue zhi yingxiang," *Mingzuo xinshang* 2 (2016): 130–33.

12. Ko, *Teachers of the Inner Chambers,* 116–17. Ni Wenjie et al., *Zuijia nüxing miaoxie cidian* (Beijing: Zhongguo guoji guangbo, 1990), gathers together and defines the terms traditionally used to describe women.

13. Xu Wenxiang, "Zhennü, cainü yu yunü—Mingdai wenren nüxingguan de goujian," *Wenxue yu wenhua* 1 (2016): 79–90.

14. Katherine Carlitz, "Lovers, Talkers, Monsters, and Good Women: Competing Images in Mid-Ming Epitaphs and Fiction," in *Beyond Exemplar Tales: Women's Biography in Chinese History*, ed. Joan Judge and Hu Ying (Berkeley: University of California Press, 2011), 177–78.

15. Leon Edel, *Writing Lives: Principia Biographica* (New York: Norton, 1984).

16. Maram Epstein, "Reflections of Desire: The Poetics of Gender in *Dream of the Red Chamber*," *Nan Nü* 1, no. 1 (1999): 89–90.

17. Tanaka Issei, "The Social and Historical Context of Ming-Qing Local Drama," in *Popular Culture in Late Imperial China*, ed. David Johnson et al. (Berkeley and Los Angeles: University of California Press, 1985), 150–52.

18. Carlitz, "Lovers, Talkers, Monsters, and Good Women," 175, 184.

19. Bettine Birge, "Chu Hsi and Women's Education," in *Neo-Confucian Education: The Formative Stage*, ed. William Theodore de Bary and John Chaffee (Berkeley: University of California Press, 1989), 325 provides an overview of this regression.

20. "Recording My Thoughts," Chang and Saussy, *Women Writers of Traditional China*, 269.

21. Zhao Cuili, "Mingdai nüxing de xiuxian shenghuo," *Zhongguo shehui jingjishi yanjiu* 1 (2009): 50–57.

CHAPTER 1

1. Elinor Ochs and Carolyn Taylor, "The 'Father Knows Best' Dynamic in Dinnertime Narratives," in *Gender Articulated: Language and the Socially Constructed Self*, ed. Kira Hall and Mary Bucholtz (New York: Routledge, 1995), 97–99.

2. Bettine Birge, "Women and Confucianism from Song to Ming: The Institutionalization of Patrilineality," in *The Song-Yuan-Ming Transition in Chinese History*, ed. Paul J. Smith and Richard von Glahn (Cambridge, MA: Harvard University Asia Center, 2003), 212.

3. Zhang Guogang, *Jiating shihua* (Beijing: Shehui kexue wenxian, 2012), 132.

4. Richard von Glahn, *The Economic History of China: From Antiquity to the Nineteenth Century* (Cambridge: Cambridge University Press, 2016), 301–2. Chang Jianhua, "Theories about the Formation of Lineage System since the Song and Ming Dynasties," *Frontiers of History in China* 3, no. 1 (2008): 43–56 discusses various theories about why lineages became so common in the Song dynasty.

5. Harriet T. Zurndorfer, "The Hsin-an Ta-tsu-chih and the Development of the Chinese Gentry Society, 800–1600," *T'oung Pao* 67, nos. 3/5 (1981): 154.

6. Chang, "Theories about the Formation of Lineage System," 62.

7. James L. Watson, "Anthropological Overview: The Development of Chinese Descent Groups," in *Kinship Organization in Late Imperial China 1000–1940*, ed. Patricia Buckley Ebrey and James L. Watson (Berkeley and Los Angeles: University of California Press, 1986), 283.

8. John W. Dardess, "The Cheng Communal Family: Social Organization and Neo-Confucianism in Yüan and Ming China," *Harvard Journal of Asiatic Studies* 34 (1974): 7–8.

9. Dardess, "The Cheng Communal Family," 45–46.

10. Deniz Kandiyoti, "Bargaining with Patriarchy," *Gender and Society* 2, no. 3 (1988): 278.

11. Zhang, *Jiating shihua*, 122.

12. Katherine Carlitz, "Desire, Danger, and the Body: Stories of Women's Virtue in Late Ming China," in *Engendering China*, ed. Christina K. Gilmartin et al. (Cambridge, MA: Harvard University Press, 1994), 105–6; Kathryn Bernhardt, "A Ming-Qing Transition in Chinese Women's History? The Perspective from Law," in *The History and Theory of Legal Practice in China: Toward a Historical-Social Jurisprudence*, ed. Philip C. C. Huang and Kathryn Bernhardt (Leiden: Brill, 2014).

13. Katherine Carlitz, "Mourning, Personality, Display: Ming Literati Commemorate Their Mothers, Sisters, and Daughters," *Nan Nü* 15, no. 1 (2013): 68.

14. Francesca Bray, *Technology and Gender: Fabrics of Power in Late Imperial China* (Berkeley: University of California Press, 1997), 60–61.

15. Allen W. Johnson and Timothy Earle, *The Evolution of Human Societies: From Foraging Group to Agrarian State* (Stanford: Stanford University Press, 1987), 6–7.

16. Penelope M. Allison, "Introduction," in *The Archaeology of Household Activities*, ed. Penelope M. Allison (London: Routledge, 1999), 1–2, 4.

17. "A Letter from My Younger Sister Arrives at the Official Residence," Chang and Saussy, *Women Writers of Traditional China*, 168–69.

18. Bray, *Technology and Gender*, 107–9, 131, 150.

19. H. Laura Wu, "Through the Prism of Male Writing: Representation of Lesbian Love in Ming-Qing Literature," *Nan Nü* 4, no. 1 (2002): 9–12, 27.

20. During the Tang, a female head of household was called a "big woman" or "great woman" (danü 大女). Deng Xiaonan, "Women in Turfan during the Sixth to Eighth Centuries: A Look at Their Activities Outside the Home," *Journal of Asian Studies* 58, no. 1 (1999): 85–103; Luo Tonghua, *Tongju gongcai: Tangdai jiating yanjiu* (Taipei: Zhengda chubanshe, 2015).

21. Li Zhiping, "Songdai nühu de tedian," *Funü yanjiu luncong* 6 (2009): 51–56; Zhang Dengcan, "Mingdai nühu de jieding ji qi shehui daiyu," *Guizhou wenshi congkan* 3 (2017): 8, 10.

22. Zhang, *Jiating shihua*, 122–23. All ages are given in *sui* 歲, which differed from the Western method or reckoning age. For a discussion of the various ways used to determine *sui* see Sanping Chen, "'Age Inflation and Deflation' in Medieval China," *Journal of the American Oriental Society* 133, no. 3 (2013): 527–33.

23. Zhang, *Jiating shihua*, 127.

24. Li Mingchen, "Shilun Mingdai hunyin falü zhidu," *Hubei Keji Xueyuan xuebao* 35, no. 6 (2015): 83.

25. G. William Skinner, "Conjugal Power in Tokugawa Japanese Families: A Matter of Life or Death," in *Sex and Gender Hierarchies*, ed. Barbara Diane Miler (Cambridge: Cambridge University Press, 1993), 236, 247–48.

26. Brook, *The Confusions of Pleasure*, 97–99; Ted. A. Telford, "Covariates of Men's Age at First Marriage: The Historical Demography of Chinese Lineages," *Population Studies* 46, no. 1 (1992): 24; Brook, *The Troubled Empire*, 145.

27. Wang Xueping, "Mingdai binü hunyin teshuxing de lishi jiedu," *Shehui kexue jikan* 3 (2010): 195–99.

28. Hu Zhongsheng, "Maishen hunshu yu Ming Qing Huizhou xiaceng shehui de hunpei he renkou wenti," in *Ming Qing renkou hunyin jiating shilun—Chen Jiexian jiaoshou, Feng Erkang jiaoshou guxi jinian lunwenji* (Tianjin: Tianjin guji chubanshe), 3, 9–11.

29. Beverly Bossler, "A Daughter Is a Daughter All Her Life: Affinal Relations and Women's Networks in Song and Late Imperial China," *Late Imperial China* 21, no. 1 (2000): 97–98; Huang Jingjing, "Ming Qing shiqi Huizhou nüzi de zeou biaozhun," *Jiamusi Daxue shehui kexue xuebao* 33, no. 2 (2015): 151–53.

30. Jiang Yonglin, trans., *The Great Ming Code / Da Ming lü* (Seattle: University of Washington Press, 2005), 82–90. Also Bian Li, "Ming Qing shiqi hunyin lifa de tiaozheng yu jiceng shehui de wending," *Anhui Daxue xuebao* 6 (2005): 115–20; Deng Qingping, *Ye shen qian zhang deng: Mingdai liangxing guanxi shi* (Xi'an: Shaanxi renmin, 2008), 48–69.

31. Katsuyama Minoru, *Chūgoku Sō—Min dai ni okeru konin no gakusaiteki kenkyū* (Tokyo: Tōhoku Daigaku shuppankai, 2007), 67–73.

32. Li, "Shilun Mingdai hunyin falü zhidu," 82–83.

33. Huang Jia, "'Chu er ke pai an jing qi' yu Mingdai hunsu wenhua," *Heilongjiang shizhi* 21 (2013): 192–93. For the origins of this idea see Niu Zhiping, *Tangdai hunsang* (Xi'an: Sanqin chubanshe, 2011), 33–37.

34. Ann Waltner, *Getting an Heir: Adoption and the Construction of Kinship in Late Imperial China* (Honolulu: University of Hawaii Press, 1990), 107, 120.

35. Pan Qing, "Yuandai Jiangnan diqu Menggu, Semu qiaoyu renhu hunyin zhuangtai de fenxi," *Xuehai* 3 (2002): 132–36.

36. Qi Wenying, "Beiming suo jian Mingdai daguan hunyin guanxi," *Zhongguo shi yanjiu* 3 (2011): 176–80.

37. Hazelton, "Patrilines and the Development of Localized Lineages," 159–61.

38. M. J. Meijer, *Murder and Adultery in Late Imperial China: A Study of Law and Morality* (Leiden: E.J. Brill, 1991), 39–40.

39. Jiang, "Legislating Hierarchical Yet Harmonious Gender Relations," 31–32.

40. Jiang, "Legislating Hierarchical Yet Harmonious Gender Relations," 32.

41. Matthew H. Sommer, "The Uses of Chastity: Sex, Law, and the Property of Widows in Qing China," *Late Imperial China* 17, no. 2 (1996): 84.

42. Jiang, "Legislating Hierarchical Yet Harmonious Gender Relations," 35–36.

43. "In Reply to Pan Jingsheng's Poem Expressing His Feelings," Chang and Saussy, *Women Writers of Traditional China*, 235.

44. Ko, *Teachers of the Inner Chambers*, 179–85.

45. Liu Junhua, *Ming Qing nüxing zuojia xiqu chuangzuo yanjiu* (Beijing: Kexue chubanshe, 2015), 90, 94–95.

46. Carlitz, "Lovers, Talkers, Monsters, and Good Women," 185; Carlitz, "Mourning, Personality, Display," 66.

47. Lynn A. Struve, "Song Maocheng's Matrixes of Mourning and Regret," *Nan Nü* 15, no. 1 (2013): 96–97. For an overview of Song Maocheng's career, see Tina Lu, "The Literary Culture of the Late Ming (1573–1644)," in *The Cambridge History of Chinese Literature*, vol. II, *From 1375*, ed. Kang-i Sun Chang and Stephen Owen (Cambridge: Cambridge University Press, 2010), 119–21.

48. Kobayashi Tetsuyuki, *Mingdai jōsei no junshi to bungaku: Haku Shoukun no kokufushi hyakushu* (Tokyo: Kyuko shoin, 2003); Wilt L. Idema, "The Biographical and the Autobiographical in Bo Shaojun's *One Hundred Poems Lamenting My Husband*," in *Beyond Exemplar Tales: Women's Biography in Chinese History*, ed. Joan Judge and Hu Ying (Berkeley: University of California Press, 2011), 230–45; Wilt L. Idema, "Bo Shaojun and Her *One Hundred Poems Lamenting My Husband*," *Nan Nü* 15, no. 2 (2013): 317–32.

49. Idema, "Bo Shaojun and Her *One Hundred Poems*," 324.

50. Hazelton, "Patrilines and the Development of Localized Lineages," 156.

51. Telford, "Covariates of Men's Age at First Marriage," 29; John Dardess, *A Ming Society: T'ai-ho County, Kiangsi, in the Fourteenth to Seventeenth Centuries* (Berkeley: University of California Press, 1996), 141. The average age of men at the time of the birth of their first child was somewhat higher, ranging from twenty-two to twenty-eight.

52. Miranda Brown, *The Politics of Mourning in Early China* (Albany, NY: State University of New York Press, 2007).

53. Norman Kutcher, *Mourning in Late Imperial China: Filial Piety and the State* (Cambridge: Cambridge University Press, 1999), 36–39; Guo Haidong, "Mingdai Zhili funü shoujie xingwei tanxi," *Changzhou Daxue xuebao* 16, no. 5 (2015): 81.

54. Lau Nap-yin, "Changes to Women's Legal Rights in the Family from the Song to the Ming," in *Modern Chinese Religion I: Song-Liao-Jin-Yuan (960–1368 AD)*, ed. John Lagerwey and Pierre Marsone (Leiden: Brill, 2015), I: 707.

55. "Sent to My Son Ting," Chang and Saussy, *Women Writers of Traditional China*, 196.

56. Hsiung Ping-chen, "Constructed Emotions: The Bond Between Mothers and Sons in Late Imperial China," *Late Imperial China* 15, no. 1 (1994): 88–93.

57. Hsiung, "Constructed Emotions," 88, 102–10.

58. Chen Yunü, *Mingdai de fojiao yu shehui* (Beijing: Beijing Daxue chubanshe, 2011), 283–321.

59. Fuma Susumu, "Seidai zenki no ikuei jigyō," in *Tō ajia seikai no seisei, hatten oyobi hoka bunmei to no kankei ni suite no kenkyū*, ed. Fuma Susumu et al. (Toyama: Toyama Daigaku Jinbun Gakubu, 1986), 9–10, 21–23, 32; Bai Hua and Zhou Youbin, "Ming Qing nibi zinü xianxjang fenxi," *Suzhou Daxue xuebao* 2 (2014): 51–60.

60. Kutcher, *Mourning in Late Imperial China,* 38–39, 277–78, 373. The author connects shifting ideas about concubines with the rise of lineages. According to Kutcher, the increasing importance of lineages led people to reassess kinship relations in general. As part of this change, they raised the status of concubines and gave them a more important place within the family.

61. Bao Hua Hsieh, "The Market in Concubines in Jiangnan during Ming-Qing China," *Journal of Family History* 33, no. 3 (2008): 262–63.

62. "Poems Written on the Wall of New Blessings Station," Chang and Saussy, *Women Writers of Traditional China*, 201.

63. For the general commoditization of women see Mao Wenfang, *Wu, xingbie, guankan: Mingmo Qingchu wenhua shuxie xintan* (Taipei: Xuesheng shuju, 2001), 47–49.

64. Bao, "The Market in Concubines in Jiangnan during Ming-Qing China," 273, 275–77.

65. He Junhong, *Danqing qipa: Wan Ming Qing chu de nüxing huihua* (Beijing: Wenwu chubanshe, 2008), 18–39, 41–48, 72–85.

66. Douglas R. White and Michael L. Burton, "Causes of Polygyny: Ecology, Kinship, and Warfare," *American Anthropologist* 90 (1988): 884.

67. Katherine Carlitz, "The Daughter, the Singing-Girl, and the Seduction of Suicide," *Nan Nü* 3, no. 1 (2001): 23.

68. Zhang Fan, *Mingdai jiachan jicheng yu zhengsong* (Beijing: Falü chubanshe, 2015), 84.

CHAPTER 2

1. Sweely, "Introduction," 1.

2. Isador Wallimann, Nicholas Ch. Tatsis, and George V. Zito, "On Max Weber's Definition of Power," *Australian and New Zealand Journal of Sociology* 13, no. 3 (1977): 231–35. For other definitions of power, see Barry Barnes, *The Nature of Power* (Urbana and Chicago: University of Illinois Press, 1988); Eric R. Wolf, "Distinguished Lecture: Facing Power—Old Insights, New Questions," *American Anthropologist*, New Series 92, no. 3 (1990): 586–96.

3. Han Lin, "Wu Zetian gushi de wenben yanbian yu wenhua neihan" (PhD diss., Nankai University, 2012).

4. Keith McMahon, *Celestial Women: Imperial Wives and Concubines in China from Song to Qing* (Lanham, MD: Rowman & Littlefield, 2016), xvii.

5. Jack Weatherford, *The Secret History of the Mongol Queens: How the Daughters of Genghis Khan Rescued His Empire* (New York: Broadway Books, 2010); McMahon, *Celestial Women*, 58–65.

6. Ellen Felicia Soullière, "Palace Women in the Ming Dynasty: 1368–1644" (PhD diss., Princeton University, 1987), 246–62; Huang Mingguang, "Mingdai nanfang zhusheng nütuguan zhizheng xianxiang yanjiu," *Guangxi Minzu Shifan Xueyuan xuebao* 30, no. 1 (2013): 21–25.

7. Rania Huntington, "Foxes and Sex in Late Imperial Chinese Narrative," *Nan Nü* 2, no. 1 (2000): 101–9.

8. Soullière, "Palace Women in the Ming Dynasty," 348–50; Jennifer Holmgren, "Imperial Marriage in the Native Chinese and Non-Han State, Han to Ming," in *Marriage and Inequality in Chinese Society*, ed. Rubie S. Watson and Patricia Buckley Ebrey (Berkeley: University of California Press, 1991), 58.

9. Soullière, "Palace Women in the Ming Dynasty," 383–84.

10. Holmgren, "Imperial Marriage in the Native Chinese and Non-Han State," 76, 88–89.

11. Soullière, "Palace Women in the Ming Dynasty," 3–4, 19; Zheng Caiyun, "Lun Xuanzong Sun Huanghou you Mingdai zhongyuan zhengzhi—jian yu Lin Yanqing xiansheng shangquan," *Nanchang Hangkong Daxue xuebao* 17, no. 2 (2015): 13–18.

12. Jiang, "Legislating Hierarchical Yet Harmonious Gender Relations," 29.

13. Zhang Shuming, "*Neixun* yu Mingdai nüxing jiaohua," *Nanfang luncong* 6 (2017): 22–26; Chang and Saussy, *Women Writers of Traditional China*, 678–81 translates the preface of *Neixun*.

14. Tang Tianhang, "Lun Mingdai renxun zhidu de feichu," *Daqing Shifan Xueyuan xuebao* 38, no. 2 (2018): 120–24.

15. Soullière, "Palace Women in the Ming Dynasty," 382–83.

16. Wang Xi, "Zhashi tuijin Mingdai gongtingshi he nüxingshi yanjiu de lizuo—ping *Mingdai gongting nüxingshi*," *Gugong xuekan* 1 (2017): 406–11 describes the official sources and informal writings regarding the history of Ming palace women.

17. Keith McMahon, "The Institution of Polygamy in the Chinese Imperial Palace," *The Journal of Asian Studies* 72, no. 4 (2013): 917–21.

18. Soullière, "Palace Women in the Ming Dynasty," 242; Ellen Soullière, "The Writing and Rewriting of History: Imperial Women and the Succession in Ming China, 1368–1457," *Ming Studies* 73 (2016): 9.

19. Liu Yu, "Mingdai huang guifei fenghao chutan," *Gugong xuekan* 2 (2016): 115–24.

20. Soullière, "Palace Women in the Ming Dynasty," 242–46; Peng Yong and Pan Yue, *Mingdai gongting nüxingshi* (Beijing: Gugong chubanshe, 2015), 71–98; McMahon, *Celestial Women,"* 80.

21. Qiu Zhonglin, "Mingdai gongren de rong yu ru—cong zhiye funü yu shehui liudong de jiaodu qieru," *Gugong xuekan* 2 (2014): 91–125; Peng and Pan, *Mingdai gongting nüxingshi*, 223–358.

22. Li Qingyong, "Mingdai nüguan laiyuan fenxi," *Qangzhou Shifan Xueyuan xuebao* 29, no. 3 (2013): 63–65.

23. Cui Jing, "Mingdai hougong yizu feipin yu Ming, Meng, Chao sanfang guanxi," *Yunnan Shifan Daxue xuebao* 46, no. 2 (2014): 151–56.

24. James Geiss, "The Cheng-te Reign, 1506–1521," in *The Cambridge History of China*, vol. 7, *The Ming Dynasty*, part 1, ed. Frederick W. Mote and Denis Twitchett (Cambridge: Cambridge University Press, 1988), 433.

25. Ray Huang, *1587: A Year of No Significance: The Ming Dynasty in Decline* (New Haven: Yale University Press, 1981), 26; Chen Chao, "Pinguan mingfu zhidu yu Mingdai funü de zongxiang shehui liudong—yi Mingren muzhiming wei yanjiu zhongxin," *Shehui kexue jikan* 6 (2010): 176–80; Chen Chao, *Ming Qing nüxing beizhuanwen yu pinguan mingfu yanjiu—yi 'siku' Mingren wenji wei zhongxin de kaocha* (Beijing: Guangming Ribao chubanshe, 2013), 32–33, 38–39.

26. Chen, *Ming Qing nüxing beizhuanwen yu pinguan mingfu yanjiu*, 84. This age is calculated as *sui*.

27. Holmgren, "Imperial Marriage in the Native Chinese and Non-Han State," 60.

28. E. Soullière, "The Imperial Marriages of the Ming Dynasty," *Papers on Far Eastern History* 37 (1988): 15, 37–38; Holmgren, "Imperial Marriage in the Native Chinese and Non-Han State," 74–75; Keith McMahon, "Women Rulers in Imperial China," *Nan Nü* 15, no. 2 (2013): 212.

29. Huang, *1587: A Year of No Significance*, 18, 39; Soullière, "The Imperial Marriages of the Ming Dynasty," 37–38; Cui Jing, "Mingdai waiqi zhuangtian chutan," *Nongye kaogu* 3 (2013): 71–75.

30. For biographies of Ming empresses and other consorts, see Ju Jixin et al., eds., *Zhongguo huanghou quanzhuan* (Jinan: Shandong jiaoxi, 1997), 819–902; Cai Shishan, *Mingdai de nüren* (Taipei: Lianjing, 2009), 2–67; Na Hai, *Ming Qing houfei de aihen wangshi* (Beijing: Gugong chubanshe, 2014). For accounts of empresses, consorts and princesses, and consort kin in the standard dynastic history, see Yi Jo-lan, "Social Status, Gender Division and Institutions: Sources Relating to Women in Chinese Standard Histories," in *Overt and Covert Treasures: Essays on the Sources for Chinese Women's History*, ed. Clara Wing-Chung Ho (Hong Kong: The Chinese University Press, 2012), 132–33. One of the most unusual empresses was Empress Ji (1451–1475), referred to as Li Tangmei in fictional works. She came from the Yao people of Guangxi and was the only ethnic Yao to become a Chinese empress.

Although she was not politically significant and has only a brief official biography, fiction authors told highly embellished stories about her.

31. Soullière, "The Writing and Rewriting of History," 7; Jiang, "Legislating Hierarchical Yet Harmonious Gender Relations," 29–30.

32. Li Min and Qian Zongfan, "Mingdai Xiaomu huang taihou: Yaozu chuanqishi nüxing Li Tangmei shiji pingyi—Yaozu lishi wenhua xilie yanjiu zhi yi," *Hezhou Xueyuan xuebao* 34, no. 1 (2018): 1–5.

33. Soullière, "Palace Women in the Ming Dynasty," 348–55, 366, 382; Soullière, "The Writing and Rewriting of History," 16–24.

34. Yu-ping Luk, *The Empress and the Heavenly Masters: A Study of the Ordination Scroll of Empress Zhang (1493)* (Hong Kong: The Chinese University Press, 2016), 24–33, 39.

35. Soullière, "Palace Women in the Ming Dynasty," 19; Xiao Jing, "Mingdai houfei kanyin fojing lunlue," *Wutaishan yanjiu* 3 (2017): 36–40; Chen, *Mingdai de fojiao yu shehui*, 102–9.

36. Cai, *Mingdai de nüren*, 68–102 provides biographies of Ming princesses. Also Soullière, "Palace Women in the Ming Dynasty," 299–302. Zhang Jingjing, "Mingdai gongzhu hunyin de 'pingminhua' quxiang," *Zhengzhou Hangkong Gongye Guanli Xueyuan xuebao* 36, no. 2 (2017): 67–68 gives a chart with the backgrounds of the husbands of princesses.

37. Yang Yaotian, "Mingdai gongzhu sangzang zhidu qianxi," *Beijing shehui kexue* 5 (2018): 23–33.

CHAPTER 3

1. Von Glahn, *The Economic History of China*, 285, 289–90, 295–96, 306.

2. Wu Renshu, *Shechi de nüren: Ming Qing shiqi Jiangnan funü de xiaofei wenhua* (Taipei: Sanmin shuju, 2005).

3. Shiga Shūzō, *Chūgoku kazokuhō no genri* (Tokyo: Sōbunsha, 1967), 50–58; Shūzō Shiga, "Family Property and the Law of Inheritance in Traditional China," in *Chinese Family Law and Social Change in Historical and Comparative Perspective*, ed. David C. Buxbaum (Seattle: University of Washington Press, 1978), 109–10; Kathryn Bernhardt, *Women and Property in China, 960–1949* (Stanford: Stanford University Press, 1999), 9–10; Birge, "Women and Confucianism from Song to Ming," 212.

4. Kutcher, *Mourning in Late Imperial China*, 38.

5. Zhang Jingwei, "Songdai caichan jicheng zhidu tanjiu," *Chifeng Xueyuan xuebao* 35, no. 1 (2014): 40–44; Yoshirō Takahashi, "Orphaned Daughters: On the So-Called Property Rights of Daughters in the Southern Song Period," trans. Matthew Raleigh, *International Journal of Asian Studies* 12, no. 2 (2015): 131–65.

6. Xu Kuoduan, "Shixi Yuandai funü zai falü zhong de diwei," *Zhongguo shi yanjiu* 4 (2000): 105.

7. Zhang, *Mingdai jiachan jicheng yu zhengsong*, 85.

8. Bernhardt, *Women and Property in China*, 2–3.

9. Jin Mei, "Tangdai hunyin jiating jicheng falü zhidu chulun" (PhD diss., China University of Political Science and Law, 2000), 155; Bettine Birge, "Inheritance and Property Law from Tang to Song: The Move away from Patrilineality," in *Tang Song nüxing yu shehui*, ed. Deng Xiaonan (Shanghai: Shanghai cishu, 2003), II: 852–53.

10. Xu, "Shixi Yuandai funü zai falü zhong de diwei," 105.

11. Bernhardt, *Women and Property in China*, 40; Chen Yingxun, *Ming Qing qiyue wenshu zhong de funü jingji huodong* (Taipei: Taiming wenhua, 2001), 25–26; Zhang Zhichao, "Mingdai funü caichan de laiyuan," *Funü yanjiu luncong* 4 (2010): 65; Zhang, *Mingdai jiachan jicheng yu zhengsong*, 85.

12. Xu, "Shixi Yuandai funü zai falü zhong de diwei," 107.

13. Zhang, *Mingdai jiachan jicheng yu zhengsong*, 77–78.

14. von Glahn, *The Economic History of China*, 291.

15. Bernhardt, *Women and Property in China*, 2–3, 47–48, 52–53, 62–63.

16. Li Jiao, "Ming Qing Huizhou funü zai tudi maimai huodong zhong de tedian—yi Huizhou wenshu wei li," *Chifeng Xueyuan xuebao* 36, no. 9 (2015): 53–56.

17. Chen, *Ming Qing qiyue wenshu zhong de funü jingji huodong*, 23–24.

18. Lau, "Changes to Women's Legal Rights in the Family," 707.

19. Zhang, *Mingdai jiachan jicheng yu zhengsong*, 84.

20. Bernhardt, *Women and Property in China*, 4–5.

21. Waltner, *Getting an Heir*, 93.

22. Mao Liping, *Qingdai jiazhuang yanjiu* (Beijing: Renming Daxue chubanshe, 2007), 7–8, 230–32.

23. Mao, *Qingdai jiazhuang yanjiu*, 234–46.

24. Stevan Harrell and Sara A. Dickey, "Dowry Systems in Complex Societies," *Ethnology* 24, no. 2 (1985): 105–20.

25. Patricia Buckley Ebrey, "Shifts in Marriage Finance from the Sixth to the Thirteenth Century," in *Marriage and Inequality in Chinese Society*, ed. Rubie S. Watson and Patricia B. Ebrey (Berkeley: University of California Press, 1991), 110–11; Mao, *Qingdai jiazhuang yanjiu*, 260–76.

26. He Deting, "Guanyu Yuandai hunyin zhidu de dutexing yu jibuxing de ruogan sikao," *Zhengfa xuekan* 21, no. 3 (2004): 103.

27. Bettine Birge, "Levirate Marriage and the Revival of Widow Chastity in Yuan China," *Asia Major* (third series) 8, no. 2 (1995): 113; Zhang, *Jiating shihua*, 108.

28. Birge, "Levirate Marriage," 114–16.

29. Bettine Birge, *Women, Property and Confucian Reaction in Sung and Yüan China (960–1368)* (Cambridge: Cambridge University Press, 2002), 263, 277; Zhang Benshun, "Songdai funü lianchan suoyouquan tanxi ji qi yiyi," *Fazhi yu shehui fazhan* 5 (2011): 88.

30. Zhang, *Mingdai jiachan jicheng yu zhengsong*, 77; Zhang, "Songdai funü lianchan suoyouquan tanxi ji qi yiyi," 88; Kathryn Bernhardt, "A Ming-Qing Transition in Chinese Women's History? The Perspective from Law," in *The History and Theory of Legal Practice in China: Toward a Historical-Social Jurisprudence*, ed. Philip C. C. Huang and Kathryn Bernhardt (Leiden: Brill, 2014), 54.

31. Mao, *Qingdai jiazhuang*, 11–13, 26–29, 147–58.

32. A Feng, *Ming Qing shidai funü de diwei yu quanli—yi Ming Qing qiyue wenshu, susong dang'an wei zhongxin* (Beijing: Shehui kexue wenxian chubanshe, 2009), 31–35 transcribes Ming and Qing dowry contracts from Huizhou.

33. A Feng, *Ming Qing shidai funü de diwei yu quanli*, 92; Liu Zhenggang, *Ming Qing diyu shehui bianqian zhong de Guangdong xiangcun funü yanjiu* (Beijing: Shehui kexue wenxian chubanshe, 2016), 54–58 describes the dowry land of Ming women in rural Guangdong.

34. Li Jiao, "Ming Qing Huizhou funü zai tudi maimai huodong zhong de tedian."

35. Zhang, "Mingdai funü caichanquan chufen," 119–20, 124.

36. Qi Bin and Wang Rimei, "Tangdai juntian zhidu xia funü buzai shoutian de yuanyin tanxi," *Xuchang Xueyuan xuebao* 31, no. 1 (2012): 96–99; von Glahn, *The Economic History of China*, 183.

37. von Glahn, *The Economic History of China*, 352–53.

38. Brook, *The Troubled Empire*, 138.

39. Timothy Brook, *The Confusions of Pleasure: Commerce and Culture in Ming China* (Berkeley: University of California Press, 1998), 66.

40. Chen Baoliang, "Mingdai funü de shehui jingji huodong ji qi zhuanxiang," *Zhongzhou xuekan* 1 (2011): 177.

41. Liu Zhenggang and Qiao Yuhong, "Ming Qing kejia nüxing de shehui xingxiang: yi Longchuan wei li," *Huanan Ligong Daxue xuebao* 5 (2008): 47.

42. Brook, *The Confusions of Pleasure*, 113–14, 194–98, 201–2.

43. Bray, *Technology and Gender*, 243.

44. Brook, *The Confusions of Pleasure*, 114, 116; Harriet T. Zurndorfer, "Cotton Textile Production in Jiangnan during the Ming-Qing Era and the Matter of Market Driven Growth," in *The Economy of Lower Yangzi Delta in Late imperial China; Connecting Money, Markets, and Institutions*, ed. Billy K. L. So (London: Routledge, 2013), 72–98.

45. Bray, *Technology and Gender*, 233, 239; Brook, *The Confusions of Pleasure*, 201–2.

46. Zhang Yuzhen, "Gui zhong hanmo: Ming Qing Jiangnan cainü de cixiu wenhua" (MA thesis, Guoli Taiwan Shifan Daxue, 2011); I-Fen Huang, "Gender, Technical Innovation, and Gu Family Embroidery in Late Ming Shanghai," *East Asian Science, Technology, and Medicine* 36 (2012): 77–129.

47. Yi Ruolan, *Sangu liupo: Mingdai funü yu shehui de tansuo* (Banqiao: Daoxiang, 2002), 42–85; Zhao Cuili, *Bei zhebi de xiandaixing: Ming Qing nüxing de shehui shenghuo yu qinggan tiyan* (Beijing: Zhishi chanquan chubanshe, 2015), 28–32.

48. Donald S. Sutton, "From Credulity to Scorn: Confucians Confront the Spirit Mediums in Late Imperial China," *Late Imperial China* 21, no. 2 (2000): 1–39.

49. Katsuyama, *Chūgoku Sō*, 67–73.

50. Qi Xin, "Mingdai nüxing chubanjia Zhou Zhibiao," *Xin shiji tushuguan* 10 (2012): 57–61.

51. Sylvia W. S. Lee, "'Co-Branding' a Cainü and a Garden: How the Zhao Family Established Identities for Wen Shu (1595–1634) and Their Garden Residence Hanshan," *Nan Nü* 18, no. 1 (2016): 49–83.

52. Brook, *The Confusions of Pleasure*, 255; Wang Xueping, "Mingdai binü hunyin teshuxing de lishi jiedu," *Shehui kexue jikan* 3 (2010): 195–99; Wang Xueping, "Mingdai chubi xianxjang de lishi wenhua yunhan—yi *Xingshi yunyuan zhuan* wei zhongxin," *Haerbin Gongye Daxue xuebao* 13, no. 6 (2011): 114–19; Wang Xueping, "Mingdai binü zhengce yu fagui de yanjin ji shehui neihan," *Dongbei Shida xuebao* 2 (2013): 55–61; Wang Xueping, "Mingdai zhufu yubi celue yu rujia lunli shijian—yi Mingdai nüxing beizhuanwen wei zhongxin," *Jianghan luntan* 11 (2013): 107–12; Wang Xueping, "Mingdai tieshen binü qunti cunzai jichu ji shengcun moshi tanwei," *Changchun Shifan Daxue xuebao* 5 (2014): 42–46; Luo Xinquan, "Ming Qing nüxing wenxue xinbian (er)—guixiu fu bi shici lungao," *Hengyang Shifan Xueyuan xuebao* 1 (2016): 77–81.

53. Brook, *The Confusions of Pleasure*, 204.

54. Zhou Jiren, "Lun Zhongguo gudai biaoyan yishu de shangpinhua wenti," *Zhongguoshi yanjiu* 15, no. 4 (1993): 44–57.

55. Brook, *The Confusions of Pleasure*, 230–31; Victoria Cass, *Dangerous Women: Warriors, Grannies and Geishas of the Ming* (Lanham, MD: Rowman and Littlefield, 1999), 25–46; Judith T. Zeitlin, "The Gift of Song: Courtesans and Patrons in Late Ming and Early Qing Cultural Production," *Hsiang Lectures on Chinese Poetry* 4 (2008): 1–46; Harriet Zurndorfer, "Prostitutes and Courtesans in the Confucian Moral Universe of Late Ming China (1550–1644)," *International Review of Social History* 56 (2011): 197–216.

56. Yan Ming, *Zhongguo mingji yishu shi* (Taipei: Wenjin, 1992), 101–7.

57. Hsu Pi-ching, "Courtesans and Scholars in the Writings of Feng Menglong: Transcending Status and Gender," *Nan Nü*, 2, no. 1 (2000): 49.

58. He, *Danqing qipa*, 18–39, 41–48, 61–72.

59. Monica Merlin, "The Nanjing Courtesan Ma Shouzhen (1548–1604): Gender, Space and Painting in the Late Ming Pleasure Quarter," *Gender and History* 23, no. 3 (2011): 630–52.

60. Judith T. Zeitlin, "The Pleasures of Print: Illustrated Songbooks form the Late Ming Courtesan World," in *Gender in Chinese Music*, ed. Rachel Harris et al. (Rochester, NY: University of Rochester Press, 2013), 41–65.

61. Daria Berg, "Amazon, Artist, and Adventurer: A Courtesan in Late Imperial China," in *The Human Tradition in Modern China*, ed. Kenneth J. Hammond and Kristin Stapleton (Lanham, MD: Rowman & Littlefield, 2007), 15–32; Daria Berg, "Cultural Discourse on Xue Susu, a Courtesan of Late Ming China," *International Journal of Asian Studies* 6, no. 2 (2009): 171–200.

62. Lara C. W. Blanchard, "A Scholar in the Company of Female Entertainers: Changing Notions of Integrity in Song to Ming Dynasty Painting," *Nan Nü* 9, no. 2 (2007): 189–246.

63. Zurndorfer, "Prostitutes and Courtesans," 209; Wang Hongtai, "Meiren xiangban—Ming Qing wenren de meise pinshang yu qingyi shenghuo de jingying," *Xin shixue* 24, no. 2 (2013): 71–130.

64. Hsu, "Courtesans and Scholars," 42–43, 45.

CHAPTER 4

1. Brook, *The Confusions of Pleasure*, 61.

2. David Johnson, "Communication, Class, and Consciousness in Late Imperial China," in *Popular Culture in Late Imperial China*, ed. David Johnson et al. (Berkeley and Los Angeles: University of California Press, 1985), 61–62, 66, 70.

3. Brook, *The Confusions of Pleasure*, 61–62.

4. Birge, "Chu Hsi and Women's Education," 356; Dorothy Ko, "Pursuing Talent and Virtue: Education and Women's Culture in Seventeenth and Eighteenth Century China," *Late Imperial China* 13, no. 1 (1992): 9.

5. Qin Haiying, *Mingdai Shandong jiaohua yanjiu* (Dalian: Liaoning Shifan Daxue chubanshe, 2011), 123.

6. Joanna F. Handlin, "Lü Kun's New Audience: The Influence of Women's Literacy on Sixteenth Century Thought," in *Women in Chinese Society*, ed. Margery Wolf and Roxanne Witke (Stanford: Stanford University Press, 1975), 13–38; Zhao Xiuli, "Mingdai daru Lü Kun de nüxingguan ji shijian," *Shangqiu Shifan Xueyuan xuebao* 2 (2008): 23–28.

7. Lü Kun, *Guifan* (Shanghai: Shanghai guji, 1994).

8. Chang and Saussy, *Women Writers of Traditional China*, 169.

9. Chang and Saussy, *Women Writers of Traditional China*, 678–81, translates the preface to *Neixun*.

10. "When I Hired a Teacher to Instruct the Girls, Someone Ridiculed Me, So as a Joke I Have Written This Retort to Explain Matters," Chang and Saussy, *Women Writers of Traditional China*, 309–10.

11. Zhang, "*Neixun* yu Mingdai nüxing jiaohua," 22–23.

12. Xie Guian, "Mingdai gongting nüjiao lunxi," *Zhongyuan wenhua yanjiu* 3 (2016): 95–102.

13. Feminist scholars refer to the effect of social perspective on knowledge as subject position. This theory casts doubt on the possibility of objective social knowledge. Charles Lemert, *Social Things: An Introduction to the Sociological Life*, 4th ed. (Lanham, MD: Rowman & Littlefield, 2008), 176–77.

14. Ellen Widmer, "The Epistolary World of Female Talent in Seventeenth-Century China," *Late Imperial China* 10 (1989): 30; Ko, *Teachers of the Inner Chambers*, 125–29; Chen Baoliang, "Mingdai de funü jiaoyu ji qi zhuanxiang," *Shehui kexue jikan* 6 (2009): 157–61; Li Guotong, *Nüzi zhi bukui: Ming Qing shiqi de nüjiao guannian* (Guilin: Guangxi Shifan Daxue chubanshe, 2014).

15. Liu Miaofen, "Zuo wei Mengxue yu nüjiao duben de Xiaojing—jian lun qi webben dingwei de lishi bianhua," *Taida lishi xuebao* 6 (2008): 1–64.

16. Yamazaki Junichi, *Kyōiku kara mita Chūgoku joseishi shiryō no kenkyū— 'josisho' to 'shinhuhu' sanbusho* (Tokyo: Meiji, 1986) analyzes the text of the four books in detail. Also Sun Xinmei, "*Nü sishu* de bianzuan yu liuchuan," *Lantai shijie* 11 (2013): 156–57; Ann A. Pang-White, "Confucius and the *Four Books for Women* (*Nü Sishu* 女四書)," in *Feminist Encounters with Confucius*, ed. Mathew A. Foust and Sor-hoon Tan (Leiden: Brill, 2016), 17–39.

17. All current editions of *Nü lunyu* are based on Ming dynasty editions. This book was repeatedly reprinted in the Ming and Qing eras. Wang Danni and Li Zhisheng, "Ming Qing shiqi *Nü lunyu* banben kaoshu," *Shandong Nüzi Xueyuan xuebao* 2 (2018): 46–55.

18. Zhang, "*Neixun* yu Mingdai nüxing jiaohua," 22–26.

19. Li Shunhua, "Nüxing duzhe yu Mingdai zhanghui xiaoshuo de xingqi," *Xueshu yanjiu* 10 (2009): 137.

20. Wang Yi, *Songdai wenxue jiazu* (Changsha: Hunan Shifa Daxue chubanshe, 2008), 376.

21. Lisa Raphals, *Sharing the Light: Representations of Women and Virtue in Early China* (Albany: SUNY Press, 1998), 113–38.

22. Ko, *Teachers of the Inner Chambers*, 29, 34–53.

23. Zhang Lijie, *Mingdai nüxing sanwen yanjiu* (Beijing: Zhongguo shehui kexue, 2009), 186–96.

24. Zhong Huiling, *Qingdai nüshiren yanjiu* (Taipei: Liren shuju, 2000), 5–6, 15.

25. Debra Spitulnik, "The Social Circulation of Media Discourse and the Mediation of Communities," in *Linguistic Anthropology: A Reader*, 2nd ed., ed. Alessandro Duranti (Chinchester, UK: Wiley-Blackwell, 2009), 93–113.

26. Widmer, "The Epistolary World of Female Talent," 29–30; Epstein, "Reflections of Desire," 85.

27. Chen Baoliang, *Mingdai shehui zhuanxing yu wenhua bianqian* (Chongqing: Chongqing Daxue chubanshe, 2014), 210–15.

28. Zhang Lijie, *Mingdai nüxing sanwen yanjiu* (Beijing: Zhongguo shehui kexue, 2009); Idema, "The Biographical and the Autobiographical," 231. Cao Hong, "Rouhan jianbi: Mingdai nüxing de wenzhang zaoyi," *Jiangxi Shifan Daxue xuebao* 43, no. 5 (2010): 106–12 describes some representative prose works by women.

29. James Hayes, "Specialists and Written Materials in the Village World," in *Popular Culture in Late Imperial China*, ed. David Johnson et al. (Berkeley and Los Angeles: University of California Press, 1985), 86; Brook, *The Confusions of Pleasure*, 186–87; Widmer, "The Epistolary World of Female Talent," 17; Ellen Widmer, "Letters as Windows on Ming-Qing Women's Literary Culture," in *A History of Chinese Letters and Epistolary Culture*, ed. Antje Richtr (Leiden: Brill, 2015), 747.

30. Wei Shuyun, *Ming Qing nüzuojia tanci xiaoshuo yu Ming Qing shehui* (Tianjin: Tianjin Shehui Kexueyuan chubanshe, 2017), 1–66, introduces the main female *tanci* authors of the Ming and Qing, and discusses the contents of their works.

31. Hua Wei, *Ming Qing funü zhi xiqu chuangzuo yu piping* (Taipei: Zhongyang Yanjiuyuan Zhongguo Wenzhe Yanzhousuo, 2003), 151–52; Liu, *Ming Qing nüxing zuojia xiqu chuangzuo yanjiu*, 5, 11.

32. Chang and Saussy, *Women Writers of Traditional China*, 686.

33. Widmer, "The Epistolary World of Female Talent," 26–27.

34. Grace S. Fong, *Herself an Author: Gender, Agency, and Writing in Late Imperial China* (Honolulu: University of Hawaii Press, 2008), 121; Wang Liyu, *Ming*

Qing nüxing de wenxue pipan (Shanghai: Huadong Shilan Daxue chubanshe, 2017). Suzanne Cahill, "Resenting the Silk Robes That Hide Their Poems: Female Voices in the Poetry of Tang Dynasty Nuns," in *Tang Song nüxing yu shehui*, ed. Deng Xiaonan (Shanghai: Shanghai cishu, 2003), II: 2, 521 puts forward a useful framework for analyzing poetry by Chinese women.

35. Yu Yi, "Lun Mingdai nüciren de huaiqinci," *Dongguan Ligong Xueyuan xuebao* 18, no. 4 (2011): 75–79.

36. Wang Meng, "Ming Qing shiqi nüxing bixia de jiemei qingyi," *Henan Jiaoyu Xueyuan xuebao* 4 (2005): 119–22.

37. "A Young Wife's Lament," Chang and Saussy, *Women Writers of Traditional China*, 251.

38. Goyama Kiwamu, "Ming Qing nüzi tibi shi kao," trans. Li Yinsheng, *Hechi Shifan xuebao* 1 (2004): 53–57.

39. Sarah Dauncey, "Bonding, Benevolence, Barter, and Bribery: Images of Female Gift Exchange in the *Jin Ping Mei*," *Nan Nü* 5, no. 2 (2003): 203–39.

40. Widmer, "The Epistolary World of Female Talent," 24; Zhong, *Qingdai nüshiren yanjiu*, 37–42; Cheng Jun, "Lun Ming Qing nüxing shishe de sanzhong leixing," *Xiamen Guangbo Dianshi Daxue xuebao* 2 (2017): 76–80, 96.

41. Zhong, *Qingdai nüshiren yanjiu*, 118–27; Wang, *Ming Qing nüxing de wenxue piping*, 23–37; Qiao Chen, "Mingdai nüzi shiwen zongji de xingbie shijiao," *Shehui kexuejia* 5 (2015): 149–53; Sufeng Xu, "The Rhetoric of Legitimation: Prefaces to Women's Poetry Collections from the Song to the Ming," *Nan Nü* 8, no. 2 (2006): 255–89. Kang-i Sun Chang, "Ming and Qing Anthologies of Women's Poetry and Their Selection Strategies," in *Writing Women in Late Imperial China*, ed. Ellen Widmer and Kang-i Sun Chang (Stanford: Stanford University Press, 1997), 147–70 describes the main anthologies of poetry by Ming women.

42. Xiaorong Li, *Women's Poetry of Late Imperial China* (Seattle: University of Washington Press, 2012), 5–6, 12, 14, 58.

43. Chang and Saussy, *Women Writers of Traditional China*, 161.

44. Yu, "Lun Mingdai nüciren de huaiqinci," 75–79.

45. "Setting Out from the Passes," Chang and Saussy, *Women Writers of Traditional China*, 287.

46. "While Traveling in Autumn, I Hear of Invading Bandits," Chang and Saussy, *Women Writers of Traditional China*, 288.

47. Clara Wing-chung Ho, "History as Leisure Reading for Ming-Qing Women Poets," *Hsiang Lectures on Chinese Poetry* 7 (2015): 27–64.

48. Li Wenshi, "Guige qingzhen: Mingdai nühuajia huihua," *Mei cheng zai jiu* 1 (2017): 62.

49. Sheng Shilan, "Ming Qing mingji de bimo biaoqing," *Shufa* 3 (2014): 42–47.

50. He, *Danqing qipa*, 41–48, 61–85.

51. He, *Danqing qipa*, 18–39, 48; Wang Weiping, "Ming Qing mushi jiaoyu suyang shulun," *Neijiang Shifan Xueyuan xuebao* 7, no. 28 (2013): 78.

52. Wu Weichun, "Yangzhou baguai yu Ming Qing cainühua zhi yuanyuan," *Weiyang Shifan Xueyuan xuebao* 5 (2010): 636–41, 645.

CHAPTER 5

1. Zhong Jinlan, "Kejia funü yu shenming chongbai—yi Ming Qing simiao beige jizai wei zhongxin de fenxi," *Jiaying Xueyuan xuebao* 30, no. 4 (2012): 13–18.

2. James L. Watson, "Standardization of the Gods: The Promotion of Ti'en Hou ('Empress of Heaven') along the South China Coast, 960–1960," in *Popular Culture in Late Imperial China*, ed. David Johnson et al. (Berkeley and Los Angeles: University of California Press, 1985), 293–94.

3. Yuan Zhoufei, "Ming Qing yilai nianhua zhong nüxing xingxiang de muti tanti," *Minsu yanjiu* 4 (2016): 114–15.

4. Li Qing, "Shilun Yuandai de Mazu chongbai," *Zhongnan Minzu Daxue xuebao* 6 (2005): 128–31; Huang Taiyong, "Yuandai Tianfei chongbai de sange wenti xintan," *Zhongguo haiyang daxue* 6 (2014): 64–68; Wang Haidong, "Yuandai haishang caoyun yu Mazu xinyang de fazhan," *Putian Xueyuan xuexiao* 23, no. 4 (2016): 1–5.

5. Pu Wenqi, "Nüxing jiazhi de zhongyang—Ming Qing shiqi minjian zongjiao zhong de funü," *Lilun yu xiandaihua* 5 (2006): 111–15 identifies forty-four goddesses.

6. Daniel L. Overmyer, "Values in Chinese Sectarian Literature: Ming and Ch'ing *Pao-chüan*," in *Popular Culture in Late Imperial China*, ed. David Johnson et al. (Berkeley and Los Angeles: University of California Press, 1985), 237, 240–41; Susan Naquin, "The Transmission of White Lotus Sectarianism in Late Imperial China," in *Popular Culture in Late Imperial China*, ed. David Johnson et al. (Berkeley and Los Angeles: University of California Press, 1985), 255–61.

7. Brook, *The Troubled Empire*, 8.

8. Luk, *The Empress and the Heavenly Masters*.

9. Xiaohuan Zhao, "Love, Lust, and Loss in the Daoist Nunnery as Presented in Yuan Drama," *T'oung Pao* 100, nos. 1–3 (2014): 80–119.

10. Overmyer, "Values in Chinese Sectarian Literature," 221, 224, 228, 230, 250.

11. Chün-fang Yü, *Kuan-yin: The Chinese Transformations of Avalokiteśvara* (New York: Columbia University Press, 2001), 295–96, 303, 311–12, 333.

12. "Seeing a Butterfly on an Autumn Day," Chang and Saussy, *Women Writers of Traditional China*, 157.

13. "Autumn Day, Village Life: Rhyming after My Father's Poem," Chang and Saussy, *Women Writers of Traditional China*, 279.

14. Chen, *Mingdai shehui zhuanxing yu wenhua bianqian*, 210–15; Lou Hansong and Wu Lin, "'Guiyin': Ming Qing zhi ji zhishi nüxing de shenfen xuanze yu jiazhi rentong," *Zhejiang shehui kexue* 2 (2016): 120–25.

15. Guo Hui, "Jianlun Mingdai biqiuni de shengcun kunjing," *Zongjiaoxue yanjiu* 3 (2013): 143; Fumiko Jōo, "Ancestress Worship: Huxin Temple and the Literati Community in Late Ming Ningbo," *Nan Nü* 16, no. 1 (2014): 31, 51.

16. Jian Ruiyao, *Mingdai funü fojiao xinyang yu shehui guifan* (Banqiao: Daoxiang, 2007), 22–29, 61–73; Chen, *Mingdai de fojiao yu shehui*, 322–39; Guo, "Jianlun Mingdai biqiuni de shengcun kunjing," 142–43.

17. Guo, "Jianlun Mingdai biqiuni de shengcun kunjing," 144.

18. Chaoying Fang, "Huo T'ao," in *Dictionary of Ming Biography, 1368–1644* (New York: Columbia University Press, 1976), 681; Brook, *The Troubled Empire*, 142.

19. Xiao, "Mingdai houfei kanyin fojing lunlue," 36–40.

20. Dardess, *Ming China 1368–1644*, 94. Chen, *Mingdai de fojiao yu shehui*, 102–9, provides a long list of the temples that she had constructed.

21. Chen, *Mingdai de fojiao yu shehui*, 381–434.

22. Jennifer Eichman, "Zhuhong's Communal Rules for the Late Ming Nunnery Filiality and Righteousness Unobstructed," *Nan Nü* 21, no. 2 (2019): 224–75.

23. B. J. ter Har, *The White Lotus Teachings of Chinese Religious History* (Honolulu: University of Hawaii Press, 1999), 139; Lin Yanqing, "Tang Sai'er," trans. Laura Long, in *Biographical Dictionary of Chinese Women: Tang through Ming, 618–1644*, ed. Lily Xiao Hong Lee and Sue Wiles (Armonk, NY: M.E. Sharpe, 2014), 392–94.

24. David E. Kelley, "Temples and Tribute Fleets: The Luo Sect and Boatmen's Associations in the Eighteenth Century," *Modern China* 8, no. 3 (1982): 361–91.

25. Zhang Li, "Ming Qing funü shenghuo yu fojiao xinyang," *Hunan Renwen Keji Xueyuan xuebao* 3 (2012): 47–51.

26. Wang Huaxu, "Ming Qing chuanqi zhong nüni nüdao juese tedian tanwei," *Jiangsu Jiaoyu Xueyuan xuebao* 29, no. 1 (2013): 118–20.

27. Brook, *The Confusions of Pleasure*, 182–84; Bray, *Technology and Gender*, 144; Song Lizhong, "Ming Qing Jiangnan funü 'yeyou' yu fengjian lunli chongtu," *Funü yanjiu luncong* 1 (2010): 40–42; Chen Baoliang, "Hao gui chong Fo: Mingdai funü de fodao xinyang ji qi yishi," *Haerbin Shifan Daxue shehui kexue xuebao* 1 (2010): 119–20.

28. Li Yongju, "Ming Qing nüxing canjia miaohui de wanhua xuqiu fenxi," *Hubei Daxue xuebao* 31, no. 5 (2004): 578–81.

29. Beata Grant, *Daughters of Emptiness: Poems of Chinese Buddhist Nuns* (Somerville, MA: Wisdom Publications, 2003), 55.

CHAPTER 6

1. Nanxiu Qian, "Milk and Scent: Works about Women in the *Shishuo Xinyu* Genre," *Nan Nü* 1, no. 2 (1999): 189–90.

2. Zhang Ping, "Mingdai caizi jiaren chuanqi zhong de nüxing yishi tanxi—yi Tang Xianzu *Mudan ting* wei li," *Zhonggong Jinan Shiwei Dangxiao xuebao* 1 (2018): 73–76.

3. Mark Stevenson, "Wanton Women in Late-Imperial Chinese Literature: Models, Genres, Subversions and Traditions," in *Wanton Women in Late-Imperial Chinese Literature: Models, Genres, Subversions and Traditions*, ed. Mark Stevenson and Wu Cuncun (Leiden: Brill, 2017), 3–26.

4. Ka F. Wong, "The Anatomy of Eroticism: Reimagining Sex and Sexuality in the Late Ming Novel *Xiuta Yeshi*," *Nan Nü* 9, no. 2 (2007): 284–329.

5. Joseph S. C. Lam, "Reading Music and Eroticism in Late Ming Texts," *Nan Nü* 12, no. 2 (2010): 215–54.

6. Yenna Wu, "The Inversion of Marital Hierarchy: Shrewish Wives and Hen-Pecked Husbands in Seventeenth-Century Chinese Literature," *Harvard Journal of Asiatic Studies* 48, no. 2 (1988): 363–82; Yenna Wu, *The Lioness Roars: Shrew Stories from Late Imperial China* (Ithaca, NY: East Asia Program, Cornell University, 1995).

7. Li Yuanyuan, "Cong *Jin Ping Mei* kan Mingdai de 'fudu' zhi feng," *Xuchang Xueyuan xuebao* 3 (2014): 70–72.

8. Liu Min, "Lun Ming Qing xiaoshuo zhong de nüxing handu wenhua—yi *Liaozhai zhiyi* zhong de 'handu fu' xingxiang wei li," *Shaanxi Xueqian Shifan Xueyuan xuebao* 31, no. 6 (2015): 57–60.

9. Bret Hinsch, *Masculinities in Chinese History* (Lanham, MD: Rowman & Littlefield, 2013), 29–46.

10. Wang Li and Li Guiyin, "Wei Jin nüxing fuchou wenxue zhuti de wenxue shiyi ji chengyin," *Suzhou Shizhuan xuebao* 18, no. 1 (2003): 4–7; Sarah M. Allen, "Tales Retold: Narrative Variation in a Tang Story," *Harvard Journal of Asiatic Studies* 66, no. 1 (2006): 106, 114, 116–20, 136; Zhang Jing, *Tangdai nüxing xingxiang shenghuo* (Lanzhou: Gansu renmin, 2007), 85–106.

11. Chen Shaoyun, "Mingdai nüxing fuchou gushi de wenhua kaocha" (MA thesis, Guoli Taiwan Shifan Daxue, 2009); Roland Altenburger, *The Sword or the Needle: The Female Knight-errant (xia) in Traditional Chinese Narrative* (Bern: Peter Lang, 2009), 127–62; Wang Li and Feng Zhihua, "Ming Qing xiaoshuo nüxing yiji Fuchou miaoxie yu shehui xinli," *Dandong Shizhuan xuebao* 24, no. 3 (2002): 1.

12. Goyama Kiwamu, *Ming Qing shidai de nüxing yu wenxue*, trans. Xiao Yanwan (Taipei: Lianjing, 2016), 465–91.

13. Zhu Yangdong and Hu Hongqiang, "Mingdai Shuihu xi nüxingguan guankui," *Yili Shifan Xueyuan xuebao* 4 (2009): 68–72.

14. Bernhardt, "A Ming-Qing Transition in Chinese Women's History?," 43–45.

15. Ping-chen Hsiung, *A Tender Voyage: Children and Childhood in Late Imperial China* (Stanford: Stanford University Press, 2005), 186–88.

16. Qin, *Mingdai Shandong jiaohua yanjiu*, 123.

17. Ronald Mellor, *Tacitus' Annals* (Oxford: Oxford University Press, 2010), 48.

18. Lemert, *Social Things*, 5, 81.

19. Julia K. Murray, *Mirror of Morality: Chinese Narrative Illustration and Confucian Ideology* (Honolulu: University of Hawaii Press, 2007), 12.

20. Katherine Carlitz, "The Social Uses of Female Virtue in Late Ming Editions of Lienü zhuan," *Late Imperial China* 12, no. 2 (1991): 117–48.

21. Raphals, *Sharing the Light*, 137.

22. Hsiung, *A Tender Voyage*, 185, 190.

23. Bray, *Technology and Gender*, 171.

24. Bray, *Technology and Gender*, 56, 59; Gao Yanyi, "'Kongjian' yu 'jia'—lun Mingmo Qingchu funü de shenghuo kongjian," *Jindai Zhongguo funüshi yanjiu* 8 (1995): 21–50.

25. Li, *Women's Poetry of Late Imperial China*, 5–6, 9, 12, 14.

26. Margery Wolf, *Women and the Family in Rural Taiwan* (Stanford: Stanford University Press, 1972), 33.

27. Song Lizhong, "Ming Qing Jiangnan funü 'yeyou' yu fengjian lunli chongtu," *Funü yanjiu luncong* 1 (2010): 40–42.

28. Halvor Eifring, "Introduction: Emotions and Conceptual History of Qing," in *Love and Emotions in Traditional Chinese Literature*, ed. Halvor Eifring (Leiden: Brill, 2004), 1–36.

29. Barbara Bisetto, "Fragments of *Qing* 情: The *Qingshi leilüe* 情史類略 and the Literary Categorization of 'Love' in the 17th Century China," in *Concepts and Categories of Emotion in East Asia*, ed. Giusi Tamburello (Rome: Carocci Editore, 2012), 164–75.

30. Katherine Carlitz, "Shrines, Governing-Class Identity, and the Cult of Widow-Fidelity in Mid-Ming Jiangnan," *Journal of Asian Studies* 56, no. 3 (1997): 617.

31. Martin W. Huang, *Desire and Fictional Narrative in Late Imperial China* (Cambridge, MA: Harvard University Asia Center, 2001), 23–27; Zhan Shiyou and Peng Chuanhua, "Cultivation (Jiaohua, 教化): The Goal of Xunzi's Ethical Thought," *Frontiers of Philosophy in China* 2, no. 1 (2007): 35, 42.

32. Goyama, *Ming Qing shidai de nüxing yu wenxue*, 52.

33. Epstein, "Reflections of Desire," 70–73

34. Bao Zhenpei, *Qingdai nüzuojia tanci yanjiu* (Tianjin: Nankai Daxue, 2008), 31–34.

35. Wu Cuncun, *Ming Qing shehui xing'ai fengqi* (Beijing: Renmin wenxue chubanshe, 2000), 59–71.

36. Huang, *1587: A Year of No Significance*, 189–221; Tamara H. Bentley, "The Rhetoric of Emotion in 17th Century China and Japan," in *Concepts and Categories of Emotion in East Asia*, ed. Giusi Tamburello (Rome: Carocci Editore, 2012), 180–81.

37. Huang, *Desire and Fictional Narrative in Late Imperial China*, 33, 39.

38. Hsu, "Courtesans and Scholars in the Writings of Feng Menglong," 52.

39. Huang, *Desire and Fictional Narrative in Late Imperial China*, 34.

40. Hsiung, *A Tender Voyage*, 199–200.

41. Carlitz, "The Daughter, The Singing-Girl, and the Seduction of Suicide," 23.

42. Handlin, "Lü Kun's New Audience," 30–31.

43. Richard G. Wang, "The Cult of *Qing*: Romanticism in the Late Ming Period and in the Novel *Jiao Hong Ji*," *Ming Studies* 33 (1994): 12–13; Epstein, "Reflections of Desire," 74; Goyama, *Ming Qing shidai de nüxing yu wenxue*, 53, 68.

44. Liu Shiyi, "Mingdai qingxing sichao yu liangxing wenxue yanbian," *Beifang luncong* 5 (2014): 31.

45. Tomoyuki Tanaka, "View of Emotions in the *Jin Ping Mei*: Perceptions of the 'Moods' and Their Expression," in *Concepts and Categories of Emotion in East Asia*, ed. Giusi Tamburello (Rome: Carocci, 2012), 213–14, 227.

46. Bentley, "The Rhetoric of Emotion," 180–81; Handlin, "Lü Kun's New Audience," 32.

47. Li Fengjian, "Ming Qing xiaoshuo zhong de jinü yu aiqing zhenjie," *Ming Qing xiaoshuo yanjiu* 2 (2005): 19–26.

48. Richard G. Wang, *Ming Erotic Novellas: Genre, Consumption, and Religiosity in Cultural Practice* (Hong Kong: Chinese University Press, 2011), 119, 125.

49. Alastair Ewan MacDonald, "Women in Erpai: The Gap Between Rhetoric and Representation," *Nan Nü* 20, no. 2 (2018): 225–55.

50. Paul Ricoeur, "Narrative Identity," *Philosophy Today* 35, no. 1 (1991): 73; Patricia Baquedano-López, "Creating Social Identities through *Doctrina* Narratives," *Issues in Applied Linguistics* 8, no. 1 (1997): 27–28.

51. Carlitz, "The Daughter, the Singing-Girl, and the Seduction of Suicide," 43; Ann Waltner, "Remembering the Lady Wei: Eulogy and Commemoration in Ming Dynasty China," *Ming Studies* 55 (2007): 80–92.

52. Liu, "Mingdai qingxing sichao yu liangxing wenxue yanbian," 32–34.

53. Harriet Zurndorfer, "Women in Chinese Learned Culture: Complexities, Exclusivities and Connecting Narratives," *Gender & History* 16, no. 1 (2014): 27.

54. "Recording My Thoughts," Chang and Saussy, *Women Writers of Traditional China*, 268.

55. Chang and Saussy, *Women Writers of Traditional China*, 193.

CHAPTER 7

1. Anne F. Broadbridge, *Women and the Making of the Mongol Empire* (Cambridge: Cambridge University Press, 2018), 10–11.

2. Wu Haihang, *Yuandai fa wenhua yanjiu* (Beijing: Beijing Shifan Daxue chubanshe, 2000), 198.

3. Henry Serruys, "Remains of Mongol Customs During the Early Ming," *Monumenta Serica* 16, nos. 1–2 (1957): 188–89; Ma Leiyin and Ren Ruping, "Lun Zhongguo gudai shouji hunzhi—yi Mingdai wei li," *Fazhi yu jingji* 7 (2014): 124–25.

4. According to the genealogy of one lineage in Tongcheng county, Anhui, detailing lineage members from 1520–1661, about 7.5 percent of these men married more than once. Telford, "Covariates of Men's Age at First Marriage," 27.

5. Xu Tuoduan, ed., *Ming shi lu leizuan: Funüshi kejuan* (Wuhan: Wuhan chubanshe, 1995), 294–424; Wang Chuanman, "Ming Qing Huizhou funü jielie xingwei de yingxiang," *Nanyang Shifan Xueyuan xuebao* 8, no. 11 (2009): 43.

6. Dong Jiazun, "Lidai jielie funü de tongji," in *Zhongguo funüshi lunji*, ed. Bao Jialin (Taipei: Daoxiang, 1988), 111–17.

7. Li Tingting, "Cong Ming Qing ni huaben xiaoshuo zhenjie lienü xiangxiang kan Ming Qing zhenjieguan de bianhua," *Hunan Renwen Kexue Xueyuan xueba* 5 (2012): 58–59.

8. Carlitz, "Shrines, Governing-Class Identity, and the Cult of Widow-Fidelity," 612.

9. Michela Bussotti, "Images of Women in Late Ming Huizhou-Printed Editions of the *Lienü zhuan*," *Nan Nü* 17, no. 1 (2015): 54–116.

10. Zhang Wenlu, "Ming Qing shiqi Wanbei nüzi xiaoxing yanjiu—yi Guangxu Shouzhou zhi, Suzhou zhi he Bozhou zhi wei kaocha duixiang," *Liupanshui Shifan Xueyuan xuebao* 30, no. 2 (2018): 61–64.

11. Guo Junjun, "Mingdai Datong zhenlie nüzi de tezheng ji qi chengyin fenxi," *Shanxi Meitan Guanli Ganbu Xueyuan xuebao* 28, no. 4 (2015): 180.

12. Liu Yan, "Mingdai Ningde lienü xingxiang yanjiu—yi Ming Jiajing shiqinian ban *Ningde xianzhi* wei li," *Luoyang Shifan Xueyuan xuebao* 35, no. 7 (2016): 57–59.

13. Wei-hung Lin, "Chastity in Chinese Eyes—Nan-Nu Yu-Pieh," *Hanxue yanjiu* 12 (1991): 13–40.

14. This technique is often called Aesopian language. Jeffries, *Grand Hotel Abyss*, 197.

15. These techniques are called iconization and erasure. Judith T. Irvine and Susan Gal, "Language Ideology and Linguistic Differentiation," in *Regimes of Language: Ideologies, Polities, and Identities*, ed. Paul V. Kroskrity (Santa Fe, NM: School of American Research Press, 2000), 36–39.

16. Carlitz, "Lovers, Talkers, Monsters, and Good Women," 177–78.

17. Lu Jianrong, "Yuanmo nüxing wei yufang shouru er zisha shijian de xingsi—xugou dangan hu, yidai youse yanjing kan wushi hu?" in *Jindai bainian chengshi shenghuo de xingbie yu quanli*, ed. Lu Jianrong (Taipei: Xin gaodi, 2019), 109–11.

18. Wang Li, "Ming Qing nüxing baozhenshu muti ji qi Yindu wenhua suyuan," *Ningxia Daxue xuebao* 1 (2007): 43–44.

19. Lin Liyue, "Xiaodao yu fudao: Mingdai xiaofu de wenhuashi kaocha," *Jindai Zhongguo funüshi yanjiu* 6 (1998): 16.

20. Qin, *Mingdai Shandong jiaohua yanjiu*, 128.

21. Waltner, *Getting an Heir*, 93–94, 113.

22. Jiang, "Legislating Hierarchical Yet Harmonious Gender Relations," 33–34.

23. Zhang, *Mingdai jiachan jiching yu zhengsong*, 77–78.

24. A Feng, *Ming Qing shidai funü de diwei yu quanli*, 174–81.

25. Sommer, "The Uses of Chastity," 78; Brook, *The Troubled Empire*, 140.

26. Lü Miaofen, "Ming Qing Zhongguo wanli xunqin de wenhua shijian," *Zhong-yang Yanjiu Yuan Lishi Yuyan Yanjiusuo jikan* 78, no. 2 (2007): 359–406.

27. Kang Xuewei, *Xian Qin xiaodao yanjiu* (Taipei: Wenjin, 1992); Luo, *Tongju gongcai*, 354–60.

28. Goyama, *Ming Qing shidai de nüxing yu wenxue*, 198–200.

29. Lin, "Xiaodao yu fudao," 1–29.

30. Katherine Carlitz, "Three Ming Dynasty Martyrs and Their Monstrous Moth-ers-in-Law," *Ming Studies* 68 (2013): 5–6.

31. Han Chenghua, "*Mingshi Lienüzhuan* de baoli, qingxu, gongjue yu nüxing xingxiang de shuxie," *Mingdai yanjiu* 32 (2019): 97–151.

32. Lu, *True to Her Word*, 43.

33. Lu, "Yuanmo nüxing wei yufang shouru er zich shijian de xingsi," 109–11.

34. Du Fangqin, "Ming Qing zhenjie de tedian ji qi yuanyin," *Shanxi Shida xuebao* 10 (1997): 41–50.

35. Meijer, *Murder and Adultery in Late Imperial China*, 39–40.

36. Sherry J. Mou, *Gentlemen's Prescriptions for Women's Lives: A Thousand Years of Biographies of Chinese Women* (Armonk, NY: M.E. Sharpe, 2004), 160–61.

37. Key Ray Chong, *Cannibalism in China* (Wakefield, NH: Longwood Aca-demic, 1990), 100–102; Lin, "Xiaodao yu fudao," 1–29; Li Fei, "Zhongguo gudai funü xiaoxingshi kaolun," *Zhongguoshi yanjiu* 3 (1994): 73–82.

38. Zhang Wenlu, "Ming Qing Wanbei funü gegu liaoqin yuanyin tanlun," *Anhui Guangbo Dianshi Daxue xuebao* 3 (2015): 105–8.

39. Lin, "Xiaodao yu fudao," 16.

40. T'ien Ju-k'ang, *Male Anxiety and Female Chastity: A Comparative Study of Chinese Ethical Values in Ming-Ch'ing Times* (Leiden: Brill, 1988), 39–69.

41. Du and Mann, "Competing Claims on Womanly Virtue," 219.

42. Wang, "On Variations in Huizhou Women's Chastity Behaviors," 46–47, 49, 51–52.

43. Carlitz, "Three Ming Dynasty Martyrs," 5; Fangqin Du and Susan Mann, "Competing Claims on Womanly Virtue in Late Imperial China," in *Women and Confucian Cultures in Premodern China, Korea, and Japan*, ed. Dorothy Ko, JaHyun Kim Haboush, and Joan R. Piggott (Berkeley: University of California Press, 2003), 231.

44. Susan Mann, "Historical Change in Female Biography from Song to Qing Times: The Case of Early Qing Jiangnan," *Transactions of the International Conference of Orientalists in Japan* 30 (1985): 71.

45. Carlitz, "The Daughter, the Singing-Girl, and the Seduction of Suicide," 26.

46. Wang Chuanman, "On Variations in Huizhou Women's Chastity Behaviors," 54.

47. Wang, "Ming Qing Huizhou funü jielie xingwei de yingxiang," 43–46.

48. Grace S. Fong, "Signifying Bodies: The Cultural Significance of Suicide Writings by Women in Ming-Qing China," *Nan Nü* 3, no. 1 (2001): 112–13.

49. Paola Zamperini, "Untamed Hearts: Eros and Suicide in Late Imperial Chinese Fiction," in *Passionate Women: Female Suicide in Late Imperial China*, ed. Paul S. Ropp et al. (Leiden: Brill, 2001), 77–104.

50. Susan Mann, "Widows in the Kinship, Class, and Community Structures of Qing Dynasty China," *Journal of Asian Studies*, 46, no. 1 (1987): 45; Carlitz, "Shrines, Governing-Class Identity, and the Cult of Widow-Fidelity," 622.

51. Fei Siyan, *You dianfan dao guifan: Cong Mingdai zhenjie lienü de bianshi yu liuchuan kan zhenjie guannian de yangehua* (Taipei: Guoli Taiwan Daxue chubanshe, 1998), 67–128.

52. Zhang Weidong, "Tangdai cishi yu jingbiao zhidu," *Jiangxi shehui kexue* 7 (2009): 146–52.

53. Guo Haidong and Niu Dongya, "Mingdai shehui nüxing sixiang kongzhi chengyin tanxi," *Heilongjiang shizhi* 13 (2010): 28–29, 33; Zhang Xiaohui, "Mingdai jingbiao zhidu chutan," *Shanxi Shifan Daxue xuebao* 25 (2011): 117; Qin, *Mingdai Shandong jiaohua yanjiu*, 127.

54. Lin, "Xiaodao yu fudao," 16.

55. Wang Weiman, "Jielie jingbiao—Ming Qing Huizhou jielie xianxiang de zhongyao yinsu," *Aba Shifan Gaodeng Zhuanke Xuexiao xuebao* 26, no. 4 (2009): 62–63.

56. Liu, "Mingdai Ningde lienü xingxiang yanjiu," 60–61.

57. Shen Haimei, *Ming Qing Yunnan funü shenghuo yanjiu* (Kunming: Yunnan jiaoyu chubanshe, 2001), 186, 189, 193; Shen Haimei, "Bianyuan wenhua zhuliuhua

zhong de funü—Ming Qing shiqi de Yunnan *Lienü qun*," *Sixiang zhanxian* 28 (2002): 66–70.

58. Liu Jingchun, "Mingdai 'jiubian' nüxing de daode jingshen yu jieji juxian—yi difangzhi 'lienü' wei zhu de kaocha," *Shaanxi Shifan Daxue xuebao* 42, no. 5 (2013): 31, 33–35.

59. Carlitz, "Desire, Danger, and the Body," 117–18.

60. Wang Chuanman, "Ming Qing shiqi zhanluan deng baoli yinsu yu Huizhou jielie funü," *Baoji Wenli Xueyuan xuebao* 6 (2008): 37–41; Zou Zetao and Li Guang-zhi, "Mingdai Dongnanhai jiang wo luan jiyi zhong de lienü gushi—yi Zhejiang fang-zhi shuxie wei zhongxin," *Zhejiang Haiyang Daxue xuebao* 35, no. 3 (2018): 6–13.

61. T'ien, *Male Anxiety and Female Chastity*, 70–89.

62. Guo and Niu, "Mingdai shehui nüxing sixiang kongzhi chengyin tanxi," 28–29, 33.

63. Hans van Ess, "Cheng Yi and His Ideas about Women as Revealed in His Commentary to the *Yijing*," *Oriens Extremus* 49 (2010): 63–77.

64. Lisa Raphals, "Arguments by Women in Early Chinese Texts," *Nan Nü* 3, no. 2 (2001): 179–81.

65. Carlitz, "The Daughter, the Singing-Girl, and the Seduction of Suicide," 24; Lu, *True to Her Word*, 40–41.

66. Carlitz, "Desire, Danger, and the Body," 102.

67. Lin, "Xiaodao yu fudao," 1–29.

68. Fan Hongjuan, "Ming Qing nüxiao xiqu chutan," *Xinyang Shifan Xueyuan xuebao* 32, no. 3 (2012): 105–10.

69. Carlitz, "Shrines, Governing-Class Identity, and the Cult of Widow-Fidelity," 631–33.

70. "Mourning the Dead: In Memory of My Husband," Chang and Saussy, *Women Writers of Traditional China*, 320.

71. Du and Mann, "Competing Claims on Womanly Virtue," 232; Ko, *Teachers of the Inner Chambers*, 185–87.

72. Fei, *You dianfan dao guifan*, 17; Paul S. Ropp, "Passionate Women: Female Suicide in Late Imperial China—Introduction," in *Passionate Women: Female Suicide in Late Imperial China*, ed. Paul S. Ropp et al. (Leiden: Brill, 2001), 17.

73. Sommer, "The Uses of Chastity," 77.

74. Mann, "Widows in the Kinship, Class, and Community Structures," 47–48.

75. Catherine Nixey, *The Darkening Age: The Christian Destruction of the Classical World* (Boston and New York: Houghton Mifflin Harcourt, 2018), 78.

76. Mann, "Widows in the Kinship, Class, and Community Structures," 49.

77. "In Imitation of the Li Sao," Chang and Saussy, *Women Writers of Traditional China*, 182.

78. Michel Verdon, "Virgins and Widows: European Kinship and Early Christian-ity," *Man*, New Series 23, no. 3 (1988): 488–505.

79. Kent Flannery and Joyce Marcus, *The Creation of Inequality: How Our Pre-historic Ancestors Set the Stage for Monarchy, Slavery, and Empire* (Cambridge, MA: Harvard University Press, 2012), 319.

80. Ebrey, "Shifts in Marriage Finance," 97.

81. Zhang Bangwei, *Hunyin yu shehui (Songdai)* (Chengdu: Sichuan renmin chubanshe, 1989), 145–61; Patricia Buckley Ebrey, "Women, Money, and Class: Sima Guang and Song Neo-Confucian Views on Women," in *Women and the Family in Chinese History*, ed. Patricia Buckley Ebrey (London: Routledge, 2003), 12–13. Jack Goody, "Inheritance, Property, and Marriage in Africa and Eurasia," *Sociology* 3, no. 1 (1969): 55–76; Jack Goody, "Inheritance, Property and Women: Some Comparative Considerations," in *Family and Inheritance: Rural Society in Western Europe, 1200–1800*, ed. Jack Goody et al. (Cambridge: Cambridge University Press, 1976), 10–36, discuss the link between virginity and dowry. Alice Schlegel, "Status, Property, and the Value on Virginity," *American Ethnologist* 18, no. 4 (1991): 719–34 explores this link in detail, demonstrating how families in different societies use dowry to attract desirable sons-in-law.

82. Du and Mann, "Competing Claims on Womanly Virtue," 231.

83. Lu, *True to Her Word*, 5, 9–10, 12–13.

CHAPTER 8

1. Pingyi Chu, "Family Instructions and the Moral Economy of Medicine in Late Imperial China," *Chinese Historical Review* 24, no. 1 (2017): 90; Su Wanling, "Jin Yuan shiqi yiliao wenhua zhong de xingbie yanjiu" (MA thesis, Fo Guang University, 2019).

2. Yi-li Wu, "Body, Gender, and Disease: The Female Breast in Late Imperial Chinese Medicine," *Late Imperial China* 32, no 1 (2011): 83–128.

3. Sun Hongzhe, "Ming Qing changpian shiqing xiaoshuo zhong nüxing de chouguai shenti," *Jilin Shifan Daxue xuebao* 2 (2011): 11–13.

4. Charlotte Furth, "Androgynous Males and Deficient Females: Biology and Gender Boundaries in Sixteenth- and Seventeenth-Century China," *Late Imperial China* 9, no. 2 (1988): 1–31.

5. For some examples see William E. Phipps, "The Menstrual Taboo in the Judeo-Christian Tradition," *Journal of Religion and Health* 19, no. 4 (1980): 298–303; Theda Perdue, *Cherokee Women: Gender and Cultural Change, 1700–1835* (Lincoln: University of Nebraska Press, 1998), 29–30, 37; Paul John Frandsen, "The Menstrual 'Taboo' in Ancient Egypt," *Journal of Near Eastern Studies* 66, no. 2 (2007): 81–106.

6. Emily M. Ahern, "The Power and Pollution of Chinese Women," in *Women in Chinese Society*, ed. Margery Wolf and Roxanne Witke (Stanford: Stanford University Press, 1975), 193–214.

7. Huntington, "Foxes and Sex in Late Imperial Chinese Narrative," 85.

8. Keith McMahon, "The Art of the Bedchamber and *Jin Ping Mei*," *Nan Nü* 21, no. 1 (2019): 1–37.

9. Timothy Earle and Kristian Kristiansen, "Introduction: Theory and Practice in the Late Prehistory of Europe," in *Organizing Bronze Age Societies: The Mediterranean, Central Europe, and Scandinavia Compared*, ed. Timothy Earle and Kristian

Kristiansen (Cambridge: Cambridge University Press, 2010), 8, 14, discusses the materialization of social identity.

10. Li Ya, *Zhongguo lidai zhuangshi* (Beijing: Zhongguo fangzhi chubanshe, 2004), 135–61; Chen Baoliang, *Zhongguo funü tongshi: Mingdai juan* (Hangzhou: Hangzhou chubanshe, 2010), 484–531.

11. Alice B. Kehoe, "A Resort to Subtler Contrivances," in *Manifesting Power: Gender and the Interpretation of Power in Archaeology*, ed. Tracy L. Sweely (London: Routledge, 1999), 24–25.

12. Howard S. Levy, *Chinese Footbinding: The History of a Curious Erotic Custom* (New York: Bell Publishing Company, 1967), 37–62; Wang Ping, *Aching for Beauty: Footbinding in China* (Minneapolis: University of Minnesota Press, 2000), 29–53; Dorothy Ko, "In Search of Footbinding's Origins," in *Tang Song nüxing yu shehui*, ed. Deng Xiaonan (Shanghai: Shanghai cishu, 2003), I: 375–414; Dorothy Ko, *Cinderella's Sisters: A Revisionist History of Footbinding* (Berkeley: University of California Press, 2005), 109–44.

13. Liu and Qiao, "Ming Qing kejia nüxing de shehui xingxiang," 47.

14. Ko, *Teachers of the Inner Chambers*, 150.

15. Mary H. Fong, "Images of Women in Traditional Chinese Painting," *Women's Art Journal* 17, no. 1 (1996): 22–27.

16. Jing Jing, "*Shijing* zhong meiren guannian dui Zhongguo shinühua de yingxiang," *Yishu baijia* 7 (2011): 223–25.

17. Scarlett Jang, "Form, Content, and Audience: A Common Theme in Painting and Woodblock-Printed Books of the Ming Dynasty," *Ars Orientalis* 27 (1997): 15.

18. Carlitz, "The Social Uses of Female Virtue," 117–48.

19. Brook, *The Confusions of Pleasure*, 128–29.

20. Jang, "Form, Content, and Audience," 3, 5.

21. Anne Behnke Kinney, *Exemplary Women of Early China: The Lienü Zhuan of Liu Xiang* (New York: Columbia University Press, 2014), 18–20.

CONCLUSION

1. Craig Clunas, *Superfluous Things: Material Culture and Social Status in Early Modern China* (Honolulu: University of Hawaii Press, 2004), 54–56.

2. Mao Hanguang, "Tangdai houbanqi houfei zhi fenxi," *Guoli Taiwan Daxue wenshizhe xuebao* 37 (1989): 175–95; Keith McMahon, *Women Shall Not Rule: Imperial Wives and Concubines in China from Han to Liao* (Lanham, MD: Rowman & Littlefield, 2013), 223.

3. Liu Guangfeng, "Songdai houfei yu diwei chuancheng," *Wuhan Daxue xuebao* 4 (2009): 429–33.

Bibliography

A Feng 阿風. *Ming Qing shidai funü de diwei yu quanli—yi Ming Qing qiyue wenshu, susong dang'an wei zhongxin* 明清時代婦女的地位與權利—以明清契約文書, 訴訟檔案為中心. Beijing: Shehui kexue wenxian chubanshe, 2009.

Ahern, Emily M. "The Power and Pollution of Chinese Women." In *Women in Chinese Society*, edited by Margery Wolf and Roxanne Witke, 193–214. Stanford: Stanford University Press, 1975.

Allen, Sarah M. "Tales Retold: Narrative Variation in a Tang Story." *Harvard Journal of Asiatic Studies* 66, no. 1 (2006): 105–43.

Allison, Penelope M. "Introduction." In *The Archaeology of Household Activities*, edited by Penelope M. Allison, 1–18. London: Routledge, 1999.

Altenburger, Roland. *The Sword or the Needle: The Female Knight-errant (xia) in Traditional Chinese Narrative*. Bern: Peter Lang, 2009.

Bai Hua 柏樺 and Zhou Youbin 周囿彬. "Ming Qing nibi zinü xianxiang fenxi" 明清溺斃子女現象分析. *Suzhou Daxue xuebao* 蘇州大學學報 2 (2014): 51–60.

Bao Hua Hsieh. "The Market in Concubines in Jiangnan during Ming-Qing China." *Journal of Family History* 33, no. 3 (2008): 262–90.

Bao Zhenpei 鮑震培. *Qingdai nüzuojia tanci yanjiu* 清代女作家彈詞研究. Tianjin: Nankai Daxue, 2008.

Baquedano-López, Patricia. "Creating Social Identities through *Doctrina* Narratives." *Issues in Applied Linguistics* 8, no. 1 (1997): 27–45.

Barnes, Barry. *The Nature of Power*. Urbana and Chicago: University of Illinois Press, 1988.

Bentley, Tamara H. "The Rhetoric of Emotion in 17th Century China and Japan." In *Concepts and Categories of Emotion in East Asia*, edited by Giusi Tamburello, 176–212. Rome: Carocci Editore, 2012.

Berg, Daria. "Amazon, Artist, and Adventurer: A Courtesan in Late Imperial China." In *The Human Tradition in Modern China*, edited by Kenneth J. Hammond and Kristin Stapleton, 15–32. Lanham, MD: Rowman & Littlefield, 2007.

———. "Cultural Discourse on Xue Susu, a Courtesan of Late Ming China." *International Journal of Asian Studies* 6, no. 2 (2009): 171–200.

Bernhardt, Kathryn. "A Ming-Qing Transition in Chinese Women's History? The Perspective from Law." In *The History and Theory of Legal Practice in China: Toward a Historical-Social Jurisprudence*, edited by Philip C. C. Huang and Kathryn Bernhardt, 29–50. Leiden: Brill, 2014.

———. *Women and Property in China, 960–1949*. Stanford: Stanford University Press, 1999.

Bian Li 卞利. "Ming Qing shiqi hunyin lifa de tiaozheng yu jiceng shehui de wending" 明清時期婚姻立法的調整與基層社會的穩定. *Anhui Daxue xuebao* 安徽大學學報 6 (2005): 115–20.

Birge, Bettine. "Chu Hsi and Women's Education." In *Neo-Confucian Education: The Formative Stage*, edited by William Theodore de Bary and John Chaffee, 361–67. Berkeley: University of California Press, 1989.

———. "Inheritance and Property Law from Tang to Song: The Move Away from Patrilineality." In *Tang Song nüxing yu shehui* 唐宋女性與社會, edited by Deng Xiaonan 鄧小南, II: 849–66. Shanghai: Shanghai cishu, 2003.

———. "Levirate Marriage and the Revival of Widow Chastity in Yuan China." *Asia Major* (third series) 8, no. 2 (1995): 107–46.

———. "Women and Confucianism from Song to Ming: The Institutionalization of Patrilineality." In *The Song-Yuan-Ming Transition in Chinese History*, edited by Paul J. Smith and Richard von Glahn, 212–40. Cambridge, MA: Harvard University Asia Center, 2003.

———. *Women, Property and Confucian Reaction in Sung and Yüan China (960–1368)*. Cambridge: Cambridge University Press, 2002.

Bisetto, Barbara. "Fragments of *Qing* 情: The *Qingshi leilüe* 情史類略 and the Literary Categorization of 'Love' in the 17th Century China." In *Concepts and Categories of Emotion in East Asia*, edited by Giusi Tamburello, 164–75. Rome: Carocci Editore, 2012.

Blanchard, Lara C. W. "A Scholar in the Company of Female Entertainers: Changing Notions of Integrity in Song to Ming Dynasty Painting." *Nan Nü* 9, no. 2 (2007): 189–246.

Bossler, Beverly. "A Daughter Is a Daughter All Her Life: Affinal Relations and Women's Networks in Song and Late Imperial China." *Late Imperial China* 21, no. 1 (2000): 77–106.

Bray, Francesca. *Technology and Gender: Fabrics of Power in Late Imperial China*. Berkeley: University of California Press, 1997.

Broadbridge, Anne F. *Women and the Making of the Mongol Empire*. Cambridge: Cambridge University Press, 2018.

Brook, Timothy. *The Confusions of Pleasure: Commerce and Culture in Ming China*. Berkeley: University of California Press, 1999.

———. *The Troubled Empire: China in the Yuan and Ming Dynasties*. Cambridge, MA: The Belknap Press of Harvard University Press, 2010.

Brown, Miranda. *The Politics of Mourning in Early China*. Albany, NY: State University of New York Press, 2007.

Bussotti, Michela. "Images of Women in Late Ming Huizhou-Printed Editions of the *Lienü Zhuan*." *Nan Nü* 17, no. 1 (2015): 54–116.

Cahill, Suzanne. "Resenting the Silk Robes That Hide Their Poems: Female Voices in the Poetry of Tang Dynasty Nuns." In *Tang Song nüxing yu shehui* 唐宋女性與社會, edited by Deng Xiaonan 鄧小南, II: 519–66. Shanghai: Shanghai cishu, 2003.

Cai Shishan 蔡石山. *Mingdai de nüren* 明代的女人. Taipei: Lianjing, 2009.

Cao Hong 曹虹. "Rouhan jianbi: Mingdai nüxing de wenzhang zaoyi" 柔翰健筆: 明代女性的文章造詣. *Jiangxi Shifan Daxue xuebao* 江西師範大學學報 43, no. 5 (2010): 106–12.

Cao Shuji 曹樹基. *Zhongguo renkou shi* 中國人口史. Shanghai: Fudan Daxuechubanshe, 2000.

Carlitz, Katherine. "The Daughter, the Singing-Girl, and the Seduction of Suicide." *Nan Nü* 3, no. 1 (2001): 22–46.

———. "Desire, Danger, and the Body: Stories of Women's Virtue in Late Ming China." In *Engendering China*, edited by Christina K. Gilmartin et al., 101–24. Cambridge, MA: Harvard University Press, 1994.

———. "Lovers, Talkers, Monsters, and Good Women: Competing Images in Mid-Ming Epitaphs and Fiction." In *Beyond Exemplar Tales: Women's Biography in Chinese History*, edited by Joan Judge and Hu Ying, 175–92. Berkeley: University of California Press, 2011.

———. "Mourning, Personality, Display: Ming Literati Commemorate Their Mothers, Sisters, and Daughters." *Nan Nü* 15, no. 1 (2013): 30–68.

———. "Shrines, Governing-Class Identity, and the Cult of Widow-Fidelity in Mid-Ming Jiangnan." *Journal of Asian Studies* 56, no. 3 (1997): 612–40.

———. "The Social Uses of Female Virtue in Late Ming Editions of Lienü zhuan." *Late Imperial China* 12, no. 2 (1991): 117–48.

———. "Three Ming Dynasty Martyrs and Their Monstrous Mothers-in-Law." *Ming Studies* 68 (2013): 5–32.

Cass, Victoria. *Dangerous Women: Warriors, Grannies and Geishas of the Ming*. Lanham, MD: Rowman & Littlefield, 1999.

Chang Jianhua. "Theories about the Formation of Lineage System since the Song and Ming Dynasties." *Frontiers of History in China* 3, no. 1 (2008): 41–77.

Chang, Kang-i Sun. "Ming and Qing Anthologies of Women's Poetry and Their Selection Strategies." In *Writing Women in Late Imperial China*, edited by Ellen Widmer and Kang-i Sun Chang, 147–70. Stanford: Stanford University Press, 1997.

Chang, Kang-i Sun, and Haun Saussy, eds. *Women Writers of Traditional China: An Anthology of Poetry and Criticism*. Stanford: Stanford University Press, 1999.

Chen Baoliang 陳寶良. "Hao gui chong Fo: Mingdai funü de fodao xinyang ji qi yishi" 好鬼崇佛: 明代婦女的佛道信仰及其儀式. *Haerbin Shifan Daxue shehui kexue xuebao* 哈爾濱師範大學社會科學學報 1 (2010): 118–25.

———. "Mingdai de funü jiaoyu ji qi zhuanxiang" 明代的婦女教育及其轉向. *Shehui kexue jikan* 社會科學輯刊 6 (2009): 157–61.

———. "Mingdai funü de shehui jingji huodong ji qi zhuanxiang" 明代婦女的社會經濟活動及其轉向. *Zhongzhou xuekan* 中州學刊 1 (2011): 176–80.

———. *Mingdai shehui zhuanxing yu wenhua bianqian* 明代社會轉型與文化變遷. Chongqing: Chongqing Daxue chubanshe, 2014.

———. *Zhongguo funü tongshi: Mingdai juan* 中國婦女通史: 明代卷. Hangzhou: Hangzhou chubanshe, 2010.

Chen Chao 陳超. Ming Qing nüxing beizhuanwen yu pinguan mingfu yanjiu—yi 'siku' Mingren wenji wei zhongxin de kaocha 明清女性碑傳文與品官命婦研究—以"四庫"明人文集為中心的考察. Beijing: Guangming Ribao chubanshe, 2013.

———. "Pinguan mingfu zhidu yu Mingdai funü de zongxiang shehui liudong—yi Mingren muzhiming wei yanjiu zhongxin" 品官命婦制度與明代婦女的縱向社會流動—以明人墓誌銘為研究中心. *Shehui kexue jikan* 社會科學輯刊 6 (2010): 176–80.

Chen, Sanping. "'Age Inflation and Deflation' in Medieval China." *Journal of the American Oriental Society* 133, no. 3 (2013): 527–33.

Chen Shaoyun 陳曉昀. "Mingdai nüxing fuchou gushi de wenhua kaocha" 明代女性復仇故事的文化史考察. MA thesis, Guoli Taiwan Shifan Daxue, 2009.

Chen Yingxun 陳瑛珣. *Ming Qing qiyue wenshu zhong de funü jingji huodong* 明清契約文書中的婦女經濟活動. Taipei: Taiming wenhua, 2001.

Chen Yunü 陳玉女. *Mingdai de fojiao yu shehui* 明代的佛教與社會. Beijing: Beijing Daxue chubanshe, 2011.

Cheng Jun 程君. "Lun Ming Qing nüxing shishe de sanzhong leixing" 論明清女性詩社的三種類型. *Xiamen Guangbo Dianshi Daxue xuebao* 廈門廣播電視大學學報 2 (2017): 76–80, 96.

Chong, Key Ray. *Cannibalism in China*. Wakefield, NH: Longwood Academic, 1990.

Chu, Pingyi. "Family Instructions and the Moral Economy of Medicine in Late Imperial China." *Chinese Historical Review* 24, no. 1 (2017): 77–92.

Clunas, Craig. *Superfluous Things: Material Culture and Social Status in Early Modern China.* Honolulu: University of Hawaii Press, 2004.

Cui Jing 崔靖. "Mingdai hougong yizu feipin yu Ming, Meng, Chao sanfang guanxi" 明代後宮異族妃嬪與明, 蒙, 朝三方關係. *Yunnan Shifan Daxue xuebao* 雲南師範大學學報 46, no. 2 (2014): 151–56.

———. "Mingdai waiqi zhuangtian chutan" 明代外戚莊田初探. *Nongye kaogu* 農業考古 3 (2013): 71–75.

Dardess, John. "The Cheng Communal Family: Social Organization and Neo-Confucianism in Yüan and Ming China." *Harvard Journal of Asiatic Studies* 34 (1974): 7–52.

———. *Ming China 1368–1644: A Concise History of a Resilient Empire*. Lanham, MD: Rowman & Littlefield, 2012.

———. *A Ming Society: T'ai-ho County, Kiangsi, in the Fourteenth to Seventeenth Centuries.* Berkeley: University of California Press, 1996.

Dauncey, Sarah. "Bonding, Benevolence, Barter, and Bribery: Images of Female Gift Exchange in the *Jin Ping Mei*." *Nan Nü* 5, no. 2 (2003): 203–39.

Deng Qingping 鄧慶平. *Ye shen qian zhang deng: Mingdai liangxing guanxi shi* 夜深千帳燈: 明代兩性關係史. Xi'an: Shaanxi renmin, 2008.

Deng Xiaonan. "Women in Turfan during the Sixth to Eighth Centuries: A Look at Their Activities Outside the Home." *The Journal of Asian Studies* 58, no. 1 (1999): 85–103.

Dong Jiazun 董家遵. "Lidai jielie funü de tongji" 歷代節烈婦女的統計. In *Zhongguofunüshi lunji* 中國婦女史論集, edited by Bao Jialin 鮑家麟, 111–17. Taipei: Daoxiang, 1988.

Du Fangqin 杜芳琴. "Ming Qing zhenjie de tedian ji qi yuanyin" 明清貞節的特點及其原因. *Shanxi Shida xuebao* 山西師大學報 10 (1997): 41–50.

Du, Fangqin, and Susan Mann. "Competing Claims on Womanly Virtue in Late Imperial China." In *Women and Confucian Cultures in Premodern China, Korea, and Japan*, edited by Dorothy Ko, JaHyun Kim Haboush, and Joan R. Piggott, 219–47. Berkeley: University of California Press, 2003.

Earle, Timothy, and Kristian Kristiansen. "Introduction: Theory and Practice in the Late Prehistory of Europe." In *Organizing Bronze Age Societies: The Mediterranean, Central Europe, and Scandinavia Compared*, edited by Timothy Earle and Kristian Kristiansen, 1–33. Cambridge: Cambridge University Press, 2010.

Ebrey, Patricia Buckley. "Shifts in Marriage Finance from the Sixth to the Thirteenth Century." In *Marriage and Inequality in Chinese Society*, edited by Rubie S. Watson and Patricia B. Ebrey, 97–132. Berkeley: University of California Press, 1991.

———. "Women, Money, and Class: Sima Guang and Song Neo-Confucian Views on Women." In *Women and the Family in Chinese History*, edited by Patricia Buckley Ebrey, 10–38. London: Routledge, 2003.

Edel, Leon. *Writing Lives: Principia Biographica.* New York: Norton, 1984.

Eichman, Jennifer. "Zhuhong's Communal Rules for the Late Ming Nunnery Filiality and Righteousness Unobstructed." *Nan Nü* 21, no. 2 (2019): 224–75.

Eifring, Halvor. "Introduction: Emotions and Conceptual History of Qing." In *Love and Emotions in Traditional Chinese Literature*, edited by Halvor Eifring, 1–36. Leiden: Brill, 2004.

Epstein, Maram. "Reflections of Desire: The Poetics of Gender in *Dream of the Red Chamber*." *Nan Nü* 1, no. 1 (1999): 64–106.

Fan Hongjuan 范紅娟. "Ming Qing nüxiao xiqu chutan" 明清女孝戲曲初探. *Xinyang Shifan Xueyuan xuebao* 信陽師範學院學報 32, no. 3 (2012): 105–10.

Fang, Chaoying. "Huo T'ao." In *Dictionary of Ming Biography, 1368–1644*, 679–83. New York: Columbia University Press, 1976.

Fei Siyan 費絲言. *You dianfan dao guifan: Cong Mingdai zhenjie lienü de bianshi yu liuchuan kan zhenjie guannian de yangehua* 由典範到規範: 從明代貞節烈女的辨識與流傳看貞節觀念的嚴格化. Taipei: Guoli Taiwan Daxue chubanshe, 1998.

Flannery, Kent, and Joyce Marcus. *The Creation of Inequality: How Our Prehistoric Ancestors Set the Stage for Monarchy, Slavery, and Empire.* Cambridge, MA: Harvard University Press, 2012.

Fong, Grace S. *Herself an Author: Gender, Agency, and Writing in Late Imperial China.* Honolulu: University of Hawaii Press, 2008.

———. "Signifying Bodies: The Cultural Significance of Suicide Writings by Women in Ming-Qing China." *Nan Nü* 3, no. 1 (2001): 105–42.

Fong, Mary H. "Images of Women in Traditional Chinese Painting." *Women's Art Journal* 17, no. 1 (1996): 22–27.

Frandsen, Paul John. "The Menstrual 'Taboo' in Ancient Egypt." *Journal of Near Eastern Studies* 66, no. 2 (2007): 81–106.

Fuma Susumu 夫馬進. "Seidai zenki no ikuei jigyō" 清代前期の育嬰事業. In *Tō ajia seikai no seisei, hatten oyobi hoka bunmei to no kankei ni suite no kenkyū* 東アジア世界の生成、発展および他文明との関係についての研究, edited by Fuma Susumu 夫馬進 et al., 5–42. Toyama: Toyama Daigaku Jinbun Gakubu, 1986.

Furth, Charlotte. "Androgynous Males and Deficient Females: Biology and Gender Boundaries in Sixteenth- and Seventeenth-Century China." *Late Imperial China* 9, no. 2 (1988): 1–31.

Gao Yanyi 高彥頤. "'Kongjian' yu 'jia'—lun Mingmo Qingchu funü de shenghuo kongjian" 空間與家—論明末清初婦女的生活空間. *Jindai Zhongguo funüshi yanjiu* 近代中國婦女史研究 8 (1995): 21–50.

Geiss, James. "The Cheng-te Reign, 1506–1521." In *The Cambridge History of China*, vol. 7, *The Ming Dynasty*, part 1, edited by Frederick W. Mote and Denis Twitchett, 403–39. Cambridge: Cambridge University Press, 1988.

Goody, Jack. "Inheritance, Property, and Marriage in Africa and Eurasia." *Sociology* 3, no. 1 (1969): 55–76.

———. "Inheritance, Property and Women: Some Comparative Considerations." In *Family and Inheritance: Rural Society in Western Europe, 1200–1800*, edited by Jack Goody et al., 10–36. Cambridge: Cambridge University Press, 1976.

Goyama Kiwamu 合山究. "Ming Qing nüzi tibi shi kao" 明清女子題壁詩考, translated by Li Yinsheng 李寅生. *Hechi Shifan xuebao* 河池師專學報 1 (2004): 53–57.

———. *Ming Qing shidai de nüxing yu wenxue* 明清時代的女性與文學, translated by Xiao Yanwan 蕭燕婉. Taipei: Lianjing, 2016.

Grant, Beata. *Daughters of Emptiness: Poems of Chinese Buddhist Nuns*. Somerville, MA: Wisdom Publications, 2003.

Guo Dongxu 郭東旭. *Songdai fazhi yanjiu* 宋代法制研究. Baoding: Hebai Daxue chubanshe, 2000.

Guo Haidong 郭海東. "Mingdai Zhili funü shoujie xingwei tanxi" 明代直隸婦女守節行為探析. *Changzhou Daxue xuebao* 常州大學學報 16, no. 5 (2015): 78–82.

Guo Haidong 郭海東 and Niu Dongya 牛東亞. "Mingdai shehui nüxing sixiang kongzhi chengyin tanxi" 明代社會女性思想控制成因探析. *Heilongjiang shizhi* 黑龍江史志 13 (2010): 28–29, 33.

Guo Hui 郭輝. "Jianlun Mingdai biqiuni de shengcun kunjing" 簡論明代比丘尼的生存困境. *Zongjiaoxue yanjiu* 宗教學研究 3 (2013): 142–47.

Guo Junjun 郭軍軍. "Mingdai Datong zhenlie nüzi de tezheng ji qi chengyin fenxi" 明代大同貞烈女子的特徵及其成因分析. *Shanxi Meitan Guanli Ganbu Xueyuan xuebao* 山西煤炭管理幹部學院學報 28, no. 4 (2015): 179–81.

Han Chenghua 韓承樺. "*Mingshi Lienüzhuan* de baoli, qingxu, tongjue yu nüxing xingxiang de shuxie" 明史列女傳的暴力，情緒，痛覺與女性形象的書寫. *Mingdai yanjiu* 明代研究 32 (2019): 97–151.

Han Lin 韓林. "Wu Zetian gushi de wenben yanbian yu wenhua neihan" 武則天故事的文本演變與文化內涵. PhD diss., Nankai University, 2012.

Handlin, Joanna F. "Lü Kun's New Audience: The Influence of Women's Literacy on Sixteenth Century Thought." In *Women in Chinese Society*, edited by Margery Wolf and Roxanne Witke, 13–38. Stanford: Stanford University Press, 1975.

Harrell, Stevan, and Sara A. Dickey. "Dowry Systems in Complex Societies." *Ethnology* 24, no. 2 (1985): 105–20.

Hayes, James. "Specialists and Written Materials in the Village World." In *Popular Culture in Late Imperial China*, edited by David Johnson et al., 75–111. Berkeley and Los Angeles: University of California Press, 1985.

Hazelton, Keith. "Patrilines and the Development of Localized Lineages: The Wu of Hsiu-ning City, Hui-chou, to 1528." In *Kinship Organization in Late Imperial China 1000–1940*, edited by Patricia Buckley Ebrey and James L. Watson, 137–69. Berkeley and Los Angeles: University of California Press, 1986.

He Bingdi 何炳棣. *Mingchu yijiang renkou ji qi xiangguan wenti* 1368–1953 明初以降人口及其相關問題, 1368–1953. Beijing: Sanlian shudian, 2000.

He Deting 何德廷. "Guanyu Yuandai hunyin zhidu de dutexing yu jibuxing de ruogan sikao" 關於元代婚姻制度的獨特性與進步性的若干思考. *Zhengfa xuekan* 政法學刊 21, no. 3 (2004): 102–4.

He Junhong 赫俊紅. *Danqing qipa: Wan Ming Qing chu de nüxing huihua* 丹青奇葩: 晚明清初的女性繪畫. Beijing: Wenwu chubanshe, 2008.

Hinsch, Bret. *Masculinities in Chinese History*. Lanham, MD: Rowman & Littlefield, 2013.

Ho, Clara Wing-chung. "History as Leisure Reading for Ming-Qing Women Poets." *Hsiang Lectures on Chinese Poetry* 7 (2015): 27–64.

Holmgren, Jennifer. "The Economic Foundations of Virtue: Widow-Remarriage in Early and Modern China." *Australian Journal of Chinese Affairs* 13 (1985): 1–27.

———. "Imperial Marriage in the Native Chinese and Non-Han State, Han to Ming." In *Marriage and Inequality in Chinese Society*, edited by Rubie S. Watson and Patricia Buckley Ebrey, 58–96. Berkeley: University of California Press, 1991.

Hsiung, Ping-chen. "Constructed Emotions: The Bond Between Mothers and Sons in Late Imperial China." *Late Imperial China* 15, no. 1 (1994): 87–119.

———. *A Tender Voyage: Children and Childhood in Late Imperial China*. Stanford: Stanford University Press, 2005.

Hsu Pi-ching. "Courtesans and Scholars in the Writings of Feng Menglong: Transcending Status and Gender." *Nan Nü* 2, no. 1 (2000): 40–77.

Hu Zhongsheng 胡中生. "Maishen hunshu yu Ming Qing Huizhou xiaceng shehui de hunpei he renkou wenti" 賣身婚書與明清徽州下層社會的婚配和人口問題. In *Ming Qing renkou hunyin jiating shilun—Chen Jiexian jiaoshou, Feng Erkang jiaoshou guxi jinian lunwenji* 明清人口婚姻家族史論—陳捷先教授, 馮爾康教授古稀紀念論文集, 1–20. Tianjin: Tianjin guji chubanshe.

Hua Wei 華瑋. *Ming Qing funü zhi xiqu chuangzuo yu piping* 明清婦女之戲曲創作與批評. Taipei: Zhongyang Yanjiuyuan Zhongguo Wenzhe Yanzhousuo, 2003.

Huang, I-Fen. "Gender, Technical Innovation, and Gu Family Embroidery in Late Ming Shanghai." *East Asian Science, Technology, and Medicine* 36 (2012): 77–129.

Huang Jia 黃甲. "'Chu er ke pai an jing qi' yu Mingdai hunsu wenhua" '初二刻拍案驚奇' 與明代婚俗文化. *Heilongjiang shizhi* 黑龍江史志 21 (2013): 192–93.

Huang Jingjing 黃靜靜. "Ming Qing shiqi Huizhou nüzi de zeou biaozhun" 明清時期徽州女子的擇偶標準. *Jiamusi Daxue shehui kexue xuebao* 佳木斯大學社會科學學報 33, no. 2 (2015): 151–53.

Huang, Martin W. *Desire and Fictional Narrative in Late Imperial China*. Cambridge, MA: Harvard University Asia Center, 2001.

Huang Mingguang 黃明光. "Mingdai nanfang zhusheng nütuguan zhizheng xianxiangyanjiu" 明代南方諸省女土官執政現象研究. *Guangxi Minzu Shifan Xueyuan xuebao* 廣西民族師範學院學報 30, no. 1 (2013): 21–25.

Huang, Ray. *1587: A Year of No Significance: The Ming Dynasty in Decline*. New Haven: Yale University Press, 1981.

Huang Taiyong 黃太勇. "Yuandai Tianfei chongbai de sange wenti xintan" 元代天妃崇拜的三個問題新探. *Zhongguo haiyang daxue* 中國海洋大學 6 (2014): 64–68.

Huntington, Rania. "Foxes and Sex in Late Imperial Chinese Narrative." *Nan Nü* 2, no. 1 (2000): 78–128.

Idema, Wilt L. "The Biographical and the Autobiographical in Bo Shaojun's *One Hundred Poems Lamenting My Husband*." In *Beyond Exemplar Tales: Women's Biography in Chinese History*, edited by Joan Judge and Hu Ying, 230–45. Berkeley: University of California Press, 2011.

———. "Bo Shaojun and Her *One Hundred Poems Lamenting My Husband*." *Nan Nü* 15, no. 2 (2013): 317–32.

Irvine, Judith T., and Susan Gal. "Language Ideology and Linguistic Differentiation." In *Regimes of Language: Ideologies, Polities, and Identities*, edited by Paul V. Kroskrity, 35–83. Santa Fe, NM: School of American Research Press, 2000.

Jang, Scarlett. "Form, Content, and Audience: A Common Theme in Painting and Woodblock-Printed Books of the Ming Dynasty." *Ars Orientalis* 27 (1997): 1–26.

Jeffries, Stuart. *Grand Hotel Abyss: The Lives of the Frankfort School*. London: Verso, 2016.

Jian Ruiyao 簡瑞瑤. *Mingdai funü fojiao xinyang yu shehui guifan* 明代婦女佛教信仰與社會規範. Banqiao: Daoxiang, 2007.

Jiang Yonglin, trans. *The Great Ming Code / Da Ming lü*. Seattle: University of Washington Press, 2005.

———. "Legislating Hierarchical Yet Harmonious Gender Relations in the *Great Ming Code*." *Ming Studies* 69 (2014): 27–45.

Jin Mei 金眉. "Tangdai hunyin jiating jicheng falü zhidu chulun" 唐代婚姻家庭繼承法律制度初論. PhD diss., China University of Political Science and Law, 2000.

Jing Jing 井菁. "*Shijing* zhong meiren guannian dui Zhongguo shinühua de yingxiang" 詩經中美人觀念對中國仕女畫的影響. *Yishu baijia* 藝術百家 7 (2011): 223–25.

Johnson, Allen W., and Timothy Earle. *The Evolution of Human Societies: From Foraging Group to Agrarian State*. Stanford: Stanford University Press, 1987.

Johnson, David. "Communication, Class, and Consciousness in Late Imperial China." In *Popular Culture in Late Imperial China*, edited by David Johnson et al., 34–72. Berkeley and Los Angeles: University of California Press, 1985.

Jōo, Fumiko. "Ancestress Worship: Huxin Temple and the Literati Community in Late Ming Ningbo." *Nan Nü* 16, no. 1 (2014): 29–58.

Ju Jixin 車吉心 et al., eds. *Zhongguo huanghou quanzhuan* 中國皇后全傳. Jinan: Shandong jiaoxi, 1997.

Kamachi, Noriko. "Feudalism or Absolute Monarchism?: Japanese Discourse on the Nature of State and Society in Late Imperial China." *Modern China* 16, no. 3 (1990): 330–70.

Kandiyoti, Deniz. "Bargaining with Patriarchy." *Gender and Society* 2, no. 3 (1988): 274–90.

Kang Xuewei 康學偉. *Xian Qin xiaodao yanjiu* 先秦孝道研究. Taipei: Wenjin, 1992.

Katsuyama Minoru 騰山稔. *Chūgoku Sō—Min dai ni okeru konin no gakusaiteki kenkyū* 中國宋—明代における婚姻の學際的研究. Tokyo: Tōhoku Daigaku shuppankai, 2007.

Kehoe, Alice B. "A Resort to Subtler Contrivances." In *Manifesting Power: Gender and the Interpretation of Power in Archaeology*, edited by Tracy L. Sweely, 17–29. London: Routledge, 1999.

Kelley, David E. "Temples and Tribute Fleets: The Luo Sect and Boatmen's Associations in the Eighteenth Century." *Modern China* 8, no. 3 (1982): 361–91.

Kinney, Anne Behnke. *Exemplary Women of Early China: The Lienü Zhuan of Liu Xiang*. New York: Columbia University Press, 2014.

Ko, Dorothy. *Cinderella's Sisters: A Revisionist History of Footbinding*. Berkeley: University of California Press, 2005.

———. "In Search of Footbinding's Origins." In *Tang Song nüxing yu shehui* 唐宋女性與社會, edited by Deng Xiaonan 鄧小南, I: 375–414. Shanghai: Shanghai cishu, 2003.

———. "Pursuing Talent and Virtue: Education and Women's Culture in Seventeenth and Eighteenth Century China." *Late Imperial China* 13, no. 1 (1992): 9–39.

———. *Teachers of the Inner Chambers: Women and Culture in Seventeenth-Century China*. Stanford: Stanford University Press, 1994.

Kobayashi Tetsuyuki 小林徹行. *Mingdai jōsei no junshi to bungaku: Haku Shoukun no kokufushi hyakushu* 明代女性の殉死と文学: 薄少君の哭夫詩百首. Tokyo: Kyuko shoin, 2003.

Kong Min 孔敏. "Tangdai xiaoshuo nüxing xingxiang dui Ming Qing wenxue zhi yingxiang" 唐代小說女性形象對明清文學之影響. *Mingzuo xinshang* 名作欣賞 2 (2016): 130–33.

Kutcher, Norman. *Mourning in Late Imperial China: Filial Piety and the State*. Cambridge: Cambridge University Press, 1999.

Lam, Joseph S. C. "Reading Music and Eroticism in Late Ming Texts." *Nan Nü* 12, no. 2 (2010): 215–54.

Lau Nap-yin. "Changes to Women's Legal Rights in the Family from the Song to the Ming." In *Modern Chinese Religion I: Song-Liao-Jin-Yuan (960–1368 AD)*, edited by John Lagerwey and Pierre Marsone, I: 643–717. Leiden: Brill, 2015.

Lee, Sylvia W. S. "'Co-Branding' a Cainü and a Garden: How the Zhao Family Established Identities for Wen Shu (1595–1634) and Their Garden Residence Hanshan." *Nan Nü* 18, no. 1 (2016): 49–83.

Lemert, Charles. *Social Things: An Introduction to the Sociological Life*. 4th ed. Lanham, MD: Rowman & Littlefield, 2008.

Levy, Howard S. *Chinese Footbinding: The History of a Curious Erotic Custom*. New York: Bell Publishing Company, 1967.

Li Fei 李飛. "Zhongguo gudai funü xiaoxingshi kaolun" 中國古代婦女孝行史考論. *Zhongguoshi yanjiu* 中國史研究 3 (1994): 73–82.

Li Fengjian 李奉戩. "Ming Qing xiaoshuo zhong de jinü yu aiqing zhenjie" 明清小說中的妓女與愛情貞節. *Ming Qing xiaoshuo yanjiu* 明清小說研究 2 (2005): 19–26.

Li Guotong 李國彤. *Nüzi zhi bukui: Ming Qing shiqi de nüjiao guannian* 女子之不朽: 明清時期的女教觀念. Guilin: Guangxi Shifan Daxue chubanshe, 2014.

Li Jiao 李姣. "Ming Qing Huizhou funü zai tudi maimai huodong zhong de tedian—yi Huizhou wenshu wei li" 明清徽州婦女在土地買賣活動中的特點—以徽州文書為例. *Chifeng Xueyuan xuebao* 赤峰學院學報 36, no. 9 (2015): 53–56.

Li Min 李敏 and Qian Zongfan 錢宗范. "Mingdai Xiaomu huang taihou: Yaozu chuanqishi nüxing Li Tangmei shiji pingyi—Yaozu lishi wenhua xilie yanjiu zhi yi 明代孝穆皇太后: 瑤族傳奇式女性李唐妹事跡評議—瑤族歷史文化系列研究之一. *Hezhou Xueyuan xuebao* 賀州學院學報 34, no. 1 (2018): 1–5.

Li Mingchen 李明辰. "Shilun Mingdai hunyin falü zhidu" 試論明代婚姻法律制度. *Hubei Keji Xueyuan xuebao* 湖北科技學院學報 35, no. 6 (2015): 82–84.

Li Qing 李倩. "Shilun Yuandai de Mazu chongbai" 試論元代的媽祖崇拜. *Zhongnan Minzu Daxue xuebao* 中南民族大學學報 6 (2005): 128–31.

Li Qingyong 李慶勇. "Mingdai nüguan laiyuan fenxi" 明代女官來源分析. *Cangzhou Shifan Xueyuan xuebao* 滄州師範學院學報 29, no. 3 (2013): 63–65.

Li Shunhua 李舜華. "Nüxing duzhe yu Mingdai zhanghui xiaoshuo de xingqi" 女性讀者與明代章回小說的興起 *Xueshu yanjiu* 學術研究 10 (2009): 137–46.

Li Tingting 李停停. "Cong Ming Qing ni huaben xiaoshuo zhenjie lienü xiangxiang kan Ming Qing zhenjieguan de bianhua" 從明清擬話本小說貞節烈女形象看明清貞節觀的變化. *Hunan Renwen Kexue Xueyuan xuebao* 湖南人文科學學院學報 5 (2012): 58–62.

Li Wenshi 李蘊詩. "Guige qingzhen: Mingdai nühuajia huihua" 閨閣情真: 明代女畫家繪畫. *Mei cheng zai jiu* 美成在久 1 (2017): 62–69.

Li, Xiaorong. *Women's Poetry of Late Imperial China*. Seattle: University of Washington Press, 2012.

Li Ya 李芽. *Zhongguo lidai zhuangshi* 中國歷代妝飾. Beijing: Zhongguo fangzhi chubanshe, 2004.

Li Yongju 李永菊. "Ming Qing nüxing canjia miaohui de wanhua xuqiu fenxi" 明清女性參加廟會的文化需求分析. *Hubei Daxue xuebao* 湖北大學學報 31, no. 5 (2004): 578–81.

Li Yuanyuan 李嫄嫄. "Cong *Jin Ping Mei* kan Mingdai de 'fudu' zhi feng" 從 '金瓶梅' 看明代的 '婦妒' 之風. *Xuchang Xueyuan xuebao* 許昌學院學報 3 (2014): 70–72.

Li Zhiping 李智萍. "Songdai nühu de tedian" 宋代女戶的特點. *Funü yanjiu luncong* 婦女研究論叢 6 (2009): 51–56.

Liang Fangzhong 梁方仲, eds. *Zhongguo lidai hukou: tiandi, tianfu tongji* 中國歷代 戶口: 田地, 田賦統計. Shanghai: Shanghai renmin, 1980.

Lin Liyue 林麗月. "Xiaodao yu fudao: Mingdai xiaofu de wenhuashi kaocha" 孝道 與婦道: 明代孝婦的文化史考察. *Jindai Zhongguo funüshi yanjiu* 近代中國婦 女史研究 6 (1998): 1–29.

Lin, Wei-hung. "Chastity in Chinese Eyes—Nan-Nu Yu-Pieh." *Hanxue yanjiu* 漢學 研究 12 (1991): 13–40.

Lin Yanqing. "Tang Sai'er," translated by Laura Long. In *Biographical Dictionary of Chinese Women: Tang through Ming, 618–1644*, edited by Lily Xiao Hong Lee and Sue Wiles, 392–94. Armonk, NY: M.E. Sharpe, 2014.

Liu Guangfeng 劉廣豐. "Songdai houfei yu diwei chuancheng" 宋代后妃與帝位傳 承. *Wuhan Daxue xuebao* 武漢大學學報 4 (2009): 429–33.

Liu Jingchun 劉景純. "Mingdai 'jiubian' nüxing de daode jingshen yu jieji juxian— yi difangzhi 'lienü' wei zhu de kaocha" 明代 '九邊' 女性的道德精神與階級局 限—以地方誌 '烈女' 為主的考察. *Shaanxi Shifan Daxue xuebao* 陝西師範大學 學報 42, no. 5 (2013): 31–38.

Liu Junhua 劉軍華. *Ming Qing nüxing zuojia xiqu chuangzuo yanjiu* 明清女性作家 戲曲創作研究. Beijing: Kexue chubanshe, 2015.

Liu Miaofen 呂妙芬. "Zuo wei Mengxue yu nüjiao duben de *Xiaojing*—jian lun qi webben dingwei de lishi bianhua" 作為蒙學與女教讀本的 '孝經'—兼論其文本 定位的歷史變化. *Taida lishi xuebao* 台大歷史學報 6 (2008): 1–64.

Liu Min 劉敏. "Lun Ming Qing xiaoshuo zhong de nüxing handu wenhua—yi *Li-aozhai zhiyi* zhong de 'handu fu' xingxiang wei li" 論明清小說中的女性悍妒文 化—以 '聊齋誌異' 中的 '悍妒婦' 形象為例. *Shaanxi Xueqian Shifan Xueyuan xuebao* 陝西學前師範學院學報 31, no. 6 (2015): 57–60.

Liu Pujiang 劉浦江. "Jindai hukou yanjiu" 金代戶口研究 2 (1994): 86–96.

Liu Shiyi 劉士義. "Mingdai qingxing sichao yu liangxing wenxue yanbian" 明代情 性思潮與兩性文學演變. *Beifang luncong* 北方論叢 5 (2014): 29–34.

Liu Yan 劉艷. "Mingdai Ningde lienü xingxiang yanjiu—yi Ming Jiajing shiqinian ban *Ningde xianzhi* wei li" 明代寧德烈女形象研究—以明嘉靖十七年版 '寧德 縣志' 為例. *Luoyang Shifan Xueyuan xuebao* 洛陽師範學院學報 35, no. 7 (2016): 57–62.

Liu Yu 劉玉. "Mingdai huang guifei fenghao chutan" 明代皇貴妃封號初探. *Gu-gong xuekan* 故宮學刊 2 (2016): 115–24.

Liu Zhenggang 劉正剛. *Ming Qing diyu shehui bianqian zhong de Guangdong xiangcunfunü yanjiu* 明清地域社會變遷中的廣東鄉村婦女研究. Beijing: Shehui kexue wenxian chubanshe, 2016.

Liu Zhenggang 劉正剛 and Qiao Yuhong 喬玉紅. "Ming Qing kejia nüxing de shehui xingxiang: yi Longchuan wei li" 明清客家女性的社會形象: 以龍川為例. *Huanan Ligong Daxue xuebao* 華南理工大學學報 5 (2008): 46–52.

Lou Hansong 樓含松 and Wu Lin 吳琳. "'Guiyin': Ming Qing zhi ji zhishi nüxing de shenfen xuanze yu jiazhi rentong" '閨陰': 明清之際知識女性的身分選擇與價值 認同. *Zhejiang shehui kexue* 浙江社會科學 2 (2016): 120–25.

Lu Jianrong 盧建榮. "Yuanmo nüxing wei yufang shouru er zisha shijian de xingsi—Xugou dangan hu, yidai youse yanjing kan wushi hu" 元末女性為預防受辱而自殺事件的省思—虛構檔案乎，抑戴有色眼睛看物事乎？ In *Jindai bainian chengshi shenghuo de xingbie yu quanli* 近代百年城市生活的性別與權利, edited by Lu Jianrong 盧建榮, 79–114. Taipei: Xin gaodi, 2019.

Lü Kun 呂坤. *Guifan* 閨範. Shanghai: Shanghai guji, 1994.

Lü Miaofen 呂妙芬. "Ming Qing Zhongguo wanli xunqin de wenhua shijian" 明清中國萬里尋親的文化實踐. *Zhongyang Yanjiu Yuan Lishi Yuyan Yanjiusuo jikan* 中央研究院歷史語言研究所集刊 78, no. 2 (2007): 359–406.

Lu, Tina. "The Literary Culture of the Late Ming (1573–1644)." In *The Cambridge History of Chinese Literature*, vol. II, *From 1375*, edited by Kang-i Sun Chang and Stephen Owen, 63–167. Cambridge: Cambridge University Press, 2010.

Lu, Weijing. *True to Her Word: The Faithful Maiden Cult in Late Imperial China*. Stanford: Stanford University Press, 2008.

Luk, Yu-ping. *The Empress and the Heavenly Masters: A Study of the Ordination Scroll of Empress Zhang (1493)*. Hong Kong: The Chinese University Press, 2016.

Luo Tonghua 羅彤華. *Tongju gongcai: Tangdai jiating yanjiu* 同居共財: 唐代家庭研究. Taipei: Zhengda chubanshe, 2015.

Luo Xinquan 駱新泉. "Ming Qing nüxing wenxue xinbian (er)—guixiu fu bi shici lungao" 明清女性文學新變 (二)—閨秀賦婢詩詞論稿. *Hengyang Shifan Xueyuan xuebao* 衡陽師範學院學報 1 (2016): 77–81.

Ma Leiyin 馬蕾吟 and Ren Ruping 任汝平. "Lun Zhongguo gudai shouji hunzhi—yi Mingdai wei li" 論中國古代收繼婚制—以明代為例. *Fazhi yu jingji* 法制與經濟 7 (2014): 123–28.

MacDonald, Alastair Ewan. "Women in Erpai: The Gap Between Rhetoric and Representation." *Nan Nü* 20, no. 2 (2018): 225–55.

Mann, Susan. "Historical Change in Female Biography from Song to Qing Times: The Case of Early Qing Jiangnan." *Transactions of the International Conference of Orientalists in Japan* 30 (1985): 65–77.

———. "Widows in the Kinship, Class, and Community Structures of Qing Dynasty China." *Journal of Asian Studies* 46, no. 1 (1987): 37–56.

Mao Hanguang 毛漢光. "Tangdai houbanqi houfei zhi fenxi" 唐代後半期后妃之分析. *Guoli Taiwan Daxue wenshizhe xuebao* 國立臺灣大學文史哲學報 37 (1989): 175–95.

Mao Liping 毛立平. *Qingdai jiazhuang yanjiu* 清代嫁妝研究. Beijing: Renming Daxue chubanshe, 2007.

Mao Wenfang 毛文芳. *Wu, xingbie, guankan: Mingmo Qingchu wenhua shuxie xintan* 物・性別・觀看: 明末清初文化書寫新探. Taipei: Xuesheng shuju, 2001.

McMahon, Keith. "The Art of the Bedchamber and *Jin Ping Mei*." *Nan Nü* 21, no. 1 (2019): 1–37.

———. *Celestial Women: Imperial Wives and Concubines in China from Song to Qing*. Lanham, MD: Rowman & Littlefield, 2016.

———. "The Institution of Polygamy in the Chinese Imperial Palace." *Journal of Asian Studies* 72, no. 4 (2013): 917–36.

———. "Women Rulers in Imperial China." *Nan Nü* 15, no. 2 (2013): 179–218.

———. *Women Shall Not Rule: Imperial Wives and Concubines in China from Han to Liao*. Lanham, MD: Rowman & Littlefield, 2013.

Meijer, M. J. *Murder and Adultery in Late Imperial China: A Study of Law and Morality*. Leiden: E.J. Brill, 1991.

Mellor, Ronald. *Tacitus' Annals*. Oxford: Oxford University Press, 2010.

Merlin, Monica. "The Nanjing Courtesan Ma Shouzhen (1548–1604): Gender, Space and Painting in the Late Ming Pleasure Quarter." *Gender and History* 23, no. 3 (2011): 630–52.

Mote, Frederick. "The Growth of Chinese Despotism: A Critique of Wittfogel's Theory of Oriental Despotism as Applied to China." *Oriens Extremus* 8 (1961): 1–41.

Mou, Sherry J. *Gentlemen's Prescriptions for Women's Lives: A Thousand Years of Biographies of Chinese Women*. Armonk, NY: M.E. Sharpe, 2004.

Murray, Julia K. *Mirror of Morality: Chinese Narrative Illustration and Confucian Ideology*. Honolulu: University of Hawaii Press, 2007.

Na Hai 那海. *Ming Qing houfei de aihen wangshi* 明清后妃的愛恨往事. Beijing: Gugong chubanshe, 2014.

Naquin, Susan. "The Transmission of White Lotus Sectarianism in Late Imperial China." In *Popular Culture in Late Imperial China*, edited by David Johnson et al., 255–91. Berkeley and Los Angeles: University of California Press, 1985.

Ni Wenjie 倪文杰 et al. *Zuijia nüxing miaoxie cidian* 最佳女性描寫辭典. Beijing: Zhongguo guoji guangbo, 1990.

Niu Zhiping 牛志平. *Tangdai hunsang* 唐代婚喪. Xi'an: Sanqin chubanshe, 2011.

Nixey, Catherine. *The Darkening Age: The Christian Destruction of the Classical World*. Boston and New York: Houghton Mifflin Harcourt, 2018.

Ochs, Elinor, and Carolyn Taylor. "The 'Father Knows Best' Dynamic in Dinnertime Narratives." In *Gender Articulated: Language and the Socially Constructed Self*, edited by Kira Hall and Mary Bucholtz, 97–120. New York: Routledge, 1995.

Overmyer, Daniel L. "Values in Chinese Sectarian Literature: Ming and Ch'ing *Pao-chüan*." In *Popular Culture in Late Imperial China*, edited by David Johnson et al., 219–54. Berkeley and Los Angeles: University of California Press, 1985.

Pan Qing 潘清. "Yuandai Jiangnan diqu Menggu, Semu qiaoyu renhu hunyin zhuangtai de fenxi" 元代江南地區蒙古, 色目僑寓人戶婚姻狀態的分析. *Xuehai* 學海 3 (2002): 132–36.

Pang-White, Ann A. "Confucius and the *Four Books for Women* (*Nü Sishu* 女四書)." In *Feminist Encounters with Confucius*, edited by Mathew A. Foust and Sor-hoon Tan, 17–39. Leiden: Brill, 2016.

Peng Yong 彭勇 and Pan Yue 潘岳. *Mingdai gongting nüxingshi* 明代宮廷女性史. Beijing: Gugong chubanshe, 2015.

Perdue, Theda. *Cherokee Women: Gender and Cultural Change, 1700–1835*. Lincoln: University of Nebraska Press, 1998.

Phipps, William E. "The Menstrual Taboo in the Judeo-Christian Tradition." *Journal of Religion and Health* 19, no. 4 (1980): 298–303.

Pu Wenqi 濮文起. "Nüxing jiazhi de zhongyang—Ming Qing shiqi minjian zongjiao zhong de funü" 女性價值的張揚—明清時期民間宗教中的婦女. *Lilun yu xiandaihua* 理論與現代化 5 (2006): 111–15.

Qi Bin 齊斌 and Wang Rimei 王日美. "Tangdai juntian zhidu xia funü buzai shoutian deyuanyin tanxi" 唐代均田制度下婦女不再受田的原因探析. *Xuchang Xueyuan xuebao* 許昌學院學報 31, no. 1 (2012): 96–99.

Qi Wenying 奇文瑛. "Beiming suo jian Mingdai daguan hunyin guanxi" 碑銘所見明代達官婚姻關係. *Zhongguo shi yanjiu* 中國史研究 3 (2011): 167–81.

Qi Xin 戚昕. "Mingdai nüxing chubanjia Zhou Zhibiao" 明代女性出版家周之標. *Xin shiji tushuguan* 新世紀圖書館 10 (2012): 57–61.

Qian, Nanxiu. "Milk and Scent: Works about Women in the *Shishuo Xinyu* Genre." *Nan Nü* 1, no. 2 (1999): 187–236.

Qiao Chen 喬琛. "Mingdai nüzi shiwen zongji de xingbie shijiao" 明代女子詩文總集的性別視角. *Shehui kexuejia* 社會科學家 5 (2015): 149–53.

Qin Haiying 秦海瀅. *Mingdai Shandong jiaohua yanjiu* 明代山東教化研究. Dalian: Liaoning Shifan Daxue chubanshe, 2011.

Qiu Zhonglin 邱仲麟. "Mingdai gongren de rong yu ru—cong zhiye funü yu shehui liudong de jiaodu qieru" 明代宮人的榮與辱—從職業婦女與社會流動的角度切入. *Gugong xuekan* 故宮學刊 2 (2014): 91–125.

Raphals, Lisa. "Arguments by Women in Early Chinese Texts." *Nannü* 3, no. 2 (2001): 157–95.

———. *Sharing the Light: Representations of Women and Virtue in Early China.* Albany: State University of New York Press, 1998.

Ricoeur, Paul. "Narrative Identity." *Philosophy Today* 35, no. 1 (1991): 73–81.

Ropp, Paul S. "Passionate Women: Female Suicide in Late Imperial China—Introduction." In *Passionate Women: Female Suicide in Late Imperial China*, edited by Paul S. Ropp et al., 3–21. Leiden: Brill, 2001.

Schlegel, Alice. "Status, Property, and the Value on Virginity." *American Ethnologist* 18, no. 4 (1991): 719–34.

Scott, Joan Wallach. "Gender: A Useful Category of Historical Analysis." *American Historical Review* 91 (1986): 1053–75.

Serruys, Henry. "Remains of Mongol Customs During the Early Ming." *Monumenta Serica* 16, nos. 1–2 (1957): 137–90.

Shen Haimei 沈海梅. "Bianyuan wenhua zhuliuhua zhong de funü—Ming Qing shiqi de Yunnan *Lienü qun*" 邊緣文化主流化中的婦女—明清時期的雲南列女群. *Sixiang zhanxian* 思想戰線 28 (2002): 66–70.

———. *Ming Qing Yunnan funü shenghuo yanjiu* 明清雲南婦女生活研究. Kunming: Yunnan jiaoyu chubanshe, 2001.

Sheng Shilan 盛詩瀾. "Ming Qing mingji de bimo biaoqing" 明清名妓的筆墨表情. *Shufa* 書法 3 (2014): 42–47.

Shiga Shūzō 滋賀秀三. *Chūgoku kazokuhō no genri* 中國家族法の原理. Tokyo: Sōbunsha, 1967.

Shiga, Shūzō. "Family Property and the Law of Inheritance in Traditional China." In *Chinese Family Law and Social Change in Historical and Comparative Perspective*, edited by David C. Buxbaum, 109–50. Seattle: University of Washington Press, 1978.

Skinner, G. William. "Conjugal Power in Tokugawa Japanese Families: A Matter of Life or Death." In *Sex and Gender Hierarchies*, edited by Barbara Diane Miler, 236–70. Cambridge: Cambridge University Press, 1993.

Sommer, Matthew H. "The Uses of Chastity: Sex, Law, and the Property of Widows in Qing China." *Late Imperial China* 17, no. 2 (1996): 77–130.

Song Lizhong 宋立中. "Ming Qing Jiangnan funü 'yeyou' yu fengjian lunli chongtu" 明清江南婦女冶游與封建倫理衝突. *Funü yanjiu luncong* 婦女研究論叢 1 (2010): 39–48.

Soullière, Ellen Felicia. "The Imperial Marriages of the Ming Dynasty." *Papers on Far Eastern History* 37 (1988): 15–42.

———. "Palace Women in the Ming Dynasty: 1368–1644." PhD diss., Princeton University, 1987.

———. "The Writing and Rewriting of History: Imperial Women and the Succession in Ming China, 1368–1457." *Ming Studies* 73 (2016): 2–29.

Spitulnik, Debra. "The Social Circulation of Media Discourse and the Mediation of Communities." In *Linguistic Anthropology: A Reader*. 2nd ed, edited by Alessandro Duranti, 93–113. Chinchester, UK: Wiley-Blackwell, 2009.

Stevenson, Mark. "Wanton Women in Late-Imperial Chinese Literature: Models, Genres, Subversions and Traditions." In *Wanton Women in Late-Imperial Chinese Literature: Models, Genres, Subversions and Traditions*, edited by Mark Stevenson and Wu Cuncun, 3–26. Leiden: Brill, 2017.

Struve, Lynn A. "Song Maocheng's Matrixes of Mourning and Regret." *Nan Nü* 15, no. 1 (2013): 69–108.

Su Wanling 蘇婉綾, "Jin Yuan shiqi yiliao wenhua zhong de xingbie yanjiu" 金元時期醫療文化中的性別研究. MA thesis, Fo Guang University, 2019.

Sun Hongzhe 孫宏哲. "Ming Qing changpian shiqing xiaoshuo zhong nüxing dechouguai shenti" 明清長篇世情小說中女性的醜怪身體. *Jilin Shifan Daxue xuebao* 吉林師範大學學報 2 (2011): 11–13.

Sun Xinmei 孫新梅. "Nü sishu de bianzuan yu liuchuan" 女四書的編纂與流傳. *Lantai shijie* 蘭台世界 11 (2013): 156–57.

Sutton, Donald S. "From Credulity to Scorn: Confucians Confront the Spirit Mediums in Late Imperial China." *Late Imperial China* 21, no. 2 (2000): 1–39.

Sweely, Tracy L. "Introduction." In *Manifesting Power: Gender and the Interpretation of Power in Archaeology*, edited by Tracy L. Sweely, 1–14. London: Routledge, 1999.

Takahashi, Yoshirō. "Orphaned Daughters: On the So-Called Property Rights of Daughters in the Southern Song Period," translated by Matthew Raleigh. *International Journal of Asian Studies* 12, no. 2 (2015): 131–65.

Tanaka Issei, "The Social and Historical Context of Ming-Qing Local Drama." In *Popular Culture in Late Imperial China*, edited by David Johnson et al., 143–60. Berkeley and Los Angeles: University of California Press, 1985.

Tanaka, Tomoyuki. "View of Emotions in the *Jin Ping Mei*: Perceptions of the 'Moods' and Their Expression." In *Concepts and Categories of Emotion in East Asia*, edited by Giusi Tamburello, 213–29. Rome: Carocci, 2012.

Tang Tianhang 唐天航. "Lun Mingdai renxun zhidu de feichu" 論明代人殉制度的廢除. *Daqing Shifan Xueyuan xuebao* 大慶師範學院學報 38, no. 2 (2018): 120–24.

Telford, Ted. A. "Covariates of Men's Age at First Marriage: The Historical Demography of Chinese Lineages." *Population Studies* 46, no. 1 (1992): 19–35.

ter Har, B. J. *The White Lotus Teachings of Chinese Religious History.* Honolulu: University of Hawaii Press, 1999.

T'ien Ju-k'ang. *Male Anxiety and Female Chastity: A Comparative Study of Chinese Ethical Values in Ming-Ch'ing Times.* Leiden: Brill, 1988.

van Ess, Hans. "Cheng Yi and His Ideas about Women as Revealed in His Commentary to the *Yijing.*" *Oriens Extremus* 49 (2010): 63–77.

Verdon, Michel. "Virgins and Widows: European Kinship and Early Christianity." *Man*, New Series 23, no. 3 (1988): 488–505.

von Glahn, Richard. *The Economic History of China: From Antiquity to the Nineteenth Century.* Cambridge: Cambridge University Press, 2016.

Walliman, Isador, Nicholas Ch. Tatsis, and George V. Zito. "On Max Weber's Definition of Power." *Australian and New Zealand Journal of Sociology* 13, no. 3 (1977): 231–35.

Waltner, Ann. *Getting an Heir: Adoption and the Construction of Kinship in Late Imperial China.* Honolulu: University of Hawaii Press, 1990.

———. "Remembering the Lady Wei: Eulogy and Commemoration in Ming Dynasty China." *Ming Studies* 55 (2007): 80–92.

Wang Chuanman 王傳滿. "Ming Qing Huizhou funü jielie xingwei de yingxiang" 明清徽州婦女節烈行為的影響. *Nanyang Shifan Xueyuan xuebao* 南陽師範學院學報 8, no. 11 (2009): 43–46.

———. "Ming Qing shiqi zhanluan deng baoli yinsu yu Huizhou jielie funü" 明清時期戰亂等暴力因素與徽州節烈婦女. *Baoji Wenli Xueyuan xuebao* 寶雞文理學院學報 6 (2008): 37–41.

———. "On Variations in Huizhou Women's Chastity Behaviors during the Ming and Qing Dynasties." *Chinese Studies in History* 45, no. 4 (2012): 43–57.

Wang Danni 王丹妳 and Li Zhisheng 李志生. "Ming Qing shiqi *Nü lunyu* banben kaoshu" 明清時期 '女論語' 版本考述. *Shandong Nüzi Xueyuan xuebao* 山東女子學院學報 2 (2018): 46–55.

Wang Haidong 王海冬. "Yuandai haishang caoyun yu Mazu xinyang de fazhan" 元代海上漕運與媽祖信仰的發展. *Putian Xueyuan xuexiao* 莆田學院學校 23, no. 4 (2016): 1–5.

Wang Hongtai 王鴻泰. "Meiren xiangban—Ming Qing wenren de meise pinshang yu qingyi shenghuo de jingying" 美人相伴—明清文人的美色品賞與情藝生活的經營. *Xin shixue* 新史學 24, no. 2 (2013): 71–130.

Wang Huaxu 王化旭. "Ming Qing chuanqi zhong nüni nüdao juese tedian tanwei" 明清傳奇中女尼女道角色特點探微. *Jiangsu Jiaoyu Xueyuan xuebao* 江蘇教育學院學報 29, no. 1 (2013): 118–20.

Wang Li 王立. "Ming Qing nüxing baozhenshu muti ji qi Yindu wenhua suyuan" 明清女性保貞術母體及其印度文化溯源. *Ningxia Daxue xuebao* 寧夏大學學報 1 (2007): 42–47.

Wang Li 王立 and Feng Zhihua 馮智華. "Ming Qing xiaoshuo nüxing yiji Fuchou miaoxie yu shehui xinli" 明清小說女性以技復仇描寫與社會心理. *Dandong Shizhuan xuebao* 丹東師專學報 24, no. 3 (2002): 1–4.

Wang Li 王立 and Li Guiyin 李貴銀. "Wei Jin nüxing fuchou wenxue zhuti de wenxue shiyi ji chengyin" 魏晉女性復仇文學主題的文學史意及成因. *Suzhou Shizhuan xuebao* 宿州師專學報 18, no. 1 (2003): 4–7.

Wang Liyu 王麗玉. *Ming Qing nüxing de wenxue pipan* 明清女性的文學批判. Shanghai: Huadong Shifan Daxue chubanshe, 2017.

Wang Meng 王萌. "Ming Qing shiqi nüxing bixia de jiemei qingyi" 明清時期女性筆下的姐妹情誼. *Henan Jiaoyu Xueyuan xuebao* 河南教育學院學報 4 (2005): 119–22.

Wang Ping. *Aching for Beauty: Footbinding in China*. Minneapolis: University of Minnesota Press, 2000.

Wang, Richard G. "The Cult of *Qing*: Romanticism in the Late Ming Period and in the Novel *Jiao Hong Ji*." *Ming Studies* 33 (1994): 12–55.

———. *Ming Erotic Novellas: Genre, Consumption, and Religiosity in Cultural Practice*. Hong Kong: Chinese University Press, 2011.

Wang Weiman 王偉滿. "Jielie jingbiao—Ming Qing Huizhou jielie xianxiang de zhongyao yinsu" 節烈旌表—明清徽州節烈現象的重要因素. *Aba Shifan Gaodeng Zhuanke Xuexiao xuebao* 阿壩師範高等專科學校學報 26, no. 4 (2009): 61–64.

Wang Weiping 王偉萍. "Ming Qing mushi jiaoyu suyang shulun" 明清母氏教育素養述論. *Neijiang Shifan Xueyuan xuebao* 內江師範學院學報 7, no. 28 (2013): 77–80.

Wang Xi 王熹. "Zhashi tuijin Mingdai gongtingshi he nüxingshi yanjiu de lizuo—ping *Mingdai gongting nüxingshi*" 紮實推進明代宮廷史和女性史研究的力作—評 '明代宮廷女性史.' *Gugong xuekan* 故宮學刊 1 (2017): 406–11.

Wang Xueping 王雪萍. "Mingdai binü hunyin teshuxing de lishi jiedu" 明代婢女婚姻特殊性的歷史解讀. *Shehui kexue jikan* 社會科學輯刊 3 (2010): 195–99.

———. "Mingdai binü zhengce yu fagui de yanjin ji shehui neihan" 明代婢女政策與法規的演進及社會內涵. *Dongbei Shida xuebao* 東北師大學報 2 (2013): 55–61.

———. "Mingdai chubi xianxiang de lishi wenhua yunhan—yi *Xingshi yunyuan zhuan* wei zhongxin" 明代廚婢現象的歷史文化蘊涵—以 '醒世姻緣傳' 為中心. *Haerbin Gongye Daxue xuebao* 哈爾濱工業大學學報 13, no. 6 (2011): 114–19.

———. "Mingdai tieshen binü qunti cunzai jichu ji shengcun moshi tanwei" 明代貼身婢女群體存在基礎及生存模式探微. *Changchun Shifan Daxue xuebao* 長春師範大學學報 5 (2014): 42–46.

———. "Mingdai zhufu yubi celue yu rujia lunli shijian—yi Mingdai nüxing beizhuanwen wei zhongxin" 明代主婦御婢策略與儒家倫理實踐—以明代女性碑傳文為中心. *Jianghan luntan* 江漢論壇 11 (2013): 107–12.

Wang Yi 王毅. *Songdai wenxue jiazu* 宋代文學家族. Changsha: Hunan Shifa Daxue chubanshe, 2008.

Watson, James L. "Anthropological Overview: The Development of Chinese Descent Groups." In *Kinship Organization in Late Imperial China 1000–1940*, edited by Patricia Buckley Ebrey and James L. Watson, 274–92. Berkeley and Los Angeles: University of California Press, 1986.

———. "Standardization of the Gods: The Promotion of Ti'en Hou ('Empress of Heaven') Along the South China Coast, 960–1960." In *Popular Culture in Late*

Imperial China, edited by David Johnson et al., 292–324. Berkeley and Los Angeles: University of California Press, 1985.

Watson, Rubie S. "The Named and the Nameless: Gender and Person in Chinese Society." In *Gender in Cross Cultural Perspective*, edited by Caroline B. Brettell and Carolyn F. Sargent, 120–33. Englewood Cliffs, NJ: Prentice Hall, 1993.

Weatherford, Jack. *The Secret History of the Mongol Queens: How the Daughters of Genghis Khan Rescued His Empire*. New York: Broadway Books, 2010.

Wei Shuyun 魏淑賓. *Ming Qing nüzuojia tanci xiaoshuo yu Ming Qing shehui* 明清女作家彈詞小說與明清社會. Tianjin: Tianjin Shehui Kexueyuan chubanshe, 2017.

White, Douglas R., and Michael L. Burton. "Causes of Polygyny: Ecology, Kinship, and Warfare." *American Anthropologist* 90 (1988): 871–87.

Widmer, Ellen. "The Epistolary World of Female Talent in Seventeenth-Century China." *Late Imperial China* 10 (1989): 1–43.

———. "Letters as Windows on Ming-Qing Women's Literary Culture." In *A History of Chinese Letters and Epistolary Culture*, edited by Antje Richtr, 744–74. Leiden: Brill, 2015.

Wolf, Eric R. "Distinguished Lecture: Facing Power—Old Insights, New Questions." *American Anthropologist*, New Series 92, no. 3 (1990): 586–96.

Wolf, Margery. *Women and the Family in Rural Taiwan*. Stanford: Stanford University Press, 1972.

Wong, Ka F. "The Anatomy of Eroticism: Reimagining Sex and Sexuality in the Late Ming Novel *Xiuta Yeshi*." *Nan Nü* 9, no. 2 (2007): 284–329.

Wu Cuncun 吳存存. *Ming Qing shehui xing'ai fengqi* 明清社會性愛風氣. Beijing: Renmin wenxue chubanshe, 2000.

Wu, H. Laura. "Through the Prism of Male Writing: Representation of Lesbian Love in Ming-Qing Literature." *Nan Nü* 4, no. 1 (2002): 1–34.

Wu Haihang 吳海航. *Yuandai fa wenhua yanjiu* 元代法文化研究. Beijing: Beijing Shifan Daxue chubanshe, 2000.

Wu Renshu 巫仁恕. *Shechi de nüren: Ming Qing shiqi Jiangnan funü de xiaofei wenhua* 奢侈的女人: 明清時期江南婦女的消費文化. Taipei: Sanmin shuju, 2005.

Wu Weichun 武維春. "Yangzhou baguai yu Ming Qing cainühua zhi yuanyuan" 揚州八怪與明清才女畫之淵源. *Weiyang Shifan Xueyuan xuebao* 淮陽師範學院學報 5 (2010): 636–41, 645.

Wu, Yenna. "The Inversion of Marital Hierarchy: Shrewish Wives and Hen-Pecked Husbands in Seventeenth-Century Chinese Literature." *Harvard Journal of Asiatic Studies* 48, no. 2 (1988): 363–82.

———. *The Lioness Roars: Shrew Stories from Late Imperial China*. Ithaca, NY: East Asia Program, Cornell University, 1995.

Wu, Yi-li. "Body, Gender, and Disease: The Female Breast in Late Imperial Chinese Medicine." *Late Imperial China* 32, no. 1 (2011): 83–128.

Xiao Jing 肖暻. "Mingdai houfei kanyin fojing lunlue" 明代后妃刊印佛經論略. *Wutaishan yanjiu* 五台山研究 3 (2017): 36–40.

Xie Guian 謝貴安. "Mingdai gongting nüjiao lunxi" 明代宮廷女教論析. *Zhongyuan wenhua yanjiu* 中原文化研究 3 (2016): 95–102.

Xu Kuoduan 徐适端. "Shixi Yuandai funü zai falü zhong de diwei" 試析元代婦女在法律中的地位. *Zhongguo shi yanjiu* 中國史研究 4 (2000): 104–16.

Xu, Sufeng. "The Rhetoric of Legitimation: Prefaces to Women's Poetry Collections from the Song to the Ming." *Nan Nü* 8, no. 2 (2006): 255–89.

Xu Tuoduan 徐适端, ed. *Ming shi lu leizuan: Funüshi kejuan* 明實錄類纂: 婦女史料卷. Wuhan: Wuhan chubanshe, 1995.

Xu Wenxiang 徐文翔. "Zhennü, cainü yu yunü—Mingdai wenren nüxingguan de goujian" 貞女, 才女與欲女—明代文人女性觀的構建. *Wenxue yu wenhua* 文學與文化 1 (2016): 79–90.

Yamazaki Junichi 山崎純一. *Kyōiku kara mita Chūgoku joseishi shiryō no kenkyū—'josisho' to 'shinhuhu' sanbusho* 教育からみた中国女性史資料の研究—'女四書' と '新婦譜' 三部書. Tokyo: Meiji, 1986.

Yan Ming 嚴明. *Zhongguo mingji yishu shi* 中國名妓藝術史. Taipei: Wenjin, 1992.

Yang Jiping 楊祭平. "Dunhuang chutu de fangqi shu suoyi" 敦煌出土的放妻書瑣議. *Ximen Daxue xuebao* 西門大學學報 4 (1999): 34–41.

Yang Yaotian 楊耀田. "Mingdai gongzhu sangzang zhidu qianxi" 明代公主喪葬制度淺析. *Beijing shehui kexue* 北京社會科學 5 (2018): 23–33.

Yi Jo-lan. "Social Status, Gender Division and Institutions: Sources Relating to Women in Chinese Standard Histories." In *Overt and Covert Treasures: Essays on the Sources for Chinese Women's History*, edited by Clara Wing-Chung Ho, 131–55. Hong Kong: The Chinese University Press, 2012.

Yi Ruolan 衣若蘭. *Sangu liupo: Mingdai funü yu shehui de tansuo* 三姑六婆: 明代婦女與社會的探索. Banqiao: Daoxiang, 2002.

Yü, Chün-fang. *Kuan-yin: The Chinese Transformations of Avalokiteśvara.* New York: Columbia University Press, 2001.

Yu Yi 余意. "Lun Mingdai nüciren de huaiqinci" 論明代女詞人的懷親詞. *Dongguan Ligong Xueyuan xuebao* 東莞理工學院學報 18, no. 4 (2011): 75–79.

Yuan Zhoufei 袁宙飛. "Ming Qing yilai nianhua zhong nüxing xingxiang de muti tanti" 明清以來年畫中女性形象的母體探析. *Minsu yanjiu* 民俗研究 4 (2016): 114–20.

Zamperini, Paola. "Untamed Hearts: Eros and Suicide in Late Imperial Chinese Fiction." In *Passionate Women: Female Suicide in Late Imperial China*, edited by Paul S. Ropp et al., 77–104. Leiden: Brill, 2001.

Zeitlin, Judith T. "The Gift of Song: Courtesans and Patrons in Late Ming and Early Qing Cultural Production." *Hsiang Lectures on Chinese Poetry* 4 (2008): 1–46.

———. "The Pleasures of Print: Illustrated Songbooks form the Late Ming Courtesan Word." In *Gender in Chinese Music*, edited by Rachel Harris et al., 41–65. Rochester, NY: University of Rochester Press, 2013.

Zhan Shiyou and Peng Chuanhua. "Cultivation (Jiaohua, 教化): The Goal of Xunzi's Ethical Thought." *Frontiers of Philosophy in China* 2, no. 1 (2007): 25–49.

Zhang Bangwei 張邦煒. *Hunyin yu shehui (Songdai)* 婚姻與社會 (宋代). Chengdu: Sichuan renmin chubanshe, 1989.

Zhang Benshun 張本順. "Songdai funü lianchan suoyouquan tanxi ji qi yiyi" 宋代婦女奩產所有權探析及其意義. *Fazhi yu shehui fazhan* 法制與社會發展 5 (2011): 79–95.

Bibliography

Zhang Dengcan 張登璨. "Mingdai nühu de jieding ji qi shehui daiyu" 明代女戶的界定及其社會待遇. *Guizhou wenshi congkan* 貴州文史叢刊 3 (2017): 8–19.

Zhang Fan 張凡. *Mingdai jiachan jicheng yu zhengsong* 明代家產繼承與爭訟. Beijing: Falü chubanshe, 2015.

Zhang Guogang 張國剛. "'Family Building in Inner Quarters': Conjugal Relationships in Tang Families," translated by Yipeng Lai. *Frontiers of History in China* 4, no. 1 (2009): 1–38.

———. *Jiating shihua* 家庭史話. Beijing: Shehui kexue wenxian, 2012.

Zhang Jing 張菁. *Tangdai nüxing xingxiang shenghuo* 唐代女性形象生活. Lanzhou: Gansu renmin, 2007.

Zhang Jingjing 張曔曔. "Mingdai gongzhu hunyin de 'pingminhua' quxiang" 明代公主婚姻的 '平民化' 趨向. *Zhengzhou Hangkong Gongye Guanli Xueyuan xuebao* 鄭州航空工業管理學院學報 36, no. 2 (2017): 67–71.

Zhang Jingwei 張經緯. "Songdai caichan jicheng zhidu tanjiu" 宋代財產繼承制度探究. *Chifeng Xueyuan xuebao* 赤峰學院學報 35, no. 1 (2014): 40–44.

Zhang Li 張麗. "Ming Qing funü shenghuo yu fojiao xinyang" 明清婦女生活與佛教信仰. *Hunan Renwen Keji Xueyuan xuebao* 湖南人文科技學院學報 3 (2012): 47–51.

Zhang Lijie 張麗杰. *Mingdai nüxing sanwen yanjiu* 明代女性散文研究. Beijing: Zhongguo shehui kexue, 2009.

Zhang Ping 張萍. "Mingdai caizi jiaren chuanqi zhong de nüxing yishi tanxi—yi Tang Xianzu *Mudan ting* wei li" 明代才子佳人傳奇中的女性意識探析—以湯顯祖牡丹亭為例. *Zhonggong Jinan Shiwei Dangxiao xuebao* 中共濟南市委黨校學報 1 (2018): 73–76.

Zhang Shuming 張書銘. "*Neixun* yu Mingdai nüxing jiaohua" 內訓與明代女性教化. *Nanfang luncong* 南方論叢 6 (2017): 22–26.

Zhang Weidong 張衛東. "Tangdai cishi yu jingbiao zhidu" 唐代刺史與旌表制度. *Jiangxi shehui kexue* 江西社會科學 7 (2009): 146–52.

Zhang Wenlu 張文祿. "Ming Qing shiqi Wanbei nüzi xiaoxing yanjiu—yi Guangxu Shouzhou zhi, Suzhou zhi he Bozhou zhi wei kaocha duixiang" 明清時期皖北女子孝行研究—以光緒 '壽州志,' '宿州志' 和 '亳州志' 為考察對象. *Liupanshui Shifan Xueyuan xuebao* 六盤水師範學院學報 30, no. 2 (2018): 61–65.

———. "Ming Qing Wanbei funü gegu liaoqin yuanyin tanlun" 明清皖北婦女割股療親原因探論. *Anhui Guangbo Dianshi Daxue xuebao* 安徽廣播電視大學學報 3 (2015):105–8.

Zhang Yuzhen 張育甄. "Gui zhong hanmo: Ming Qing Jiangnan cainü de cixiu wenhua" 閨中翰墨: 明清江南才女的刺繡文化. MA thesis, Guoli Taiwan ShifanDaxue, 2011.

Zhang Zhichao 張志超. "Mingdai funü caichan de laiyuan" 明代婦女財產的來源. *Funü yanjiu luncong* 婦女研究論叢 4 (2010): 64–72.

Zhao Cuili 趙崔莉. *Bei zhebi de xiandaixing: Ming Qing nüxing de shehui shenghuo yu qinggan tiyan* 被遮蔽的現代性: 明清女性的社會生活與情感體驗. Beijing: Zhishi chanquan chubanshe, 2015.

———. "Mingdai nüxing de xiuxian shenghuo" 明代女性的休閒生活. *Zhongguo shehui jingjishi yanjiu* 中國社會經濟史研究 1 (2009): 50–57.

Zhang Xiaohui 張曉輝. "Mingdai jingbiao zhidu chutan" 明代旌表制度初探. *Shanxi Shifan Daxue xuebao* 山西師範大學學報 25 (2011): 114–17.

Zhao, Xiaohuan. "Love, Lust, and Loss in the Daoist Nunnery as Presented in Yuan Drama." *T'oung Pao* 100, nos. 1–3 (2014): 80–119.

Zhao Xiuli 趙秀麗. "Mingdai daru Lü Kun de nüxingguan ji shijian" 明代大儒呂坤 的女性觀及實踐. *Shangqiu Shifan Xueyuan xuebao* 商丘師範學院學報 2 (2008): 23–28.

Zheng Caiyun 鄭彩雲. "Lun Xuanzong Sun Huanghou you Mingdai zhongyuan zhengzhi—jian yu Lin Yanqing xiansheng shangquan" 論宣宗孫皇后與明代中葉 政治—兼與林延清先生商榷. *Nanchang Hangkong Daxue xuebao* 南昌航空大學 學報 17, no. 2 (2015): 13–18.

Zhong Huiling 鍾慧玲. *Qingdai nüshiren yanjiu* 清代女詩人研究. Taipei: Liren shuju, 2000.

Zhong Jinlan 種晉蘭. "Kejia funü yu shenming chongbai—yi Ming Qing simiao beige jizai wei zhongxin de fenxi" 客家婦女與神明崇拜—以明清寺廟碑刻記載 為中心的分析. *Jiaying Xueyuan xuebao* 嘉應學院學報 30, no. 4 (2012): 13–18.

Zhou Jiren 周繼仁. "Lun Zhongguo gudai biaoyan yishu de shangpinhua wenti" 論 中國古代表演藝術的商品化問題. *Zhongguoshi yanjiu* 中國史研究 15, no. 4 (1993): 44–57.

Zhu Yangdong 朱仰東 and Hu Hongqiang 胡洪強. "Mingdai Shuihu xi nüxingguan guankui" 明代水滸戲女性觀管窺. *Yili Shifan Xueyuan xuebao* 伊犁師範學院學 報 4 (2009): 68–72.

Zou Zetao 鄒賾韜 and Li Guangzhi 李廣志. "Mingdai Dongnanhai jiang wo luan jiyi zhong de lienü gushi—yi Zhejiang fangzhi shuxie wei zhongxin" 明代東南海 疆倭亂記憶中的烈女故事—以浙江方志書寫為中心. *Zhejiang Haiyang Daxue xuebao* 浙江海洋大學學報 35, no. 3 (2018): 6–13.

Zurndorfer, Harriet T. "Cotton Textile Production in Jiangnan during the Ming-Qing Era and the Matter of Market Driven Growth." In *The Economy of Lower Yangzi Delta in Late Imperial China; Connecting Money, Markets, and Institutions*, edited by Billy K. L. So, 72–98. London: Routledge, 2013.

———. "The Hsin-an Ta-tsu-chih and the Development of the Chinese Gentry Society, 800–1600." *T'oung Pao* 67, nos. 3/5 (1981): 154–215.

———. "Prostitutes and Courtesans in the Confucian Moral Universe of Late Ming China (1550–1644)." *International Review of Social History* 56 (2011): 197–216.

———. "Women in Chinese Learned Culture: Complexities, Exclusivities and Connecting Narratives." *Gender & History* 16, no. 1 (2014): 23–35.

Index

ASIAN VOICES
An Asia/Pacific/Perspectives Series
Series Editor: Mark Selden

I'm Married to Your Company! Everyday Voices of Japanese Women
   by Masako Itoh, edited by Nobuko Adachi and James Stanlaw
Sisters and Lovers: Women and Desire in Bali
   by Megan Jennaway
Moral Politics in a South Chinese Village: Responsibility, Reciprocity, and Resistance
   by Hok Bun Ku
Queer Japan from the Pacific War to the Internet Age
   by Mark McLelland
Behind the Silence: Chinese Voices on Abortion
   by Nie Jing-Bao
Rowing the Eternal Sea: The Life of a Minamata Fisherman
   by Oiwa Keibo, narrated by Ogata Masato, translated by Karen Colligan-Taylor
The Scars of War: Tokyo during World War II, Writings of Takeyama Michio
   edited and translated by Richard H. Minear
War and Conscience in Japan: Nambara Shigeru and the Asia-Pacific War
   edited and translated by Richard H. Minear
Growing Up Untouchable in India: A Dalit Autobiography
   by Vasant Moon, translated by Gail Omvedt, introduction by Eleanor Zelliot
Exodus to North Korea: Shadows from Japan's Cold War
   by Tessa Morris-Suzuki
Hiroshima: The Autobiography of Barefoot Gen
   by Nakazawa Keiji, edited and translated by Richard H. Minear
China Ink: The Changing Face of Chinese Journalism
   by Judy Polumbaum
Red Is Not the Only Color: Contemporary Chinese Fiction on Love and Sex between Women, Collected Stories
   edited by Patricia Sieber
Sweet and Sour: Life-Worlds of Taipei Women Entrepreneurs
   by Scott Simon
Dear General MacArthur: Letters from the Japanese during the American Occupation
   by Sodei Rinjirō, edited by John Junkerman, translated by Shizue Matsuda, foreword by John W. Dower
Unbroken Spirits: Nineteen Years in South Korea's Gulag
   by Suh Sung, translated by Jean Inglis, foreword by James Palais
Hidden Horrors: Japanese War Crimes in World War II, Second Edition
   by Yuki Tanaka
Zen Terror: The Death of Democracy in Prewar Japan
   by Brian A. Victoria

No Time for Dreams: Living in Burma under Military Rule
    by Carolyn Wakeman and San San Tin
A Thousand Miles of Dreams: The Journeys of Two Chinese Sisters
    by Sasha Su-Ling Welland
Dancing in Shadows: Sihanouk, the Khmer Rouge, and the United Nations in Cambodia
    by Benny Widyono
Voices Carry: Behind Bars and Backstage during China's Revolution and Reform
    by Ying Ruocheng and Claire Conceison